Historical events  working with man, trying to teach us to love Him and one another. The Bible is the record of God's interactions. When we read it we see his loving character. He uses miracles and fulfillment of prophecies to demonstrate His power so we will know he exists. God sent his son, Jesus, to institute a way for us to have an eternal life. Jesus fulfilled everything that God had foretold including his sacrificial death so we would know Him and His love for us. Further proof is received when we commit to them and receive the Holy Spirit. God communicates with us through the Holy Spirit and the Bible.

Upon accepting God and Jesus in your life, you want to know more about them. As a result, you start searching the Bible for acquiring information. This caused me to start taking notes so I could have a thorough understanding of the various subjects. While reading the parable of the sower (Matthew 13:1), I realize we all need to take root. Taking root can be difficult. Sometimes, we need further information to fully accept his Lordship and commit to his will. If we do not take root, we can be choked and lose our chance of an eternal life.

As I took my notes, I realized the bountiful information that proves God's existence and his character. My notes have been beneficial to me as I continue my journey in loving and understand God and Jesus. Sometimes, we need more complete understanding before we can put our total faith in them. I know my notes helped my understanding. It is my hope that my book will lead you to a stronger understanding of God and Jesus so we will all be together in their eternal Kingdom.

The book is organized by various subjects with extensive indexes for quick reference. There are charts, maps and other information that will aid your understanding. They were gathered from an expanded version of the New King James Bible, The New International Version translation of the Bible, Halley's Bible Handbook, Holman Bible Atlas Guides to the Bible, The Time chart of Biblical History, Who's who in the Bible, and Webster's Dictionary. I wrote my notes and referenced the scriptures used in preparing the notes. You can look up the references for better understand and verification of the validity of the notes. I think it would be beneficial for you to take notes. You can refer to them later when you might need them. If there are any questions between these notes and the Bible, always use the word of God. It is my hope that these notes will be aid in your relationship with God and Jesus while strengthening your faith and see God's love and will for you.

Copyright 2015 by Michael Conrad

Written by Michael Conrad

All rights reserved. No part of this book may be reproduced or transmitted in any form or by any means, electronic or mechanical, including photocopying, recording or by an information storage and retrieval system, without written permission from the author.

This book is a collection of notes gathered various sources. Thus, it is a mixture of the author's writings and quotes from other sources. As these notes were gathered prior to being placed in this book some of the sources are not delineated. We are sorry for this situation because a reader may desire to go to the original authors work for further information. There are many Bible scriptures referenced in this book. They were taken from the NIV translation.
I encourage you to go to any of the references so you are assured of the truth and understanding of the original authors.

Table of Contents

Facts about the Bible	1
Basic Bible Notes	8
Prophecies / Fulfillment	168
Miracles	196
Books of the Bible	213
Books of the Bible-written	220
Bible Books (*Descriptions*)	225
Special Events in the Bible	307
Notes from Bible Scholars	313
Special Scriptures	329
Time line of the Bible	347
Prominent People in the Bible	355
Words of the Bible	379
Maps of Bible Times	387
Subject index	397

Facts about the Bible

The Bible has been around for many centuries. However, as time passes, some people have lost sight of the greatness of this book. We seldom go to the Bible for our answers. For many people it is rarely read except for a few verses on Sundays.

We need to be reminded that the Bible is a wondrous, special life-giving book. Many of the great men of recent times have described how they felt that this book.

Following are some of these quotes.

George Washington: "It is impossible to rightly govern the world without God and the Bible."

Abraham Lincoln: "I believe the Bible is the best gift God has ever given to man. All the Good from the Savior or the world is communicated to us through this Book."

Daniel Webster: "If there is anything I my thought or style to commend, the credit is due to my parents for instilling in me an early love of the Scriptures. If we abide by the principles taught in the Bible, our country will go on prospering and to prosper; but if we and our posterity neglect its instructions and authority, no man can tell how sudden a catastrophe may overwhelm us and bury all our glory in profound obscurity."

Horace Greeley; "It is impossible to enslave mentally or socially a Bible-reading people. The principles of the Bible are the Ground work of human freedom."

U. S. Grant: "The Bible is the sheet-anchor of our

liberties."

Napoleon: "The Bible is no mere book, but a living Creature, with a power that conquers all that opposes it."

Robert E. Lee: "In all my perplexities and distresses, the Bible has never failed to give me light and strength.

Sir Isaac Newton: "There are more sure marks of authenticity in the Bible that in any profane history.

John Quincy Adams: "So great is my veneration for the Bible that the earlier my children begin to read it the more confident will be my hope that they will prove useful citizens of their country and respectable members of society. I have for many years made it a practice to read through the Bible once every year."

As you can see Great men from many walks of life have always held the Bible in high regards. We need to continue this tradition.

What is the Bible?

The Bible is a written message from God to all men. It records his promises and instructs us on how we can live a righteous life. It tells us how we can have an eternal life in his kingdom by believing in him and loving him as he loves us. God gives us many guidelines on how we can have a better life. Using these guidelines we can acquire wisdom, knowledge, understanding, strength for our life, fellowship with others and reconciliation with God
As you read through the Bible, you realize that God has given proof of his existence and his plans for us He

always tells us what he is going to do in the future, so we will know he exists and is understanding, powerful and loving God. In reviewing how God interacts with man in the Bible you will see that he is a loving God.

How did the Bible come into existence?

God selected special people from his believers and inspired them to write the scriptures. First, he used servants from his chosen people. They recorded his covenants, promises, miracles, guidance, prophesies, righteousness, blessings and judgment. God also sent Jesus, his son, to earth as his representative, so that we could know him. Jesus' followers were inspired by God thru the Holy Spirit recorded Jesus' life so we could have a better understanding of God. They also, explained God's love and plan for our salvation and how we can obtain eternal life.

Why does God use a Bible?

God does not want to force his Lordship on us. He uses the Bible so that man can read and learn about him and his love for us. It explains his deity, righteousness, love, judgment, faithfulness and his plans for man in his eternal kingdom. God wants us to know and understand him and be willing to accept him as our Lord. When we see his love and righteousness, then we will want to do his will. In doing his will, we will have love and harmony in his eternal kingdom.

God uses the Bible so that man can learn about him and his love for us. It explains his deity, righteousness, love, judgment, faithfulness and his plans for man in his eternal kingdom. God wants us to know and understand

him and be willing to accept him as our Lord.
If he just appeared to us in his majesty and power we would probably fear him and accept him as Lord. However, we would not understand him and we would lose the desire to do his will. Then when things didn't go our way, most likely we would rebel as the devil did. God wants us to know him and be willingly to choose him as Lord so we will want to do his will rather being forced to do his will. When we see his love and righteousness as it is presented in the Bible then we will do his will.

When and where did the Bible come about?

As God chose Abraham to start the People of Israel, most of the Old Testament was written in Hebrew. It started with Moses writing the Pentateuch. Later it was expanded by prophets and others who were telling their history and God's will for man. Some of these later books were written in Aramaic. The formation of the Old Testament was gathered after the Israelites returned from Babylon. It was regarded as the work of the Great Assembly associated with Ezra in the latter part of the 5th century B.C. As the political and acceptance language changed the Old Testament was translated to Greek by 70 Jewish scholars. This translation was completed at approximately 250 years before Christ and it was called the Septuagint. This is significant in that prophesies concerning Christ were in record before he was born. The next version was the Peshitta. There were many other translations and it was finally canonized by the rabbinical Council of Jamnia around A.D. 90.

The New Testament was written by the apostles and followers of Christ. Greek was the main language for the people of the Mediterranean, so most of it was written in

Greek. These books were completed in the first century A.D. The Books were first canonized in 180 A.D.by the Cannon Moratoria. The Bible, as we now know it, was standardized and canonized by the Council of Carthage in 397 A.D. Since then there have been many translations to aid people with different languages. All these translations have tried to maintain the meaning of the original writings.

In this wonderful book, we can find; history, great literature, poetry, answers to life's problems, and how to live with one another. We learn that God is in command through his fulfillment of his promises and prophecies. It shows how God loves his creation and has guided it for centuries. He has done this through his chosen people and his nation Israel. Later he wanted to extend his love and guidance to all his creations, so he sent us Christ to show his will to all of his creations. We now have the Holy Spirit to put God's will in our hearts. By accepting Jesus and allowing God's will to enter our hearts, we may obtain salvation through Christ and live in God's eternal kingdom.

Everyone should read the Bible form cover to cover. By doing this we can understand God's guiding hand. We can learn how to obtain an eternal life in Heaven.

After reading the entire Bible, we have an overwhelming appreciation for God, his will and his teachings. However, most have difficulty in remembering text and where to find various events and teachings. Further studying brings this understanding. As beginners in reading the scriptures, we need references to help us find which scriptures we need. Because of this difficulty, I went back through the Bible and took these notes and

later placed them in **Notes for Bible 101**. I also added information and in other sections of the book
The sections of the book are as follows

Basic Bible notes section. This is the collection of my notes grouped by subjects. I have referenced the scriptures where I obtained the information for the notes so you can assure your understanding of the subject. Some of these are: God, God's covenants with man, Jesus, Jesus' Parables, Miracles Apostles, Crucifixion, Resurrection, Born Again, Holy Spirit, Heaven and Hell, Prophecy, Faith ,love, Grace, Baptism, Communion, Christmas, Marriage, Divorce, Sexual immorality, Gospel with the components of salvation., Easter, Prayer, The Genealogy of Christ, Tribulation, Millennium, End time prophecies, coming, Rapture, Judgment, Facts concerning the Hebrews. For the location of a specific note see the **subject index.**

Books of the Bible section furnishes information about each of the 66 books of the Bible. It explains the subjects covered in the Book, their authors, background concerning time and time of its writing.

The **Prophecies** section of these notes is God's prophecies and their fulfillment. They explain where and when the prophecies were given and their fulfilment. Prophesies in the Bible are proof of God's hand in the world. These prophecies were written over 400 years before his birth. They were fulfilled in his life on earth and recorded by his eyewitness. Some of the Major Prophecies concerning Jesus are also listed in the notes.

Miracles This section lists many events that prove

God's existence, power, and love for aiding his people.

Special Events of the Bible. Many great events in the Bible are described but are hard to find until you have read them many times. In this section, the events are listed along with their location in the Bible.

Notes from Bible Scholars section is where notes come from interesting scholar statements. These statements are their conclusion from their study of the Bible. However, scholars sometimes disagree about dates and facts that are not specifically related in the Bible. In review of these statements, it is advisable that you should review the referenced text and compare it to the Bible and determine if you agree.

Special Scriptures section lists many scriptures that Christians commonly refer to. When reading the Bible, you know that there are many special scriptures that affect us. People quote scriptures, which affect them in their life with God. I encourage you to record your favorite scriptures.

Prominent People of the Bible section is a listing of people that were involved in special events noted in the Bible. It is arranged in alphabetical order for ease of information. Bible reference and dates are furnished for your understanding of their situation.

Words of the Bible section is a listing of some of these words and their definitions that are commonly used among Christians. Sometime Christians use words that are not common to all. For a better understanding they are Included with these notes.

Time Line of the Bible section furnishes historical time of major events of the past for a better understanding of the time and relationship of the events of the Bible, **Maps** are also included to give you an idea where these events took place.

Basic Bible Notes

When we hear and believe in God and his son, Jesus, we naturally accept their lordship.
With our acceptance of their lordship, we are born again and are given the Holy Spirit. The Holy Spirit aids us by placing Gods laws for righteousness in our hearts. We can have an eternal life with God and Jesus as long as we abide in them.

As Christians, Jesus told us to reach out to others so they could have eternal life. God and Jesus knew that we would need to have a source of information to pass this opportunity on to others so he gave us his scriptures. Thus, we now have the Bible. This Bible and the fellowship of other believers enable us to mature in our Christian living.

In our lives we have many distractions and earthly desires that keep us away from reading the Bible. The Bible is the greatest teacher. It will aid us through our lives, trials, and tribulations.

These **basic Bible notes** are just a beginning in understanding the great truths that God. A search of scripture can be used to explain God's truths. These study notes help you understand God and why he sent Jesus so we can to have salvation and life with him.

With each subject discussed you will find referenced scriptures which were used to prepare the notes. Everyone needs to use this kind of practice to learn more about God and our savior Jesus. There are many ways that you can find scripture for these studies and make you own notes. There are Study Bibles, Christian theme search books and indexes and concordance in some Bibles. Use whatever method is available to find scriptures that apply for your study. Write your understanding of the scriptures. This will help you remember and understand God's will for us.

Following are my scriptural notes that describe God Jesus, and the Holy Spirit and their direction for our lives. As you read them you will see their deity, power and love for us. God's commandments, covenants and Bible historical record of His and Jesus's interaction with their followers down through the century's shows us God's will for us.

The scriptures concerning Jesus, informs us about God's new covenant called the Gospels which benefits all men who want to accept their Lordship. Jesus brought a better understanding of God's will for man and how we should conduct our lives. Jesus taught his disciples about God and his will for man. They passed this information in their writings of the New Testament.

In my notes I have tried to gather information from various parts of the Bible for a specific subject. I referenced the scriptures where I obtained my information so the reader can review them for a further understanding and due a validation of my notes.

It is my hope that these notes will give the reader a better understanding and ease of finding answers to their questions.

They are intended to shed light on life issues we need to follow to support one another. Some of these subjects are Being Born again, being a new creation, baptism, prayer, church, communion, salvation, sin, repentance, God's grace, marriage, divorce and sexual immorality.

Some notes give us a glimpse of what God plans for the future and what we need to do for eternal life in God's kingdom. These subjects are: rapture, great tribulation, the sign and second coming of Christ, millennium, judgment, heaven, hell and prophecies.

History seems to repeat in one way or another. Many lessons concerning man and God are found in the scriptures. A review of some of the following subjects can give us a better understanding of God and what he expects of man. These can be found in: creation, Noah and the flood, Tower of Babel, the fall of Jerusalem, and Israel's captivity.

There are also cultural elements relevant to historical aspects about God's chosen people that will aid us in understanding them. These items are; Hebrew calendar, festivals, celebrations, 12 tribes of Israel, Ten Commandments, and God's silent years, the tabernacle and the Ark of the Covenant.

The works contained herein are just a sampling of discovery I have found. Hopefully this start will inspire and fuel you own search for your work and understanding.

God

God is omnipotent (all powerful), omnipresent (everywhere at all times) and omniscient (all wise and knowing). He is eternally existent in spirit and rules in the three persons (Trinity): Father, Son, and Holy Spirit.

The Bible has not given us a complete description of who God is or where he came from. As God said that he made man in his image, we know that he may look like. However, He is Spirit and we are flesh.

The Bible lets us learn about God through his actions and interactions with his creations. As you read about God's interaction with his people we learn about him. We see his nature, power, glory and his will for us. For our understanding, he sent Jesus his beloved son, so we could get to know him and his will for us. Jesus said in John 14:7 "If you really knew me, you would know my Father as well. From now on, you do know him and have seen him." Through this we can learn more about God. After Jesus died, on the cross, for our sins, He also demonstrated how we could be resurrected in to God's world.

We are given another view of God by the actions of the Holy Spirit. The Holy Spirit was actively showing glimpses of God to us. When we take Christ and God as our personal Lord and are baptized, the Holy Spirit comes to us and helps us understand God and his will for us.

In the scriptures of Exodus, you can see how God has shown his majesty and strength to his people.
He had Isaiah, Jeremiah, Ezekiel and Daniel reminds his people of the lessons of the past and for tells them their future. He showed his power by assuring the future happens as foretold. This was especially true about the life of Christ and the rise and fall of nations. This shows his majesty and guidance in the world and the ability to control this world. In Exodus, he also gave commandments and made covenants for us to prepare for his kingdom.

God's nature is shown in the way he has always helped his people. He is called Father because his nature is that of a father. A father loves, is concerned, forgiving, tender and unselfish. God is eternally true. You see his love and concern for his people by the way he has taken care of the Hebrews even though they would not live by his covenants (Exodus, Kings and Chronicles). God's forgiveness is revealed by the way he made future provision for his people after they broke his covenants and stopped acknowledge him. He disciplined them like a father and told them he would make things better later (predictions by Daniel and Jeremiah). He made provisions for his people to return to Jerusalem and rebuild their land by having the Persian King allow the return and the rebuilding (Ezra and Nehemiah) of their city and temple.

God wants to be the center of our lives and wants us to worship him as he is worshiped in his kingdom. In return for this, he gives us his love, provides for our needs and teaches us to be righteous so we can live with him in his future kingdom. He is so forgiving and loving that he made it easier to be accepted into his spirit kingdom. He sent Jesus to implement his new covenant and show us that there is a second life. Our sins are forgiven through Jesus sacrifice and our faith and acceptance of his Lordship.

Names of God

God referred to himself as, The Lord God of your fathers, the God of Abraham, Isaac and Jacob, I am I cause to be. I shall be present."

The people of Israel did not think it was proper to use the name of God, so they forbid it in their Torah. Other names for God are Yahweh, Oh that one! El Shaddai, Elyon Olamelohe Yisrael, Rock, Father, Shield ,Redeemer, Judge, Shepherd, The living God, The First and the Last, Alpha and Omega, Rider of Clouds, God of Israel. As Jesus was his son he was called by many of the name used for God.

Names of God

Elohim	God	God power and might

Yahweh	The lord	Proper name for divine person
E. Elyon	God Most High	Above all gods
El Roi	God who sees	Oversees creation & people
El Shaddai	God Almighty	God is all powerful
Yahweh Yireh	Lord will provide	God will provide our needs
Yahweh Nissi	Lord is may banner	Remember God her helping
Adonai	Lord	God alone is the head
Yahweh Ellohe Yisrael	Lord God of Israel	The God of Israel
Yahweh Shalom	Lord of peace	God gives us peace
Oedosh Yisrael	Holy one of Israel	God is morally perfect
Yahweh Saboth	Lord of Heaven's armies	God is protector
El Olam	Everlasting God	God is eternal
Yahweh Tsidkenu	Lord of righteousness	God of good behavior He can make us righteous

| Yahweh Shaah | The Lord is there | God is always present |
| Attiq Yomin | Ancient of days | God is ultimate authority |

God's appearances

God communicated with man by appearing to them (Adam and Even), Talked to man with a voice (Noah, Moses Abraham, Elisha, Joshua, the Judges and prophets.). As objects (Moses and the burning bush and a fiery cloud on top of Mount Sinai), he used angels as messengers (Abraham, Lot, Joshua before battle of Jericho and for the announcement of the birth of Jesus), and gave dreams and visions to men (Joseph, Jacob Isaiah, Jeremiah, Ezekiel, Daniel).

Event	Bible Reference
Creation	Genesis 1
Great Flood with Noah	Genesis 7
Destruction of the Tower of Babel	Genesis 11
God selects Abram as father of his people	Genesis 12
Destruction of Sodom and Gomorrah	Genesis 19

Birth of Isaac late if life of Abraham and Sarah	Genesis 21
Abraham's family is moved to Egypt through Joseph	Genesis 39
God calls Moses at the miraculously burning bush	Exodus 3
God delivers the Israelites for Egypt with 10 Plagues, including the "Pass Over."	Exodus 7
God opens the Red Sea	Exodus Genesis 114
God destroys the Egyptians as they try to cross the Red Sea.	Exodus 14
Manna (food) is sent to the People of Israel daily for 40 years	Exodus 16
God furnished water from rock for the people	Exodus 17
God appears to Moses on Mount Sinai. The people see the thundering the lightning flashes, the sound of the trumpet and the mountain smoking. God furnishes the 10 commandments.	Exodus 20
God fills the Tabernacle with His Glory	Exodus 40:34
Miraculous crossing of the Jordan	Joshua 3
Destroying the walls of Jericho	Joshua 6
Miraculous Birth of Samson and his strength	Judges 13
God aided David to defeat	I Samuel 17

Goliath	
Elijah taken to heaven in a fiery chariot	II Kings 4
Shadrach, Meshach and Abend-Nego and an angle survive the fiery furnace	Daniel 3
Supernatural placement of handwriting on the wall	Daniel 5
Daniel saved in the Lion Den	Daniel 5
Jonah and the whale (great fish)	Jonah 1
Destruction of Assyria By God	Isaiah 10
God does miracles for Elisha (Widow's oil, Shunammite's son, Deadly Stew Healing of Mammon, Floating Ax Head, Gods' Chariots and Horses, Syria's Army Blinded)	2 Kings 4 & 5
God does miracles for Elijah (Miracle of Drought, Miracle of Food, Miracle of resurrection of the Gentile son, Fire on Mount Carmel, Rain,	I Kings 17 & 18
God also prepared the way for Jesus and assured that all his prophecies concerning Jesus came true.	See Jesus section on his prophesies and the miracles of completion.
The Resurrection of Christ	Matthew 28,

	Mark 16, Luke 24, John 20

Scriptures references to support these notes

Genesis 1:1, Genesis 1:26, Isaiah 40:28, John 4:24, Romans 1:20, 1 John 1:5, Daniel 6:26, Exodus 3: 14, Exodus 34:5, 2 Corinthians 6:16, Psalms 100:5, John 3:16-18, John 4:7, 1 John 4:12, Matthew 18:12, Deuteronomy 7:8, 2 Chronicles 7:14, Revelation 1:8, John 14: 7

Gods' Attributes

All knowing (Omniscient)
Hebrews 4-13, 2 Sam 17:14, Exodus 11:1, 1 John 3:20, Matt. 23:5-7, Job 7:17-18 Job 12:13

All powerful
Romans 1:20, 1 Chronicles 16:30-33, Exodus 13:3.

All Present (Omnipresent)
Jeremiah 23:23-24, Job 24:22-25, Hebrew 13:5-6, Jeremiah 23:23-24,

Eternal
Daniel 6; 26, Ecclesiastes 3:10-11. Luke 1:32-33, Revelation 1:8, 1 Timothy 6:15-16

Faithful
Hebrews 10:22-23, 1Timothy 5:23-24, Luke 1:68-79.

Forgiving
Psalms 130:3-40, Jeremiah 50:20, 2 Chronicles 7:14 Hebrews 8:13

Good
James. 1:17, Luke 18:19, Jeremiah 32:40, 1Timothy

4:4, Psalm 145:9.
Holy
Revelation 4:8, Ezekiel 36:21, Exodus 15:11, 1Peter 1: 14, Joshua 24:19, Isaiah 6:3
Infinite
Revelation 22:13, 1Kings 8:27, Psalms 90:1, Isaiah 40:12.
Just
James 4:12, Romans 2:3, Deuteronomy 32:3.
Loving
1 John 4:7, Romans **8:38, John 3:16, Romans.05:5, Laminations 3:22.**
Merciful
1 Peter 1:3, Titus 3:5, Peter 1-3, Matthew 5:7 Romans 9:15, Luke 1:48, Titus 3:5.
Patient
2 Peter 3:9, Zechariah 1:12, Psalms 88:15.
Righteous
Psalm 71:19, Jeremiah 9:23, Psalms 145:17 Psalms 71:19, 2 Timothy 4:8.
Self-sufficient
Jeremiah 10:6 Acts 17:24, Daniel 4: 35.
Sovereign
Daniel 4:7, 2 Samuel 24:1, Acts 23-10-11, Daniel 2:21, Ephesians 1:5, Luke **2:27.**
True
Romans 15:8, John **17: 17, John 1:14, 2 Corinthians 5:6, Isaiah 65:16.**
Unchanging
Hebrew 13-8, Malachi 3:6, James 1:17, Hebrews 6:13.
God's covenants with Israel
Genesis 2: 15, Genesis 3:16, Genesis 6:18, Genesis 9: 8, Genesis **12:2, Genesis 15:18, Genesis 17:2 Exodus 19:5, Deuteronomy. 30:16, 2 Samuel 7:12,** Jeremiah **31: 31, I Kings 9:5.**

God has always communicated with man. Sometimes man doesn't listen or react to God's messages. This was quite evident after Solomon's kingdom. His people stated disobeying His covenants which forced Him to take his promised actions against them. He stopped His blessings and finally forced them from their promised land. During this time he increased his communication by sending more messages to his prophets. Later, He stopped communicating through prophets for 400years. Some people call this a time of silence.

During this time God was not silent He was communicated with man through actions rather than words. He fulfilled prophecies and returned his people to their promised land. Many of His fulfilment were for the preparations for the implementation of his new covenant. He fulfilled his prophecies concerning changing of world Empires.as He prophesized in Daniel Chapter 2. The Persians ruled Israel until 331 BC. Persia was tolerant with the Jews way of life. The Greek Alexander the Great defeated Persia. Greek world was changed when Alexander died in 323 BC. Then Greek rule was divided in to four groups; Ptolemy's took rule of Israel 321. Rule for this empire was in the city of Alexander. Until 250 B.C It should be noted that the Hebrew portion of the Bible was translated to Greek (Septuagint 250 to 130 BC.) so all men could read it and be assured that God was the one who fulfilled his prophecies when they occurred. This included prophecies of the coming Messiah which provided the proof that God sent Jesus to implement the new covenant at the end of these 400 years (Daniel Chapter 9). Rome overtook Israel 63 B.C. Rome continued to rule for several centuries

These events brought a common language (Greek) and one political (Roman) empire so that all the people in the area would be able to speak to one another and move

through different countries. These actions also prove Gods existence and power. (For further understandings see _God's preparation for the Gospel section_
The 400 year silence was broken when the Angel Gabriel told the priest Zacharias he would have a son John and later told of the birth of the Messiah. From that time on Jesus and the Holy Spirit communicated with man and God's teaching was recorded in the New Testament

Jesus

God prepared the world for Jesus. He sent prophecies concerning his life. He let the known world, be conquered by one nation. There was a universal language so the whole world could converse. Events could be recorded and passed on to the rest of the world. God brought all these events together to match with the time that Daniel's prophecy of Jesus' triumphal entry into Jerusalem.

The Israelites were expecting a Messiah. Jesus, the Messiah, came to the Lord's people near the end of their time and starting of the time of the Gentiles. This was done because Jesus was to be a light to the Gentiles. After the time of the Gentiles, he will return to a New Israel.

God wanted us to know him and his will for us. He sent Jesus, his only son, as an example in an earthly body. He did it in a way that would prove Jesus was from God. He sent many prophecies about Jesus to his believers for them to record. Some of these were Born of a virgin **(Isaiah 7:14)** in the city of Bethlehem **(Micah 5: 2)** even though his parents lived elsewhere. The wise men came to his birth due to prophecy by way of a special star. He lived in Egypt **(Hosea 11: 1)** and Nazareth **(Matthew 2: 23)**. He was of the family of King David **(Isaiah 9: 6)**. The coming of his public life would be announced. **(Isaiah 40:3, Malachi 3: 1**. His mission would include the Gentiles **(Isaiah 42: 1)**. He would teach by Parables **(Psalms 78: 2)**. He would have a triumphal entry into Jerusalem **(Zechariah 9: 9)**. He would be crucified **(Isaiah 53, Psalms 22** for our sins. After 3 days he would be resurrected **(Matthew 12: 40)** to prove there is a life after death for those who have faith in him. All these prophecies were fulfilled during his life and witnessed to by many people. The Gospels (Matthew, Mark Luke and John) in the New Testament is devoted to the Life of Christ. See them for more description of Christ.

Jesus trained disciples to spread the Gospel. He sent them to make other disciples to carry the Gospel throughout the world. **(Matthew 28:18)**. He foretold of a second coming when he would return again. **(Matthew 25: 31)**

Jesus proved he was the promised Messiah. He did this by living the life prophesied by God's prophets. He showed us the true nature of God. He gave better understanding of what God's will was for man.

One of the prophecies was, he would be a light to the Gentiles and the Word of God would be taken to the ends of the earth. The giving of the great commission is fulfilling this prophecy.

In God's changing world, there were less people with access to animals for sacrifice. God was turning the judgment of man over to Jesus. God now accepts Jesus' blood as a sacrifice for all sin. If we have faith in Jesus and his sacrifice, and repent, our sins forgiven.

Jesus told us that God would send the Holy Spirit to place God's law and will in our hearts. With our hearts connected to God we now can govern ourselves in Gods will and prepare ourselves for his kingdom. If we sin, we may go directly to God and Jesus for our forgiveness. The resurrection and ascension of Jesus demonstrated the future of the saints at the 2nd coming of Jesus.

The apostle Paul describes Jesus in **Colossians 1:15** He is the image of the invisible God, the first born over all creation. For he created all things that are in heaven and that are on earth, visible and invisible, whether thrones or dominions or principalities or powers, All things were created through him and for him. And he is before all things and in him all things consist. And he is the head of the body, the church, who is the beginning, the firstborn from the dead, that in all things he may have the preeminence. For it pleased the father, that in Him all the fullness should dwell, and by him to reconcile all things to himself, by him, whether things on earth or things in heaven, having made peace through the blood of his cross. And you, who once were alienated and enemies in you mind by wicked works, yet now He has reconciled in the body of his flesh through death to present you holy, and blameless, and irreproachable in His sight.

Names of Jesus

Jesus was his personal name.
Other names for Jesus are: The Messiah (Hebrew) or The Christ (Greek), meaning the Anointed One of God

to redeem the rule of the world. The Son of God (name used for his deity) God called him "BELOVED SON, KING OF KINGS, EMMANUEL, SAVIOR". In Isaiah 9 v 6 God told Isaiah His name will be called Wonderful, Counselor, Mighty God, Everlasting Father, and Prince of Peace.

Other names were. The Son of God (name used for his deity), Everlasting Father, Price of Peace, Redeemer, Wonderful Counselor, Mighty God, Faithful Witness, Deliver, The Great high Priest, The Captain of our Salvation. The Alpha and the Omega, First and the Last or beginning and the end, Our Advocate, The Son of God, The son of Man. The Holy one of God, Only Begotten Son, Lord of All, Lord of Glory, Lord of Kings Prince of Life, Prince of Peace, The Son of David. The Branch of Root of David. Shiloh, Star,

Jesus named himself (as noted mainly in John). I am the Truth, I am the Way, I am the door, I am the Bread of Life, I am the life, and I am the resurrection.

Jesus is the Son of God.

Before he was conceived an angel told Mary that she was well favored by God and that she would bear a child sent by God. The Holy one sent by God will be called the Son of God and be named Jesus. (Luke1:35)

At Jesus baptism, the Holy Spirit in a bodily form, landed on him like a dove and a voice from heaven said "You are my dearly loved Son, and you bring me great joy (Luke 3:21). John the Baptist testified that Jesus was the son of God. He was told earlier to baptize, in water, and the one that the Holy Spirit came down on would baptize with the Holy Spirit and he was the Son of God.

(John 1:33-34)

When Jesus asked his disciples who do you say that I am? Peter with the aid of the Holy Spirit said "You are the Messiah sent from God. Jesus' disciples knew he was the Messiah and the son of God. (Luke 9:18) Jesus took Peter, John and James to pray and Moses and Elijah appeared and Jesus clothes were transfigured to a dazzling white. A voice came from the cloud and said "This is my son, my chosen one. Listen to him. (Mathew 17:5 & Luke 9:35)

Jesus claims his son ship to God and let it be known that he was one with the father (God). He proved this by the work he did in the Fathers' name. He tells that the works he does are from the father. When you believe his works then you may know and believe that the Father is in him, and he is in the Father. He and the Father are one. (John 10:25-30).

Jesus proved he was the son of God because he fulfilled prophesies that were put in scriptures telling what would happen to the messiah. He also told us he was the Messiah and that he was sent by God (John 7:28). Jesus fulfilled the prophecy of bring the new covenant of salvation to men through his sacrifice on the cross (*See section dealing with major Prophecies about Jesus.*) The Roman officer and the other soldiers at the crucifixion after watching Jesus, having an earthquake, and other things that were done, feared exceedingly, said "truly this man was the Son of God."

Jesus also showed that he was one with the father because he did miracles in the name of the father. He healed people, raised people from the dead, multiplied food and controlled the weather. *(See section on Miracles performed by Jesus)* A prophesized Son of God would be superior to others. Jesus is superior to prophets and angels, Moses and the Priesthood of Aaron. (Hebrews 1-7)

After Jesus was sacrificed, bringing the new salvation, he was resurrected to prove he was giving us a way to eternal life with the father. After being with his father he returned to let us know that he was given all authority in heaven and earth. (Matthew 28:18) Jesus informed us that he was going to sit at the right hand of the Father and he would return on the clouds of heaven. When this happens there will be no doubt that he is the Son of God. (*Mathew 24:30 Jesus also called himself the Son of man*)

Jesus' teaching Parables (extended Metaphors)

Parables are stories or sayings that had double meanings. They are stories to illustrate truths. They tell truths in such a way that those who believed would understand and others would not. Jesus told many metaphors and Parables to explain God's will and plans for us through Jesus. Jesus said (Mark 4:11) "To you (disciples) it has been given to know the mystery of the kingdom of God; but to those who are outside, all things come in parables, Lest they should turn, and their sins be forgiven them."

Parable of the Sower   Matt. 13: 1-23
Mark4: 1, Luke 8: 4
This tells of the reception of the Gospel. Some will not listen and some will accept it but soon disregard it. Some will hold on in various degrees and some to the end.

Tares and the Net　　　　　　　Matt. 13: 24,
Even with The Gospel there will be good and evil to the end. God will separate the Good to Heaven and evil to Hell. (Explanation of the parable Matt 13:36)

Mustard seed and the Leaven　　Matt.13: 31, Mark 4:30, Luke 13: 18
Christ's kingdom has a small beginning and later become large. It is worth giving up everything even life to obtain kingdom of heaven.

Land Owner and his vineyard　　Matt. 21: 33, Mark 12:1, Luke 20: 9
Land Owner (God) sent sons to his vineyard and they were killed. Aimed at Israel, The kingdom would be taken away and given to others bearing the fruits of it. Christ is the rejected corner stone.

Parable of the marriage Feast　　Matthew 22:2
It is similar meaning as the Land Owner parable. The King wants to have a wedding feast and send invitations to the guests and they ignore it and kill some of the servants. He responds and cast them into outer darkness. Many called but few are chosen. Some think it also was telling of the chosen people betrayal of God so he was going to destroy their kingdom and go else ware to get guests for his kingdom

Growing seed　　　　　　　　　Mark 4: 26
It is a description on the kingdom using a planting and harvesting example.

Rich man and Lazarus　　　　　Luke 16: 19
It shows the gulf between Heaven and Hell and your choices, which lead to the respective place.

The Rich Fool   Luke 12:16
It is the story of a man who was laying up his treasures on earth and not toward God then he was to die before he could use them. This show you need to be more concerned about God and not the enjoyment of this life.

Crucifixion

Some people ask "Why did Jesus have to be crucified?" It seems this was a harsh thing to do to one's son.

God wanted us to love and believe in him, so He sent Jesus to implement His Good News covenant (See the Gospel section for more information). This covenant saves us in the world through atonement for sin by the blood of Jesus. This atonement allows us to be forgiven. This proves that God loved us enough to sacrifice Jesus.

God's law required that nearly everything be cleansed with blood and without the shedding of blood there is no forgiveness. Jesus said; "This is my blood of the covenant, which is poured out for many for the forgiveness of sins. Sins and lawless acts I will remember no more."
Jesus set aside the first sacrifices and established the second in the new covenant. We have been made holy through the sacrifice of the body of Jesus Christ.
When, we are forgiven and repent, we are on the road to learning about God's righteousness plan and his will for us. We should be glad that God gave us this tool to learn his righteousness.

God wanted us to know that he was sending Jesus to implement his Good News plan. He told his prophets in advance about many of the upcoming events of Jesus life. Many of them were associated with the crucifixion. In doing this we have proof God sent Jesus.

There were over 30 prophecies concerning the events of the crucifixion. They tell how Jesus would suffer at the hands of man before crucifixion; His pain during it, His last words and how and why His atoning sacrifice was for the forgiveness of sin. *(See the prophecies section for these prophecies.)*

Events of the crucifixion

This is my understanding of the trial and crucifixion.

Even from the start of His arrest Jesus was concerned about making sure that his life would be lived as God had planned. It stared out by being forsaken by Judas for 30 pc. of silver. He told the religious leaders "This has all taken place that the writings of the prophets might be fulfilled."

At the time of the arrest a disciple cut off the ear of a servant of the high priest. Jesus healed the ear and was taken prisoner. Then all the disciples deserted him and fled.

Before the Sanhedrin

The High priest asked Jesus was the messiah, son of God. Jesus admitted he was God's Messiah.

Then the high priest declared Jesus spoke blasphemy and asks the gathering what they though. They answered "He is worth of death." Then they spit in his face, blindfolded him and struck him with their fists.

While this was going on Peter disowned knowing Jesus three times just as Jesus said. "Before the rooster crows, you will disown me three times." And he went outside and wept bitterly

Early in the morning, they took him to Governor Pilate to have him killed as they had planned for some time.

Before Pilate

Very early in the morning the chief priest, elders and the whole Sanhedrin bound Jesus and handed him over to Pilate. The chief priest accuses Jesus of many things but, Jesus made no reply. Because he made no reply, Pilate told Jesus that he had authority over his life. Jesus still didn't answer the charges of the chief priest. However, He explained that his kingdom is not of this world and he was born to testify to the truth. Everyone on the side of truth listens to me. Pilate then knew it was a religious argument and found no fault with Jesus. From then on, Pilate tried to set Jesus free. The Jewish leaders kept trying to have Jesus crucified. They told him he was creating problems in Galilee and now in Judea. Upon Pilate finding out that Jesus was from Galilee he tried to have Herod take the responsibility for this trial.

Jesus was sent to Herod who was in Jerusalem. Herod questioned Jesus but Jesus remained silent. Herod had his soldiers ridicule and mock him. Dressing him in an elegant robe then sent him back to Pilate. He called the Chief priest, the rulers and the people and told them he found no basis for their charges against him and he released him and sent him back to Pilate.

Pilate then called together the chief priest, the rulers and the people. He told them that he or Herod could not find Jesus guilty worthy of death so he would punish him and then release him.

It was the custom at the Feast to release a prisoner whom the people requested.
The crowd came up and asked Pilate to do for them what he usually did. Pilate asked "Do you want me to release to you the king of the Jews?" The chief priests stirred up the crowd to have Pilate release Barabbas instead and cried to "crucify Jesus"

Wanting to satisfy the crowd, Pilate released Barabbas to them. He had Jesus flogged, and handed him over to be crucified.

The soldiers led Jesus away to the palace (that is, the Praetorium) and called the whole company of soldiers. They mocked him as king of the Jews. They made a crown of thorns put it on his head and pressed to head. They flogged (Scrooged) and struck him on his face and head with a staff and spit on him. It is believe flogging was done in the manner that the Romans used at the time of crucifixion, in their horrible whipping with flagrum. It was one of the most feared dreaded instruments of the time. It can cause rib facture, bruising of the lungs, bleeding in chest cavity with a lot of blood loss. The constant hitting of Jesus face made him unrecognizable.

Crucifixion

By the time He arrived at Calvary, Jesus was in exquisite pain, struggling to breathe and suffering from blood and fluid loss. Jesus fell several times on the way and to keep him alive for the crucifixion they had Simon of Cyrene help carry the crosspiece. His body, mental state, and hydration must have already brought him close to death.

On the way to the cross, a large number of people followed him who mourned and wailed for Him. Jesus told them not to mourn for him. He warned them they and their children were also going to have bad times.

At the third hour (9:00 AM present time system) they arrived at the place called Golgotha. They offered him wine mixed with Myrrh but he refused it.

The solders mounted him on a cross. They drove nails through his hands on the cross beam. And then his feet were nailed below on the center beam. This in itself would be horribly painful. They them dropped the cross in a hole so it would stand up right. This added more pain and cause it harder to breath. Jesus said, "Father, forgive them, for they do not know what they are doing.

They crucified him with two other criminals' one on each side with Jesus in the middle. Pilate had a notice prepared and fastened to the cross. It read **"JESUS OF NAZARETH, THE KING OF THE JEWS"**. It was written in Aramaic, Latin and Greek. The Chief priest did not want the sign to say King of the Jews. He wanted to say this man claimed to be the King of the

Jew. Pilate said he would not change it "what I have written, I have written".

When the soldiers crucified Jesus, they took his clothes, dividing them into four shares. However, the undergarment was seamless, woven in one piece from top to bottom. They decided to determine the ownership by tossing lots. This happened that the scripture might be fulfilled which said "they divided my garments among them and cast lots for my clothing."

In an hour or so, People started passing by and shouting abuse, shaking their heads in mockery. They said such things as: "You can destroy the Temple and build it again in three days, Can You? "He saved others let him save himself if he is the Christ of God, the chosen one". The chief priest and the teachers mocked him among themselves. "He saved others, "they said "but he can't save himself "Let this Christ, the King of Israel, come down now from the cross, that we may see and believe." Even the soldiers mocked him. They offered him a drink of sour wine and called out to him "If you are the King of the Jews, save yourself?"

Jesus looked down and saw his mother and his beloved disciple. He wanted his mother to be taken care of after he was gone. So he said "Dear woman, here is your son" indicting he was to take care of her. And he told the disciple "Here is your mother". From then on the disciple took her into his home.

Around noon, darkness came over the whole land for three hours. During this time Jesus cried out in a loud voice *"Eloi, Eloi, lama sabachthani?"*—which means, "My God, my God, why have you forsaken me?" This is a reminder of Psalm 22 where there were prophecies concerning Jesus's crucifixion.

When Jesus realizes the end of his sacrifice is near completion. He says "I'm Thirsty". He was given some wine vinegar. . After the drink He said "It is finished" and bowed his head and gave up his spirit. At that moment the curtain of the temple was torn from top to bottom. The earth shook and the rocks split. Tombs broke open and the bodies of many holy people who had died were raised to life. They came out of the tombs, and after Jesus' resurrection they went into the holy city and appeared to many people.

When the centurion and those with him who were guarding Jesus saw the earthquake and all that had happened, they were terrified, and exclaimed, "Surely he was the Son of God!"

It was the day of preparation and the next day was to be a special Sabbath. Jewish law forbids a body to be left on the crosses during the Sabbath so they asked Pilate to have the legs broken and the bodies removed.

The soldier broke the legs of the criminals. When they came to Jesus he was already dead so they didn't break his legs to assure he was dead, one of the soldiers pierce Jesus' side with a spear, bringing a sudden flow of blood and water. This fulfilled the scriptures that said "Not one of his bones will be broken" and, "they will look on the one they have pierced.

As evening approached, Joseph of Arimathea, a prominent member of the Council, who had become a disciple of Jesus went boldly to Pilate and asked for Jesus's body. When Pilate found out that Jesus was dead he gave the body to Joseph. He was accompanied by Nicodemus, the man who earlier had visited Jesus at night. Nicodemus brought a mixture of myrrh and aloes, about seventy-five pounds. Taking Jesus' body, the two of them wrapped it, with spices, in strips of linen. This was in accordance with Jewish burial customs.

At the place where Jesus was crucified, there was a garden, and in the garden a new tomb, in which no one had ever been laid. Because it was the Jewish day of Preparation and since the tomb was nearby, they laid Jesus there. Then he rolled a stone against the entrance of the tomb.
The women who had come with Jesus from Galilee followed Joseph and saw the tomb and how his body was laid in it. Then they went home and prepared spices and perfumes. But they rested in obedience of the Sabbath commandment.

After the preparation Day, the Chief Priest and Pharisees went to Pilate and told him that Jesus said he would rise again in three days. They asked him to guard the tomb during this time because his disciples may come and steal the body and tell the people that he was raised from the dead. This would make the situation worse than it was before.

As a result, Pilate ordered them to take a guard and secure the body for three days. So they went and made the tomb secure by putting a seal on the stone and posting the guard.

The crucifixion of Christ was done as predicted by the prophets 400 years before the occurrence. Jesus reminded them of these prophecies when he quoted the first line of Psalm 22." My God, My God, why have you forsaken me?" This psalm tells of his crucifixion with, pain, trust, deliverance and praise of the Lord. It also tells of the Lord's future ruling of the nations. Jesus prayed to God as his father. He said" Father forgive them for they know not what they do". He asked God to forgive their sin as he was sacrificed for our sins. He told the sinner alongside of him on the cross that his sins were forgiven when he said" today thou shall be with me in paradise". Knowing this, acknowledges his relation with God. He acknowledged the completion of the sacrifice and forgiveness of sin when he said "Father (Jesus was the Son of God) into your hand I commit my spirit".

The detailed description of the arrest, crucifixion and death of Jesus are found in the following book of the Bible.

Matthew Chapters 26 through 27:56-61,

Mark   Chapters 14:43 through 15:47

Luke   Chapters 22:47 through 23:49-56

John   Chapters 18 through 19:42

Following are the main scriptures associated with the prophesized crucifixion. Isaiah 52:13-53:12 Psalms 22:1-31.

Resurrection

The resurrection of Christ is very significant to all souls and a victory for believers. It proves that we will not remain dead. We will be resurrected to an eternal life. It also proves that Jesus is the Messiah, Son of God, and God has power of resurrection. Jesus' resurrection was God's way of letting us know that if we live in accordance to His New Covenant, we will be resurrected. Jesus' resurrection proves God's love and desire for us to be in his kingdom.

God sent prophecies concerning the resurrection to prove his involvement. Some of them were: Jesus' resurrection would occur three days after Jesus' sacrificial death. He would not be recognized because of his beating. God told about how he would later resurrect man as he did Jesus. Jesus would be a light to the world. Seeing God's power over death and how he fulfilled prophecies proves how much God loves us. It also gives us assurance of our belief and knowing we can now look forwards to God's promises. *(You can find these prophecies and their fulfilment in the prophecies list section.)*

After the resurrection, God gave us a glance of what a spiritual body might be like. He sent angels, which had the appearance of men. They gleamed like lightning and dressed in white robes. Jesus resurrected body also showed us that some traces of his physical body were in his spiritual body. His physical characteristics were noticeable in his spiritual body. He was recognized by his voice, nail holes in his hands and feet. After returning from his father, He was easily recognized by

his apostles.
Some other astounding facts were; Jesus also talked and ate with his disciples. He had the ability to appear from one place to another with no effect on the surroundings. This and God's promise for us to be in his kingdom, gives us insight and assurance that our present bodies will be changed to the imperishable resurrected bodies in his heaven, where they will never perish, spoil or fade.
Events of the Resurrection

This is my understanding of the scriptural events which occurred in our Lords' resurrection.
The Sabbath was now over and it was early in the morning of the 1st day of the week. There was a violent earthquake, for an angel of the Lord came down from heaven and, going to the tomb, rolled back the stone and sat on it. His appearance was like lightning, and his clothes were white as snow. The guards at the tomb were so afraid of the angel that they shook and became like dead men. Later, some of the guards went to the chief priest and reported what happened. The chief priest and the elders devised a plan to rebuke the resurrection. They gave the soldiers a large sum of money telling them. "You are to say, his disciples came during the nights and stole him way. If this report gets to the governor, we will satisfy him and keep you out of trouble. The guard didn't want to get in trouble so they took the money and did as instructed. This account of deception was widely circulated among the Jews.

Soon after Jesus' resurrection, many holy dead people came out of the tombs, and went into the Holy City and appeared to many people. Their resurrection gives us further hope for our resurrection.
Mary Magdalene, Mary the mother of James, and

Salome bought spices so that they might go to anoint Jesus' body for a proper burial. They went to the tomb and saw that the large stone had been rolled way. Upon entering the tomb, they were alarmed to see a young man siting dressed in a white robe, don't be alarmed," he said. "You are looking for Jesus the Nazarene, who was crucified. He has risen! He is not here! Remember how he told you, while he was still with you in Galilee: 'The Son of Man must be delivered into the hands of sinful men, be crucified and on the third day be raised again." Then they remembered his words.

There were two men in clothes that gleamed like lightning beside them. The women bowed down with their faces to them. Their appearance seems to be that of angels. Mary turned and saw Jesus standing there but did not recognize him. He said to her "Mary" Then she recognized his voice called him teacher. Jesus told her "Do not hold on to me, for I have not yet returned to the Father. Go instead to my brothers and tell them, "I am returning to my Father and your Father, to my God and your God". So the women hurried away from the tomb, afraid yet filled with joy, and ran to tell his disciples.

Upon arriving where the disciples were, the women told Simon Peter and the other disciples what happened in the tomb. The disciple s didn't believe the women, because their words seemed to be nonsense. However, Peter and another disciple got up and ran to the tomb. When Peter went in he saw the burial cloth that had been around Jesus' head. The cloth was folded up by itself, separate from the linen. The other disciple, who had reached the tomb, first, also went inside. He saw and believed. They still did not understand from Scripture that Jesus had to rise from the dead.

During the day, Cleopas and another disciple were on their way to a village near Jerusalem. They were discussing what had happened to Jesus. Jesus appeared and walked with them. He asked about what they were talking about. They didn't recognize him so they told him about what happened to their prophet powerful in word and deeds before God and all the people. They also told him how the chief priests and rulers handed him over to be crucified and now after three days women had gone to the tomb and said he had risen but, he was not found there. Jesus responded and said "How foolish you are, and how slow of heart to believe all that the prophets have spoken! Did not the Christ have to suffer these things and then enter his glory?"
The disciples neared the city and felt good with Jesus, so they asked him to stay with them. They started to eat and Jesus took bread gave thanks, broke it and began to give it to them. Then their eyes were opened and they recognized him, and he disappeared from their sight. They were amazed that their hearts burned while he talked and opened the scripture. They immediately returned to Jerusalem to tell the other disciples. Saying "It is true, the Lord has risen and has appeared to Simon." That evening while they were still talking about this, Jesus himself stood among them and said to them, "Peace be with you." "Why are you troubled, and why do doubts rise in your minds? Look at my hands and my feet. It is I myself! Touch me and see; a ghost does not have flesh and bones, as you see I have." He said to them, "This is what I told you while I was still with you: Everything must be fulfilled that is written about me in the Law of Moses, the Prophets and the Psalms." Then he opened their minds so they could understand the Scriptures. He told them, "This is what is written: The Christ will suffer and rise from the dead on the third day,

and repentance and forgiveness of sins will be preached in his name to all nations, beginning at Jerusalem. You are witnesses of these things.

Thomas one of the disciples was not at the evening meeting, so he didn't receive the proof that Jesus was alive and was a doubter. A week later his disciples were in the house again and Thomas was with them. Though the doors were locked, Jesus came and stood among them and said, "Peace be with you!" Then he said to Thomas, "Put your finger here; see my hands. Reach out your hand and put it into my side. Stop doubting and believe." Thomas said to him, "My Lord and my God!" Then Jesus told him, "Because you have seen me, you have believed; blessed are those who have not seen and yet have believed."

.Eight of Jesus' disciples decided to go fishing. They went out in a boat but could not catch any fish. Jesus appeared on shore and asked them if they had caught any fish. They answered no. Jesus then told them to, "Throw your net on the right side of the boat and you will find some."
When they did, they had so many fish they could not haul in all the fish.
One of the disciples' remembered that Jesus had done this before. He told Peter and Peter put on his clothes and swam to see Jesus. Jesus ate breakfast with them. This was the third time Jesus met with his disciples.
.

When Jesus met Mary he asked her to tell his disciples to go to Galilee. He later met with them and told them "All authority in heaven and on earth has been given to me. Therefore, go and make disciples of all nations, baptizing them in the name of the Father and of the Son and of the Holy Spirit, and teaching them to obey everything I have commanded you. And surely I am with you always, to the very end of the age."

On one occasion, while he was eating with them, he gave them this command: "Do not leave Jerusalem, but wait for the gift my Father promised. John baptized with water, but in a few days you will be baptized with the Holy Spirit. You will receive power when the Holy Spirit comes on you; and you will be my witnesses in Jerusalem, and in all Judea and Samaria, and to the ends of the earth. "When he had led them out to the vicinity of Bethany, he lifted up his hands and blessed them. He said to them: "It is not for you to know the times or dates the Father has set by his own authority. But you will receive power when the Holy Spirit comes on you; and you will be my witnesses in Jerusalem, and in all Judea and Samaria, and to the ends of the earth. "In in a newer version the Gospel of Mark He said. "Go into all the world and preach the good news to all creation. Whoever believes and is baptized will be saved, but whoever does not believe will be condemned. And these signs will accompany those who believe: In my name they will drive out demons; they will speak in new tongues; they will pick up snakes with their hands; and when they drink deadly poison, it will not hurt them at all; they will place their hands on sick people, and they will get well." As this was not in the earlier version its authenticity may be questioned. However, it may have been added to later revisions. In any case, we can see

the truths of the statement. The believers had the signs mentioned. They drove out demons, spoke in new tongues, not harmed by poisonous snakes (Paul), and healed sick people.
After he said this to the disciples, He was taken up to heaven.

They were looking intently up into the sky as he was going, when suddenly two men dressed in white stood beside them. "Men of Galilee," they said, "why do you stand here looking into the sky? This same Jesus, who has been taken from you into heaven, will come back in the same way you have seen him go into heaven.

Jesus spent 40 days of presenting himself to over 500 people, so they would be witnesses of his resurrection. It was reported that many of witnesses lived a full life while continuing their witnessing his resurrection. During this time he also gave his disciples instruction on how to implement the New Covenant.

After these 40 days Jesus went to sit at the right hand of his Heavenly Father. Forty nine days after the Passover He sent the Holy Spirit to his disciples as he had promised. This completed the implementation of the New Covent (Good News/ Gospel).

Now we all have God's promise. "I will put my law in their minds and write it on their hearts. I will be their God, and they will be my people. No longer will a man teach his neighbor, or a man his brother, saying, 'Know the LORD,' because they will all know me, from the least of them to the greatest," declares the LORD. "For I will forgive their wickedness and will remember their sins no more."

The forty ninth week after the Passover is very significant. It is the celebration of the giving of God's laws (Tora) during their exodus for Egypt. . It was called the festival of Shavuot or Pentecost. It appears that God sent the Holy Spirit on this anniversary date because he was replacing his teaching method so all men can know him and have salvation which leads to His eternal kingdom. It is now a time, where we can know and love God and be reconciled to God through Jesus' atonement blood for of sins, be forgiven and have salvation for our eternal life.

For further information concerning the "New Covenant see the Gospel- Good News section.

Scriptures references to support these notes

The events of the Resurrection are found in the following scriptures. **Matthew 28:1-15, Mark 16:1-13, Luke 24:1-53,John 20:1through 21:14 ,Acts. 1:4-11, 2:1-13**.

Jesus's raised the dead. **Matthew 9:18-26, Mark 5:21-24, 35-43, 5:22-43, Luke 8:41-56.Hebrews 8:8-Titus 3:3-7 ,1 Peter 1:51-52   Corinthians 15:6-1 Corinthians 15: 51-52   1 Peter 1:3 Acts 1:7-11 1 Thessalonians 4:13-18**

God sent several prophecies concerning the resurrection. The fulfillment of these prophecies lets us see how God works for our love. The prophecies were: Jesus would be resurrected 3 days after his sacrificial death; He would not be recognized because of his beating. He also told about how he would also later resurrect man; He would send the Holy Spirit to man: Jesus would be a light to the world. *(You can find these prophecies and heir fulfilment in the prophecies section.)*

There are many proofs of Jesus' death and resurrection. The apostles and others were witness who spread the news of the resurrection and it was accepted. Christians believed in the resurrection so strong that they give up their lives rather than their belief. Most of them could have just renounced their belief and they would have lived. Instead they remained faithful and died horrible deaths at the hands of the Romans in the colosseum and other places. This fight of ideals continued to such an extent that the Romans destroyed the Jewish homeland (prophesized), thinking that it would stop the uproars in their society.

The Christian religion is the only religion where its founder, transcended death and promises the same for his believer. Other religions founders ended in their death and was not resurrected.

Jesus' Deity and Humanity
Ever since Jesus returned to his father in heaven, skeptics and non-believers questioned his humanity and deity. Some say he was a prophet and not a deified being of God. Some question in his humanity did he have the same emotion, thoughts and the body like ours.
When I hear these opinions, I feel that these people are not reading or understanding Jesus as explained in God's

historical Bible. The Gospels and the epistles tell about Jesus and how he was a human being with the same deity as his father.

Jesus had a human mother and a spiritual father. This made him different than us in one respect. However, he set aside his deity and became a man. He did this to accomplish his goal of understanding man and serving man by presenting God's promised new covenant. With this new covenant we all will have the ability to have an eternal life with him in his kingdom.

When you read the scriptures you see his humanity. They recorded his emotions of Anger, Grief, Affection, Wept, Grew weary, Tempted, and felt Anguish.

His physical traits can be seen when you read the Gospels. He was born and grew strong. Jesus had to walk from place to place and talk to people. He needed sleep and eat to survive. He learned the occupation of a carpenter. He faced being hungry, thirsty, suffered pain and death.

He grew in wisdom and stature in favor with God and men. Men were amazed at his understanding and answers to situations.

When his human trials were so strong, he would pray to his father for aid in facing his prophesied life. This shows how strong his humanity was. When you look at this information there is no doubt Jesus lived a human life.

Deity

God is the ruler of the universe, eternal, creator and a supreme being who is worshiped and adorned. A deity is the estate of rank of a God. That has the character and nature of a supreme being.

To assure we see Jesus' deity, we need to look for his

eternal life, assuring he is a supreme being that is worshipped and adorned.

Scripture tells us that he was around before man and he is still alive. Having faith in him, we can see that the resurrection further proves he is Eternal. A final proof of this is foretold in scripture when we see his return to earth as the supreme ruler.

While Jesus was on earth as a man, he gave us evidences that he was a Supreme Being. He lived the foretold life, taught us everlasting truths, performed miracles, and predicted future events.

God gave Jesus Authority over man. We will see further examples of this when he judges the living and the dead upon his return to earth.

Jesus is Adorned and Worshiped every day by Christians. Worshipers are found in all the countries on earth.

With this information we can see Jesus' deity. However, some people may need additional information for their understanding. Following are some additional facts.

God told his prophets that he was going to send his Messiah (Jesus) four hundred years in advance of the event. He describes the future events of Jesus' life in great detail so that we would know that Jesus was His Messiah. (See Prophecies concerning Jesus in Prophecy section.)

Jesus came and fulfilled these prophecies proving he was the messiah and sent by God. He performed miracles which man cannot do. He instantly healed people, drove (exorcism) out demons, calmed storms, walked on water and raised people from the dead (See the Miracles Section).

Twice, with witnesses, God proclaimed that Jesus was

his son and he was proud of him (Jesus' Baptism and the transfiguration).
Jesus is God's eternal son and appointed heir. Sons usually have the characteristics of the father. Some of the characteristics are love (*He gave his life so we could have salvation*), righteousness (*he taught righteousness throughout his ministry*) being eternal (*he was resurrected and continues a spirit life.*). Men worship him (*Christians*). He prophesized the destruction of the Israelites Temple *(destroyed in 70 A.D.)*.
The future will provide much more proof of His Deity. Prophecies will come about concerning the rapture of the saints, Jesus returns with power and great glory to rule the earth, his judgement of the living and the dead, and his ruling during the millennium.

Scriptures that support Jesus Deity

Hebrews 1:1-4 , Colossians 2:9-10, Psalms 110:1-4,Hebrews 5:7-10, Jerimiah 31:31-34, John 6:38-40. John 2:11, Acts 10:42, Philippians **2:5-11, John 1:1-3, John 20:30-31, Collations 2:9-10, John 1:14, Matthew 11:4-5, John 5:20, Revelations 12:10, John 17:2-3 Matthew 28:18-19,** Hebrews **4:14-16, and Revelations 12:10**

Humanity

God had several reasons for sending Jesus to us as a human. In his love he was sending his new covenant for our salvation. As part of this, he had to have his son become a human sacrifice for our sins and be reconciled to Him.

As Jesus was going to be His Messiah, he wanted him to have an understanding of the ways of man, so he could become an excellent judge of man when he returns to earth as our Lord.

Jesus was born of a human mother and grew up with humans and learned their ways. During his life he grew up emotionally and physically. He gained wisdom and stature in favor with God and man. He amazed men and grew in wisdom and stature. He used these attribute and those from his father he when he performed his ministry, He had the emotions like men. He walked, became hungry and thirsty, slept and became angry. He was affectionate concerning others. He was tempted, had anguish faced humility, suffered pain and died.

Following are Scriptures that reflect his humanity.

Luke 1:34-35, Hebrews 2:14-15, Luke 2:5-6, Luke 2:40-52, Luke 4:22, Matthew 26:39,

Human emotions
Mark 3:5-6 anger, Luke 4:1-3 tempted, Luke 22:41 anguish, **Luke 19:41, John 21: loved. Matthew 4:2-3 hungry. John 19:28 thirsty, John 4:6 tired, Matthew 8:24 sleeping, John 19:1-3 (suffered) flogged, and Luke 23:44 Died breathed his last**

Jesus' Apostles (Messenger)

Mathew 10:2, Mark 3: 13, Luke 6; 14, Acts 1: 13

Name, Occupation   Death
(Bible and other records)

1. **Simon named Peter**, fisherman, Crucified Upside down Rome
2. **Andrew** (Peter's brother), fisherman, Crucified in

Greece

3. **James (Son of Zebedee)**, fisherman, Beheaded

4. **John (the brother of James)**, fisherman, John dies 97AD

5. **Philip from Bethsaida**, Martyred in Turkey

6. **Bartholomew** from Cana, Crucified Armenia

7. **Matthew**, Tax collector, unknown

8. **Thomas**, from Galilee, Martyred in India

9. **James (son of Alphaeus)**, The younger, Beheaded

10. **Thaddaeus / Judas** (son of James Jude), Martyred in Persia

11. **Simon** (the Canaanite) Zealot,, Martyred in Persia

12 **Judas Iscariot,** betrayer, Hung himself

Matthias Replacement for Judas (Acts 1:26)

Paul (Saul), Pharisee, Beheaded in Rome

Just before Jesus died he warned the disciples "they will put some of you to death

Apostolic Age

Jesus gave the apostles the great commission.

Matthew 28:19 Therefore go and make disciples of all nations, baptizing them in the name of the Father and of the Son and of the Holy Spirit, and teaching them to obey everything I have commanded you. And surely I am with you always, to the very end of the age."

The apostles went out into all the nations to fulfill Jesus' commission. This was done from 30 AD to 101AD. Following are some of the major events timing of this period.

Date (AD) - Event

30AD Holy Spirit fills the faithful at Pentecost. Peter Preaches (Acts 2:1)

32AD Stephen stoned to death Acts 7:1

Paul (Saul) meets the risen Christ on the read to Damascus and converts him. Acts 9:1

43AD Paul visits Antioch Acts 13:14

47AD Paul's first missionary trip

48/53AD Galatians was written

48AD Peter in Antioch Gal 2:11-16

49AD Apostolic Council in Jerusalem Acts 5:1

50AD Paul's second missionary journey Acts 15:36

51/52AD, The book of 1& 2 Thessalonians

53AD Paul's third missionary journey Acts. 18:23

54/56AD Paul writes the books of 1&2 Corinthians

55/57AD Paul writes the book of Romans

56AD Paul is arrested and imprisoned Acts 21:-28

60AD Epistle of James is written

The books of Philemon, Luke, Colossians and Ephesians were written during the rest of the 60's Matthew and Hebrews were written.

61AD Acts Colossians and Philippians was written

62AD The books of Mark, 1Timothy and Titus were written
      Paul was freed, visits Macedonia and Crete
      James is martyred
      Peter went to Rome

63AD Paul was taken to Rome.
I Peter was written

64AD Peter and Paul were Martyred

63/66AD The books of 2 Timothy, Titus and 2 Peter were written

60-70AD   The book of Jude was written. The book of John was written between 66 and 68AD

70 AD   Jerusalem was destroyed.

80-90AD   The book of Revelation, John 1, 2 and 3, were written

97AD   The Last apostle (John dies) ending the age of the apostles.

Jesus' Family

Father   Joseph
Mother   Virgin Mary
Brothers   James, Joses, Jude and Simon
Sisters   Salome and Mary

Genealogy of Jesus (Names are listed in order of birth.)Genesis 5,1 Adam, Seth, Enosh, Kenan, Mahalalel, Jared, Enoch, Methuselah, Lamech, Noah, Shem, Arphaxad, Shelab, Eber, Pleg, Reu, Serug, Nahor, Terah, and Abraham.

Matthew 1 Abraham, Isaac, Jacob Judah Perez Hezron Ram Amminadab, Nahshon, Salmon, Boaz ,Obed Jesse, David, Solomon, Boaz, Obed Jesse David, Soloman, Rehoboam, Abijah, Asa Jehoshaphat, Joram, uzziah, Jotham, Ahaz, Hezekiah, Manasseh, Amon, Josiah, Jeconiah, Shealtiel, Zerubbabel, Abiud, Eliakim0, Azor, Zadok, Akim, Eliud0, Eleazar0, Matthan, Jacob, Joseph and Jesus.

Holy Spirit

The Holy Spirit has been with God and Jesus since the Creation. He is part of the trinity. Jesus relied on him when he was on earth. Jesus told us that the Holy Spirit would be with his followers and gives them strength from the time of his leaving to his second coming. God can send the Holy Spirit to us when he knows our heart is in the right relationship with him. When you believe, and confess he is Lord, you are given the promise of the Holy Spirit. Then we have the Holy Spirit in us, it teaches us to be more like Jesus. When Jesus was baptized the Holy Spirit descended on him. When you believe in the Gospel of your salvation you have the promise of as the Holy Spirit. When it is in us, it is there forever and it helps us become more like Christ. Our bodies become a temple for the Holy Spirit.

With the Holy Spirit in us we obtain many benefits for our spiritual lives. We receive a washing and a renewal of our soul. Our lives are changed and we become a new creature. God puts his laws in our hearts, and writes them on their minds so we will know the truth and promote righteousness for the Day of Judgment. The Holy Spirit or counselor teaches us all things. The Holy Spirit convicts us guilt due to sin, righteousness and judgment. When we are aware of our sinful nature, we can repent and be forgiven and start anew. We must never grieve the Holy Spirit.

We also should get rid of bitterness, rage anger brawling slander and any other forms of malice. We need to be kind and compassionate to each other.

The Holy Spirit gives gifts to those who received him. It is different with each one of us.

Some of the gifts are wisdom, knowledge, faith, healing miraculous powers prophecy, discernment, tongues and interpreting tongues. With gifts and the guidance of the Holy Spirit our lives are changed and others will see the fruits of the spirit. These fruits are love, joy, peace, longsuffering kindness, goodness faithfulness, gentleness, and self-control.

Scriptures references to support these notes

John 14:26, Ephesians 1:13, 1 Corinthians 6:19, John16:8, John 14-16, Hebrews 10:16, Acts 15:8 . **John 16:13, John 14:26, Titus 3:5. 1 Corinthians 6:19, Acts 10:47, Ephesians 4: 30, 1 Corinthians 12:8, Galatians 5:22, Matthew 12:32.**

Gifts of the Holy Spirit
1. The word of wisdom
2. The word of knowledge
3. Faith.
4. Gifts of healing
5. Working of miracles
6. Prophecy
7. Discerning of spirits.
8. Different kinds of tongues
9. Interpretation of tongues

Fruits of the Holy Spirit.

Paul told us we could recognize Christians who had the Holy Spirit by their fruits.

I Corinthians Chapter 12, and Galatians 5: 22.

1. Love (1 Corr. 13) (1 John3: 14)
2. Joy (John 15: 11)
3. Peace (beyond human understanding. (Phil 4:6)
4. Longsuffering (Romans 5: 3)
5. Kindness (2 Tim 2: 24)
6. Goodness (Matt. 5: 8 & Titus 1: 16)
7. Faithfulness (1 Cor.4: 2)
8. Gentleness. (1 Cor.13: 5)
9. Self-Control (Eph. 5: 15 & Matt. 5: 16)

The works of the flesh oppose the works of the Holy Spirit. They are: adultery, fornication, uncleanliness, licentiousness, idolatry, sorcery, hatred, contentions, and jealousies, outbursts of wrath, selfish ambitions, dissensions, heresies, envy, murders, drunkenness, and revelries. Those who practice these things will not inherit the kingdom of God.

Satan, Devil, Lucifer, Evil One

Satan is God's advisory who attacks God's plans and people because he desires to destroy Gods kingdom and establish his own. The Bible describes many of his attacks on Gods' people.

Satan has done extra ordinary attacks and has received other names as a remembrance of the incident. These names tell about his personality and his mode of operation. He is known and referred to by the following names: Satan, Devil, Evil One, the Enemy, Tempter, Lucifer, Dragon, Beast, ancient serpent, Prince of this world, Liar, Father of lies and Murder. Other places in the Bible Satan is referred to as the,

Prince of Demons, Perverter of the Scriptures, the God of this world, Seducer, Slander, Adversary and the Blinder the Minds. He considers himself as an Angel of light. Jesus referred to him, as an angel that he saw fall from heaven.

Satan is from the spirit world and he has access to God. He is a spiritual being that we cannot see, but we sense his presence as he attempts to influence our lives. He has greater power than man but less than God. The Bible tells us of miracles he has performed in the book of Job and future miracles that are prophesied in Daniel and Revelations. His main influence is deceiving men and trying to turn them from God's will.

He is not alone; there are fallen angels and demons that serve him. He and his followers disguise themselves as servants of righteousness to distract us from God. They scheme using slander, lies, seduction, temptation, perversion, murder, deception, manipulation. Satan and his followers are continually roaming the earth looking for ways to destroy our belief in God and his son Jesus.

Satan uses us as part of his spiritual warfare. He and his demons continually work against the church and Christ's followers. They use temptation and lies to turn us away from God's love.
His evil attacks cause many problems in our lives in order to dissuade us from believing in God and his righteousness.

The Bible describes some of the scheming events that Satan uses against God and his people. He started first with Adam and Eve in the garden. He then worked on Cain and convinced him to murder Abel. He also attacked God's special people using temptation and persecution (Job, Joseph, David, Paul and Jesus and his Apostles). When you look at his schemes it appears that he also may have used them against God's chosen people in the wilderness and the destruction of the Hebrew kingdoms.

It is important to know that Satan's rule is temporary. Jesus has authority over Satan's workers. Jesus proved this when he rebuked the demons while healing people and performing miracles. The Bible (book of Revelation) describes how God and Jesus will use their authority to destroy Satan and his followers. Meantime, we need to resist Satan's schemes.

The Bible tells us to gather God's strength over Satan's schemes by being alert and putting on God's armor and praying for God's assistance in resisting Satan. Then Satan will flee. We need to stand firm in Gods' truth and righteousness by reading his word and receive sanctification through the Gospel. Resisting Satan, loving God and Jesus and practicing the gospel can assure us of eternal life with God and his son Jesus.

God has warned us for centuries about Satan's efforts during the great tribulation. Satan will have strength and authority for the seven years during the tribulation. *(See the tribulation section for more information)*. He will control men with a world government for seven years. He will perform miracles and ask to be worshiped as a God. Two of his major miracles during tribulation reign are healing one of his beasts from a mortal wound (Revelation 13) and killing God's two witnesses (Rev. 11:3-12). During this time, all men living on the earth must decide between the loving the God of the Bible or Satan. Everyone who chooses God during the tribulation will lose their earthly life but they will have an eternal life. Those that choose Satan will be destroyed with him at the final judgement. Knowing about this tribulation makes me so glad to know that those who have already committed their life to our heavenly father and Jesus our lord will be caught up in heaven, to be with Jesus during the great persecution in tribulation *(for additional information see the section on the rapture)*.

At the end of the seven year tribulation, Jesus will return and set up his kingdom and Satan will be placed in chains during Jesus millennium reign. At the end of the Millennium, Satan will be released and gather armies from God and Magog to attack Gods people and Fire comes down and destroys the army and Satan and his prophet are defeated and are thrown into the lake of burning sulfur. They will be tormented day and night forever and ever.

Scripture references supporting Satan

Book of Job, Book of Revelation, Genesis chapters 3,4, Luke 10:18, Matthew 12:26, 25:41, Matthew 13:28, Matthew 4:3, Matthew1:24, Matthew 4:4, Matthew 16:18, Acts 26:18 , John 8:24, John 12:30-32, 2 Corinthians 4:4, Revelation 2:9-12, 1 Peter 5:8, 2 Corinthians 4:4, 2 Corinthians and 11:14, 2 Thessalonians 2:9-12, 1 Timothy 4:1 Revelations chapters 12-13, Ephesians. 2:1-3, Ephesians 6:14-17, 2 Corinthians 2:10-12, Ephesians 6:10-18, 1 Peter 5:8-11, 1 John 3:7-8, 1 John 5:18, James 4: 1-10, John 8:44, Matthew 4:1-11, Revelation 13: 14-15 and Revelation 20:7-11

God's Covenant with his people and Nation

God said to Abram "I will make you a great nation, I will bless you" (**Genesis 12:2**). Within a few generations, he sent his children to Egypt. Later the Egyptians persecuted them, so God freed his children and formed them as a nation of people. He took them under his wing and made a covenant with them. ***Exodus 19:5*** Now if you obey me fully and keep my covenant, then out of all nations you will be my treasured possession. Although the whole earth is mine, you will be for me a kingdom of priests and a holy nation.' He then gave his nation the 10 Commandments (Exodus 20). However, the people did not keep his commandments and worshiped Idles. Moses interceded with God for the people so God does not destroy them. A new covenant was made with God's nation. God will be with them if they destroy their (enemies) alters, break their sacred pillars and cut down their wooden images (for you shall worship no other God, for the Lord whose name is Jealous, is a Jealous God **(Exodus 34:10)**. He warns them of making covenants with the inhabitants of the land, and they play the harlot with their gods and make sacrifice to their gods, and one of them invites you and you eat of his sacrifice, and you take of his daughters for your sons, and his daughter play the harlot with their gods

God's people still feared the people in the Promised Land and did not put their trust in God and refuse to enter the Promised Land. God was angered and didn't allow those who don't trust in him to go into the Promised Land. He has them wonder in the wilderness for 40 years, until that generation dies. **(Numbers 14:27)** God wanted the people to remember him. He explains that he did it to humble them, allow them to know that Man shall not live with bread alone; but man lives by every word that proceeds from the mouth of the Lord. He also wanted them to know that in their hearts that as a man chastens his son, so the Lord your God chastens you. Therefore you shall keep the commandment of the Lord your God, to walk in His ways and to fear him **(Deuteronomy 8)**.

Before the new generation enters the land, Moses reminds them of the covenant **(Deuteronomy 4 & 5)** God command that the laws be observed and taught to the Children. **(Deuteronomy 6:4-10)** He tells them he will bring them in the land of which he swore to Abraham, Isaac, and Jacob to give them large and beautiful cities which they did not build. God tells them that victory in the new land depends upon obedience. **(Deuteronomy 11:22)**

God foretells that Israel will have a King as the other countries. **(Deuteronomy 17:14)**

God expands the covenant with his people prior to entering the Land **(Deuteronomy 28-30)**. He tells the promises of blessings for obedience and curses for disobedience. God tells the people to love him and abide by his statues he will bless them in the land, But if their heart turn away and worship other gods and serve them he will punish them and perish and not prolong their days in the land.

When the people are getting ready to enter the Promised Land, Moses reminds the people of the covenant of obeying God's statues. The people reconfirm the covenant. Moses then dies and Joshua take over the leadership of the nation. He takes the Israelites in the Promised Land. As they are obeying God, he aids them in defeating the major armies of the land. Joshua is getting old he relinquishes control of the nation. He gives the land allotments to the various tribes. Before he dies he reminds the people how God has brought them out of bondage and that blessing come through obedience. He renews God's covenant **(Joshua 24)**. However, not all the enemies of the land were taken out of the land. God would continue to help them with the promised blessings if they continued in obedience. However, the people were split up and lost their complete faith and did not continue in God's will. They failed to completely conquer the land. Their failures are listed in Judges 1. An angel of the Lord came to them and reminded them of the covenant which they had broken. He said *(***Judges 2:3** *)* Now therefore I tell you that I will not drive them out before you; they will be thorns in your sides and their gods will be a snare to you. This is the way it was. However, when they would cry out to the Lord he would send a deliver. This was God way of helping them. He raised a leader (Judge) again and again to help them.

This continued through the period of the judges. Samuel was the last of the judges and he became a prophet. God called him, during turbulent times of the Judges. He was confirmed as a prophet at a time when the word of the Lord was seldom heard. Even with many great acts of Samuel, the people wanted a king to unify them and protect them from nearby kingdoms. God decide that he would give them a king. He picked Saul. He had Samuel anoint him and declare him king. God helped Saul with battles and the people accepted him as king.

Saul is disobedient to God. This angers God and he decides to anoint David to be King of Israel. Saul is still King and David defeats Goliath and becomes a national hero. Later, Saul recognizes that David is a threat to his kingdom and tries to kill David. David flees and gathers followers. With Saul's disobedience, God doesn't give him blessings and his rule becomes less effective. Eventually Saul is killed in battle. David the takes charge of the Judah. David Obey God and continues with God's blessings and later becomes a righteous King of Israel. However, as with many men, David sins in the eyes of the lord with adultery and murder. David marries the women of his adultery. A child came from this act of adultery. God take the life of their child. David repents for his sin. God gives another son to the couple. His name was Solomon. David's disobedience caused God to stop giving special blessing to David. There were troubles in the remaining reign of David.

God still loved David and made a covenant **(2 Samuel 7)** with him. He promised David when he dies "I will set up your seed after you, who will come from your body, and I will establish his kingdom. He shall build a house for My name, and I will establish the throne of this kingdom forever. I will be his Father, and he shall be my son. If he commits iniquity, I will chasten him with the Rod of men and with the blows of the sons of men. But my mercy shall not depart from him, as I took it from Saul, who I removed from before you." **(2 Samuel 7: 12.)**

Solomon became king after David. God gives the blessing to Solomon as he promised David. He obeys God and God gave him many blessings. He made him a great king. The Nation became very prosperous. However, Solomon kept striving to have a more powerful kingdom. He made alliance with other countries by marrying other king's daughters. He ended up having 700 wives and 300 concubines. Some of these wives served other Gods of their countries. They started drawing him away from God. His pride grew and faith in God diminished. He started doing many things that God told his people not to do. So God started chastening him. From this point on, God Chastised Solomon and the kingdom (**I Kings 11: 14**). God still kept his promise and the kingdom was maintained until Solomon died. Now every king would be accepted or cursed according to his obedience.

Solomon's son Rehoboam was to be king after Solomon. He took the advice of his younger piers and decided that he would rule with force and hardship on the people. There had always been a rivalry between Judah and the northern tribes of Israel.
The northern tribes decided that they did not want to follow Rehoboam. They Chose Jeroboam to be their king. There was fighting between Israel and Judah from then on until Israel was defeated by the Samaria. God's nation was divided from 922 B.C. to 722BC, when Samaria defeated and took Israel captive. Judah Continued until the Babylonian empire took Jerusalem and destroyed the temple (586 BC). During this time God still gave blessings to the ones that obeyed and curses to those who didn't obey. When God felt that his nation was not obeying him he set it aside. He sent them into exile to chasten them and show that he was their God.

Looking a history, you can see that God aided and gives blessings to those nations that follow his obedience. When nations were disobedience, he chastens the nations. He will even use evil nation to chasten in order to try to get nations back to obedience.

God makes plans for redeeming his people and nations. He will continue his covenant with people and nations. He also gives them a new assistance in obedience. He had prophets foretold his people of their Messiah and his life (see notes section on Major prophecies about Jesus). He then sent the Messiah (Christ) as an example of how to be obedient and the Holy Spirit to remind us to be obedient in our daily life.
God promises a new nation of his people. This will be the promised second coming of Jesus the Messiah

The Second coming of Christ

God keeps his covenants. He expects us to keep them. If we do, we will be with him in his kingdom. If we do not keep the covenants we become sinners. As you can see, even God's chosen fall short and sin. God realize this and gave us a savior. Jesus, our Savior, will help us to be with the father in his kingdom. To do this we must turn away from disobedience and toward obedience and have faith in Jesus. We must have a spiritual rebirth. With this spirit, we gain the assistance of the Holy Spirit. Even if we fail from time to time, we can repent and become more obedient. This process leads to obedience and, through Jesus, and the grace of God, we will one day be in God's perfect kingdom.

God's new covenant with man

God gave a new covenant for salvation. This covenant is for anyone that loves God and wants to submit to the Lordship. When you are spiritually reborn God gives is the Holy Spirit and he puts his laws in our hearts. He allowed his son to be sacrificed for atonement of our sins. God no longer wanted to be worship in an earthly temple; he wanted to be worship through Jesus. Jesus is now the Holy temple of God. He appointed his Son as an eternal High Priest as a mediator of this covenant. We now can go directly to God in the name of Jesus and ask for forgiveness of sin. With our trust in Jesus through this covenant we become heirs of his everlasting kingdom.

To understand this we should be aware of the following events.

God planned to give us the New Covenant many centuries before it became effective. He told Isaiah over 450 years before Jesus was born that he would be sacrificed. His sacrifice would be atonement the sin of many and make intercession for the transgressors. God told Jeremiah over 450 year before the birth of Jesus that he would write his laws in the minds and hearts of his people. Jeremiah recorded this in Jeremiah 31. This writing of the laws in our hearts and minds is done through the Holy Spirit

When the people of Israel wanted to have atonement from sins, they would go before the High Priest to have him ask God for forgiveness. However, the priesthood was inherited within the family of Levi. The priest were man, thus they had their faults and died. The Priest head changed due to the various men and their ways. God recognized the inconsistencies and wanted to have an understanding and consistent High Priest.

Under the new covenant, Jesus was assigned as our High Priest. He is qualified to help us because he lived a life which gave him mercy and faithful to be the High priest.

Jesus was resurrected after he was crucified proving he was an eternal being. When we realize our sin, we change so we will not sin again. We now can go to our eternal High Priest in prayer and receive atonement. Christ atonement helps us receive the promise eternal inheritance by setting us free from the sins committed under the first covenant. . Jesus will always be an everlasting High Priest to mediate our judgment.

Additional information concerning this covenant is found in the Gospel section

<u>Following are some scriptures which should aid your understanding.</u>

***Isaiah* 53** Who has believed our message and to whom has the arm of the LORD been revealed? He grew up before him like a tender shoot, and like a root out of dry ground. He had no beauty or majesty to attract us to him, nothing in his appearance that we should desire him. He was despised and rejected by men, a man of sorrows, and familiar with suffering. Like one from whom men hide their faces he was despised, and we esteemed him not. Surely he took up our infirmities and carried our sorrows, yet we considered him stricken by God, smitten by him, and afflicted. But he was pierced for our transgressions, he was crushed for our iniquities; the punishment that brought us peace was upon him, and by his wounds we are healed. We all, like sheep, have gone astray, each of us has turned to his own way; and the LORD has laid on him the iniquity of us all. He was oppressed and afflicted, yet he did not open his mouth; he was led like a lamb to the slaughter, and as a sheep before her shearers is silent, so he did not open his mouth. By oppression and judgment he was taken away.

And who can speak of his descendants? For he was cut off from the land of the living; for the transgression of my people he was stricken. He was assigned a grave with the wicked and with the rich in his death, though he had done no violence, nor was any deceit in his mouth. Yet it was the LORD'S will to crush him and cause him to suffer, and though the LORD makes his life a guilt offering, he will see his offspring and prolong his days, and the will of the LORD will prosper in his hand. After the suffering of his soul, he will see the light of life and be satisfied: by; his knowledge my righteous servant will justify many, and he will bear their iniquities. Therefore I will give him a portion among the great, and he will divide the spoils with the strong, because he poured out his life unto death, and was numbered with the transgressors. For he bore the sin of many, and made intercession for the transgressors.

Scriptures references to support these notes

Jeremiah 31-31, Acts 2:38, Hebrews 9:15, Ezekiel 16:62, 2 Corinthians 3:12

Born of the spirit

Many ask" how can anyone be born again?" The second birth is a spiritual one. We have to recognize there is an eternal spiritual world. One way, we can see this world exists is to acknowledge that someone had to design the universe. Another way is to see the fulfillment of prophecies down through the centuries and realize that someone was in control. When we see how God's love and righteousness has always benefited men, then it is natural to accept him as the Lord of our life.

That is the first step in being born again. With belief you soon have faith in God and his son, Jesus. To affirm your faith and publicly announce your commitment to God, you need to be publicly baptized so that there is witnesses to you commitment to the Lord. The Holy Spirit will write God Laws on you heart. Now you have been born in the spirit. This is only the beginning. You will spend the rest of your life becoming a mature Christian.

John3:3 In reply Jesus declared, "I tell you the truth, no one can see the kingdom of God unless he is born again. **John 3:5** Jesus answered, "I tell you the truth, no one can enter the kingdom of God unless he is born of water and the Spirit. Flesh gives birth to flesh, but the Spirit gives birth to spirit. You should not be surprised at my saying, 'you must be born again **1 Peter 1:23** For you have been born again, not of perishable seed, but of imperishable, through the living and enduring word of God. **1John 3:9** No one who is born of God will continue to sin, because God's seed remains in him; he cannot go on sinning, because he has been born of God **1John 5:18** We know that anyone born of God does not continue to sin; the one who was born of God keeps him safe, and the evil one cannot harm him.

God's preparation for the Gospel

God loves man and wants us to be part of his eternal kingdom. He wants men who love him, honor him, and accept his lordship and will live in peace and harmony. He knew that this would mean that each person would need to believe and have faith in his lordship before he would be allowed into his kingdom.

As man lives on earth and God lives in a larger spiritual universe, we cannot see him or his spiritual world. We also cannot see the wind. However, we can see the effects of the wind. We see the effects of God in our world. God communicates with man in various ways proving his power to govern in love and authority. When we look at the early recording of history in the Bible, we can see his attempt to communicate with man. Those that receive communication and responded received many blessings. Those who did not respond did not receive the blessings or were disciplined.

God set up a systematic way contacting man and a method of passing on the knowledge from generation to generation. God chose Abram, who he later called Abraham, to start this special communication. He set him apart from others and gave him promises. He promised that he would be the father of believers who trusted in him. From this time on, God used him and his descendants to communicate with man. In these communications God furnished evidence of his love, power and will for man.

The Israelites or Abrahams descendants were the holders of God's laws, and history of Gods actions and blessings and prophecies. They recorded this information in their scriptures preserving it for future generations. Now all people can know about God, his will, power and future plan.
In these scriptures, you can read many prophecies and their fulfillment. This was done to help later generation see Gods power and will for man. These prophecies also included a plan for expanding a relationship with all men on earth through the spreading of the Gospel.

God brought many things together to implement the Gospel. He would have prophecies fulfilled, set the world stage in order to accept the Gospel and present a new covenant with man. He set the implementation date when he told Daniel about the 70 week prophecy 530 years before the event. In the 69th week the messiah, Jesus would come to the earth. God brought the fulfillment of prophecy by sending his son to earth to represent him. God's son, Jesus, was the center of Gods plan for the Gospel. To let man know that Jesus was his son, he had prophecies recorded about him in the Israelites scriptures. He had several of his prophet's record events in the upcoming life of Jesus. He later fulfilled these prophecies to assure all men knew that Jesus was his son (for details: see the section concerning Jesus' prophecies and their fulfillment).

God knows that we need to understand him, before we can believe and trust in him. Jesus told us that if you have seen him, you have seen the father. Jesus told us about the father and his kingdom with parables. He lived a life that the father was well pleased. Jesus taught us about God's will for us. He explained that we no longer were judged by the letter of the law but the attitude of our hearts. Jesus and his teachings are part of the Gospel. That is probably why parts of the Bible that describe his life are called the Gospel. Jesus demonstrated his and God's power by performing many miracles. These miracles showed how God had the power of life, weather, matter, health, agriculture and all things he created. Jesus gathered his apostles around his and taught them so when he returned to the father; they could send the Gospel to the rest of the world.

God wants us to learn how to live with each other. In

order to impress upon us that we are doing something wrong (sin) he asks us to change our ways (repent) and ask for forgiveness. God uses sin to teach us how we can make our life better by letting us know that we have done something wrong.

He will forgive us, if we repent and change our way. Forgiveness has always been granted through blood atonement. With the Gospel, this atonement was changed from being done with animal sacrifice. God let his son, whom he loved, be sacrificed and Jesus' blood became atonement for all sin. Forgiving our sin teaches us how to live in God's will. It also prepares us for our eternal life in god's kingdom.

The Gospel offers eternal life in God's kingdom. In order for man to realize and believe in an eternal life, God showed that there is life after an earthly death by resurrecting Jesus from the dead. This resurrection was witnessed by more than 500 wittiness.

The Gospel has a new covenant which God would replace the old covenants. This covenant was prophesied by Jeremiah approximately 600 years before the event. God said "This is the covenant I will make with the house of Israel after that time, declares the Lord. I will put my laws in their minds and write them on their hearts. I will be their God, and they will be my people" This was the sending the Holy Spirit to the believers. This would be for all men because when men believe in God they are adopted in to Gods family which is the house of Israel. The Holy Spirit would be with the believer and give power to the evangelist to show God's power and authority so that they would believe.

God instructed Isaiah to record many prophesizes

concerning events of the coming Gospel. One was that "I, the LORD, have called you in righteousness; I will take hold of your hand." " I will keep you and will make you to be a covenant for the people and a light for the Gentiles." He was a light to the gentiles through his prophecies about Christ. Christ is the center of the Gospel. His life, teachings, sacrifices and resurrection are examples for the Gospel. Isaiah told about God putting the sins of all men on Jesus and Jesus would intercede for all men's sins. These prophecies and their fulfillment tell us that all people with faith in Jesus can have eternal life due to the Gospel.

For the Gospel to be spread to the Gentiles there had to be a common language and a political system that would allow people to go from one region to another without being hassled by country differences. The Greek language was spread over the known world and the Romans had conquered it at the time. It appears that God brought guidance from the spiritual world, fulfillment of prophecies, world situations, actions of men, together at one time so that his new plan for the Gospel would succeed.

Jesus knew for the Gospel to be successful for future generations it would need to be passed on by loyal men down through the generations. Jesus gathered his apostles around him and taught them so when Jesus returned to the father; they could follow his great commission. Of course, they did even through many trails. Christ's church was born and taken to the ends of the earth.

Scripture concerning preparation for the Gospel

Genesis 12:2, Galatians 3:8, Hebrews 8:13, Daniel

9:25, Acts 3:24, Isaiah 53:10, Luke 22:.20 Exodus 30:10, Luke 24:25, Romans 3:25, Romans 16:25, Matthew 28:18, Jeremiah 31:33.

Gospel—Good News --Gods' plan for salvation and Reconciliation

In man's beginning, God told man not to eat from the tree in the middle of the Garden. Man rebelled against God by eating from the tree. God told man that he would die and not have eternal life because his disobedience. When we are born we have a free will that is centered on ourselves. We gratify our cravings by following our desires and thoughts. Our self-centeredness causes us to disobey God. God wants us to love and obey him. He wants us to love our fellow men.

Even though God forsake man for his sins, he predestined him to be conformed to the likeness of his son Jesus. God had a plan to save his people from the consequences of their rebellion. God loves us so he gave us a plan of salvation which delivers us from our sin and reconciles us. This plan is called the Gospel

Gospel is a Greek verb to announce the Good News. The Good News is that God made and new plan of salvation so that you can be heirs to his kingdom. God loves us and wants our fellowship. So in his grace he provided the Gospel. The Gospel tells everyone in every nation, tribe, tongue and people that they can have salvation and an eternal life. The most important part of the Gospel is that Christ died, was buried and raised on the third day according to the scriptures. In Gods' salvation plan Jesus died for our sins and was raised again to show us that there is an eternal life which can be shared with God.

He let this plan first be known when he told Abraham that he would bless all people (including the gentiles) through him. God continued to foretell his plan through his prophets. They recorded God's word in their writings. This was done to prove that the Gospel was from God. Most of these prophecies were made over 700 years before Christ was born. The scriptures of Isaiah announced the future coming of the Christ and how he would be atonement for all sin. . Isaiah also told that God had a plan for calling of all people. As Jesus was the main part of his plan, he foretold all the major events of his life. He told of his crucifixion where Jesus' blood gave forgiveness and atonement of sin. Jesus came and lived the prophesied live. His life shows us an example of God and his love for us. The fulfillment of the prophecies proved Jesus divinity and that God the father had sent him.

To make this new covenant supersede the old one Jesus had to be sacrificed in accordance with the scriptures for the atonement of all sins and be resurrected. Jesus is our savior, who destroyed death and has brought new life of immortality. Jesus completion of these prophesied events proved there is an eternal life awaiting those that believe and put their faith in Christ. Our proof of the resurrection is that it was witnessed by more than 500 people before Christ went to his father in heaven. Jesus showed us how to live a life that was in God will. He did this even though he was tempted by his adversary the devil concerning preservation of life (hunger), worshiping the devil rather than God (earthly power), and not testing God (taking action to make God serve him)

The scriptures of Jeremiah announced the coming of Holy Spirit into minds and hearts of man. God sends the Holy Spirit in to our hearts when we accepted the Lordship of Christ. The Holy Spirit puts Gods Laws in our minds and writes it on our hearts. With the Holy Spirit in our hearts, we know that we need a closer relation to God. The new covenant is of the spirit and thus it requires more communication between us and God. Now we can freely communicate directly with him in prayer. With the use of prayer we can discuss our spiritual problems with God. As we are not perfect and still sin, we now can repent form our sin and ask Jesus our High Priest to forgive our sins and we will be forgiven. Thus, we are assured of our salvation and rest knowing that we are followers of Christ

How do we obtain salvation in accordance with his plan? First we need to hear about God and realize he is the creator and ruler of the universe. Look at his love and will for us, then decide if he is the one we want to follow. God also offers an eternal life.
Many people on earth live by passion and pleasure, which hurts others by their action. Those who chose drugs, alcohol, sex, power, and violence are ruled by their choices. When you chose someone or something it causes you become part of it and you serve it like a slave. The ways of the world are not loving or fair to everyone. When you believe in God and Jesus his son, you trust and give them your loyalty and obedience. As you do this, you become more reliant on God and you put your faith in him and his son Jesus. Accepting God as our lord makes you a new creation and you live in God's will.

Man has not always followed him and has sinned against God. Man's disobedience has made it so that all men must be judged before they are allowed to live with him in his eternal kingdom. God still wants his creation, man, to live with him. So he allows us to call on him with our hearts are in proper order he will call on us through the Holy Spirit to use his salvation plan. You need to confess with our mouth that Jesus is Lord of your life and believe in your heart that he is Gods' son and He raised him from the dead. God gave Jesus all authority over us, so we must remember that Jesus is the only way that we are saved by this salvation plan. When you accept Christ as you savior and lord, you will want to be baptized so that you will publicly announce your loyalty to God. When we do this, we are committing to new way of life, which is furnished through the death and resurrection of Christ. In accepting this new life you are reconciled with God and your salvation is assured.

Of course, we have not completed our life here on earth. God wants us to be prepared for our life in his kingdom. He wants us to become more spiritually mature like his son. God asks us to have faith in him and Jesus and accept his lordship with obedience. He then will unconditionally love us and adopts us in to his family. He sends us the Holy Spirit who writes his laws on our hearts so we will know his will for us. He allows us to be reborn in the spirit and we then have a new nature. He puts our name in the Book of Life. He shields us from the evil one. As Christ died as an atonement of our sins, he forgives us our sins when we repent of them. We have Jesus, who has lived earthly life, be our High Priest and mediator in regard to our judgment. With all this in mind, we can have confidence that we are in Gods' family and we will have an eternal life with him in his glory.

After receiving our salvation there are many benefits for us.. We have been saved and justification by faith in Christ and we are reconciled with God. We lose our self-centeredness and become a new creation. You are born again in the spirit and receive the Holy Spirit in your life. The Holy Spirit will live within you and guide you and comfort you. He writes Gods laws in our hearts so we will know Him. God has adopted us as his children to live with him in his eternal life. We are no longer judged as men in regard to body, but our life according to the spirit.

However, we must remember to stay firm in our belief and not allow the evil one to remove our belief. The parable of the sowing of the seed tells us that the evil one is always trying to destroy our faith in God. Even though we have been saved, we will still sin and have trying times. Remember that our sins can be forgiven as long as we repent and ask for forgiveness. God and the Holy Spirit will aid us through the rough times. If we remember that we are now trying to live a spiritual life, we should put the rough times in respect to our spiritual life in Christ.

Scriptures regarding the Gospel

Hebrews 8:8-13, Genesis 1:1, Revelation **4:11,
Romans 8:28, Ephesians 2:3, Romans 6:16-17,
Romans 10:13, Matthew 7:7, Acts 2:39,** Romans
**16:25, Titus 3:3, John14:6, Romans 3:22, John 3:16, 1
Corinthians15:3, Hebrews 5:8   Isaiah 53:5,
Hebrews 9:22,Hebrews 9:28, I Peter 1:3, Matthew
26:26, Acts 2:38, 1 Corinthians 15:1, Ephesians 1:13,
1 Corinthians 6:11, I Peter 1:8, Hebrews 6:4,
Ephesians 4:22, 2 Corinthians 5:17, John1:12, Mark
16:15, Ephesians 1:1 3, Hebrews 9:28**

*Should you want to have more detail information
concerning hearing of the word, believing, faith,
forgiveness, born of the spirit, The Holy Spirit, Baptism,
Heaven and Hell? You will find additional information
following in their respective heading.*

Hear the word of God.

The first step is hearing the word of God and believing
it. If you have not heard the word of God it will be
brought by someone else. Today, most of these people
will be the followers of Jesus. The word of God was
recorded in the Old Testament's, God's son Jesus
brought more of the word of God which was placed in
the New Testament. When we are believers and have
faith in God and are baptized we will also know the
word of God by the means of the Holy Spirit.
The word of God is living and active. It divides soul and
the spirit. It is a guide for the thoughts and the attitudes
of the heart. If we believe we will hear and understand
the word. However, if we do not believe then we will
not understand the word of God. When we obey the
word of God, God blesses us.

Scriptures for hearing

John 14:26, Luke 8:21, John 8:47, John 11:42, Acts 15:5, **Romans 10:14, Revelation 1:3,** Luke **8:10, Luke 11:28, Acts 13:46, Hebrews 4:12,** John 14:24, Romans 10:14.

Believe

Most leaders want a commitment to them before they accept you into their group. God loves us so much that he asks that we believe. He sent his son to show us his character and his will. When we hear the word of God and know it is from him and not of man, we understand God's love and we will believe in him. God knows if you believe in him, we will have faith in him and want to serve and obey him in his kingdom

God plan was to send Jesus to establish his new covenant. Jesus was to the main part of the covenant. Jesus was to live among man, demonstrate God's character and be atonement for man's sin. God wants us to believe in Jesus as his son and representative. When you believe in Christ, you believe in God. God sent Jesus from the spirit world to our world so that we understand him. Jesus' life provided fulfillment of scriptures, examples of how to live, miracles, sacrifice and his resurrection so we could believe. When you look at Jesus life and see these examples, it gives you proof that leads to belief that he is the way and truth. .

In order to have salvation in accordance with the new covenant or Gospel, you need to believe in Jesus, who was sent by the father and crucified for the atonement of your sins.

Believing and faith comes from hearing the word of God and believing in Christ and his resurrection. When you believe in Jesus you also believe in God. The Scripture declares that the whole world is a prisoner of sin and if we do not receive and believe in Jesus we will not be part of the new covenant (Gospel) and we will be condemned and not have eternal life. When you believe in Jesus with your heart that God raised Jesus from the dead you will be saved and will have the promise of resurrection and your spirit will never die. For it is with your heart that you believe and are justified.

To confirm your believe, you should confess with your mouth that you believe in Jesus. In this belief, you show your trust and hope in Jesus and give him your loyalty and obedience. God wants us to believe in the name of his Son, Jesus Christ, and to love one another. The scriptures also say "Whoever believes shall not perish and will have eternal life." With belief in Jesus, we become part of Gods family.

Scriptures references to support these notes

John 3:16, Mark 16:16, Mark 1:15, John 3:18, John 6:29, John 8:24, John 12:44, John 14:10, John 20:29, Romans 6:8, Galatians 3:7, Galatians 3:22, 1Thessalonians 2:13, 1 Peter 1:8, 1 John 3:23, Acts 15:11, Matthew 28:18, Romans 10:9, John 11: 25.

Faith

Faith is being sure of what you hope for and being certain of what we cannot see. Faith comes from hearing the word of God and believing in Christ and his resurrection. In believing in Christ, you believe in God so your hope and faith are in God. Trust and faith in Christ justifies us with God and credits us with righteousness. When we have faith we receive God's grace and he justifies us without our works. He then adopts us as his children. Without faith it is impossible to please God, because anyone who comes to him must believe that he exists and that he rewards those who earnestly seek him. When we live with faith we earn a greater assurance. Jesus told us to have faith in God. He demonstrated his faith in God by living his predicted life which caused him shame and pain of the cross. Jesus' faith enabled him to live his life giving glory to the Father. He now sits at the right hand of God

God's rewards us with grace and peace because of our faith. We can now rejoice in the hope of Gods glory. In remembering Christ's faith, we believe in God who resurrected Jesus. Salvation through faith in Jesus Christ is given to believers and righteousness comes from God. We are redeemed and acquired the promise given to Abraham when we have Faith in Jesus. We are adopted into Gods family. Faith gives us many benefits in strengthening our walk with God. The righteous will live by faith. Grief and trials come so that your faith may be proved genuine and result in praise to Christ. Anyone who has faith in Jesus will do what he did because of his great example. Even with a small amount of faith many things may be done. As faith grows, we are able to accomplish more for the kingdom.

Scriptures concerning faith
Hebrews 11:1, Romans 19-17, Romans 1:17, Hebrews 11:6, John 14:12, Matthew 17:20, Acts 26:17, Romans 3:22, Romans 4:4, Romans 5:1, Ephesians 2:8, Hebrews 11:6, Hebrews 12:2, Galatians 3:23, Galatians 3:26 , 1 Peter1:7, Romans 5:,1 Romans 1:17, 1 Peter 1:9

Love

To a believer, love is the center of the universe. When you look at God's relationship with man you can't help seeing his love for his creation. God's love endures and he keeps sending his instructions so we can love him and our fellowmen.

Men's desires were overriding the love that God wanted for his creation. As a result, He decided to start and new nation with one man. He told this man, Abram, to go to another country so he would be away from his culture and be reliant on Him. He showed his love to this family by helping them through their struggles. They struggled and learned God's love, and then God sent them to a great nation where they could multiply and learn skills that would be needed to transfer his instructions to future generations.

When the leaders of the nation felt God's people were becoming a problem, they persecuted God's people. God decided to free them and start their own nation. By this time, they knew language and writing skills. They started making records of God's instructions so future generations would have the benefit of using God's love. God gave them the Ten Commandments and other laws that would aid them from then on. Later, with his great

love, he sent his only son to live with man so they would have a better knowledge of him. We know this was done out of love because the scriptures tell us so.
John 3:16 "For God so loved the world that he gave his one and only Son, that whoever believes in him shall not perish but have eternal life". God's only son Jesus summarized the 10 commandment as follows. **Matthew 22:37-40** "Love the Lord your God with all your heart and with all your soul and with all your mind. This is the first and greatest commandment. And the second is like it: 'Love your neighbor as yourself.' All the Law and the Prophets hang on these two commandments". With this statement, you can see that love is from God and he wants us to love one another.

The scriptures are full of references about God's love for his followers and he wants man to love one another. He started putting Love in the scriptures from the very first and it continued through the completion of the Bible. Paul the apostle tried to describe Love and recorded it in the Bible. **1 Corinthians 13:3-8** "If I give all I possess to the poor and surrender my body to the flames, but have not love, I gain nothing. Love is patient, love is kind. It does not envy, it does not boast, it is not proud. It is not rude, it is not self-seeking, it is not easily angered, it keeps no record of wrongs. Love does not delight in evil but rejoices with the truth. It always protects, always trusts, always hopes, always perseveres. Love never fails." He also recorded it on Romans 9. God's commands for love are found in most all books of the Bible. They were put there so all can see that love is needed from generation to generation.
He went further by describing how we could do this as Christians in **Romans 12**. He told us to be sincere, cling to good, and be devoted to one another in brotherly love.

Live in harmony with one another and live at peace with everyone. Do not repay evil with evil. He also tells us that of faith, hope and love that love is the greatest. Love does not delight in evil but rejoices with the truth. It always protects, always trusts, always hopes, and always perseveres. Love never fails. The reason the world does not know love as we do is because they do not know our Heavenly Father.

God gave us instruction on how to love. Following are some of these instructions

God is eternal and his love endures forever. This is proven because with all his problems with man he still loves those who love him. He is so animate about wanting us to love him that he wants us to love him with our heart and soul. We can show our love to him by walking in love and obeying his instructions**.** He always supported those that kept his commandments.

God wants you to love your neighbor as yourself. He gave us instructions in the fourth through the tenth commandments. He knows if we love each other we will be righteous to each other. This kind of love comes from God, and with it, we know we have been born again and people will know that we are his followers. He wants us to meet together so we may spur one another toward love and good deeds. God will support love by purifying your heart and those of your descendants so love will abound in your life. When we love one another, it helps cover up a multitude of sins. Jesus knew that God was going to spread the Gospel to the unbelievers so he told us to love our enemies because they might someday want to be part of God's kingdom. He even went so far as tell, us to pray for our enemies and treat them fairly.

Benefits of loving one another

Even though we have not seen God, we know he lives because he gives us his spirit so we will love him and one another. With this love, we honor the fourth through tenth commandments of the Ten Commandments. God keeps his covenant of love with those who love and obey his commands.

God is love and we can rely on him when we abide in him. We then are assured that goodness and love will follow us. By standing firm in his love to the end, we will be saved and be confident on the day of judgement.

God shows his love.
God shows his love by being compassionate, slow to anger, faithful, gracious and forgiving of our transgressions. With all these qualities, you can call on the lord and he will respond to you and let him into your life. He loves you so much, he becomes your heavenly father and he will rebuke and discipline you so you will learn to repent and receive salvation and have an eternal life.

God warns us of things that ruin love for one another.
God warns us to stand firm against wickedness and obey his commandments. If you do not, they will draw you away from his love. Seeking revenge or bearing a grudge will also cause you to lose love.

Scriptures concerning Love

Romans 12:9-19, Romans 13:10, 1 Corinthians 13-13, 1 John 3:1, Matthew 5:43-48,.1 John 4:16-21, John 14:21, 1John 1:6, 1 John 4:10-13, Ephesians 3:16-19, Exodus 34:6-7, 1 Chronicles 16:34, Nehemiah 1:5,

Nehemiah 9:17, Deuteronomy 30:6, Jeremiah 33:11, Psalms 23:6 Daniel 9:4, Matthew 5:44-48, Luke 6:27-28 ,Luke 6:35, Colossians 3:13-15, Hebrews 10:24-25, 1Peter 4:8, 1 John 4:7, John 13:34-35, Matthew 24:12-13, Revelation 3:19-20, Matthew 24:12-13, Leviticus 19:18.

Sin

The origin of sin is in man himself. Man has the freedom to choose, and he carries with him the responsibility of that choice. God wants us to love and care for him and our fellowmen. Any infraction is an offense against God will and it is defined as sin. God uses sin to let us know that he has a better way for our lives. He wants us to turn back to his teaching and then he will forget our sin.

Scriptures regrading sin
I John 1:8, Ecclesiastes 7:20, John 2:1.

Repentance

Repentance means to turn away from one's actions when regretting doing wrongs. We need to repent so we will not do it again. We must humble ourselves, acknowledge and confess our sins and then change our mind and turn away from sin. We must cease to do evil and take steps of doing Gods' will. Through repentance we can be forgiven.
Scriptures concerning repentance
II Corinthians 7:10, Luke 13:3, II Peter 3:9, Psalms 32:5.

Forgiveness

When we understand the righteousness of God and his will for us, we know that we a need forgiveness for our sins. In accepting the Lord, we can now repent and change our ways and we will be forgiven for our transgression against him.

God stated that blood was the life of a creature and it is to be used for the atonement of sin. Down through the centuries it has been used for atonement. It was used in the first sacrifice when Abraham did it for his son Isaac. It was used at the Passover when the Israelites left Egypt. The sacramental atonement for sin was set up when God sent his laws to the Israelites.
The prophets of Israel recorded Gods promise that everyone who believes in Jesus receives forgiveness of sins through Jesus name prior to his birth.

The Father offered his son as a sacrifice of blood for all of man's sins. As Jesus' blood atoned for all, God no longer requires sacrifice of blood for atonement of sins. We are justified freely by grace through the redemption that came by Jesus.

In the new gospel plan of salvation, God wants us to repent our sins, so we can change our lives and ask be forgiven. Then with our faith in Jesus, will be forgiven...On the Day of Judgment Jesus will not remember our sins if we have repented and asked for forgiveness.

Scriptures concerning Forgiveness

Leviticus 17:11, Hebrews 9: 20, Exodus 30:10, PSALM 32:5, ACTS13:38, Matthew 26:28, Matthew 18:21, I

John 1:9, Acts10:42, Ephesians 1:7, Hebrews 9:14, Hebrews 10:17.

Baptism
After Jesus resurrection and just before he ascended to heaven he announced that he had been given authority in heaven and on earth. Then he told the disciples to go and make disciples of all nations, baptizing them in the name of the Father and of the son and the Holy Spirit. He told his disciple this so that all people could have salvation in accordance with this new salvation plan. Believing, repenting and being baptized in the name of Jesus Christ you receive salvation and are given eternal life. As a result, you are now born again in the spirit and are assured of eternal life with God. If you do not believe, repent you are condemned. If you receive the Holy Spirit from God because of your believing, you should be baptized to let other now that you are a follower of God and Jesus.

Baptism is a simple ceremony which includes a public announcement by the person being baptized that they are renouncing his old life and the devil. They are repenting their sins and requesting forgiveness and are making a commitment of faith to the father God, Jesus Christ and the Holy Spirit. They are then immersed in water or water is put on their body. Baptism is done in the Name of the Father, the Son and the Holy Spirit. Baptism is a symbol of our death to the old way of life and our beginning of a new life in Jesus. Jesus said that whoever believes and is baptized will be saved. The Holy Spirit then places Gods' laws in your heart so you will know gods' will.
Following are scriptures that support baptism.
Scriptures references to support these notes

Matthew 28:19, Mark 16:16, Acts 2:38, I Corinthians 12:13, Galatians 3:26, Acts 1:5, Romans 6:3.

New Creation
When we receive salvation and start living for God and Christ we are changed. We are now looking for an eternal life and our goal change from earthly thing to heavenly things. Yes, we are still here on earth but our desires are put in order with our heavenly goals. Our obedience to God and righteousness directs us to a different life which leads to our loving God and fellow men. We no longer strive to gain our power but to use Gods' power for the good of all. This new creature is reconciled with God through his plan for salvation. Our life and love for God now makes us want to help him. Christ gave the Great commission to gather others to God and warn others that they are condemned if they do not believe. We want to spur one another on toward love and good deeds and sanctify each other with the truth.

2 Corinthians 5:17-19 Therefore, if anyone is in Christ, he is a new creation; the old has gone, the new has come! All this is from God, who reconciled us to himself through Christ and gave us the ministry of reconciliation: that God was reconciling the world to himself in Christ, not counting men's sins against them. And he has committed to us the message of reconciliation.

Spiritual Maturing
Once we have become children of God we need to

mature to life like Jesus. When we do this there will be more harmony in the eternal kingdom. It is not easy for us. We have to work at it. The forgiveness of sin is part of the process. When we sin the Holy Spirit lets us know and we ask for forgiveness and change our ways. Here on earth we will never be perfect, but we will become more mature and live more in Gods will and he will be please.

Scriptures references to support these notes
Ephesians 4-12, Philippians 3:14, Hebrews 5-13, James 1:3, and Luke 8:14.

Prayer

To make an earnest request or beseech of God for a favor, thanks, confess sin for forgiveness. Prayer is a communication with God's in his spirit world. The Bible tells us that we should not be anxious about anything and take everything in prayer. Some things that are mentioned in the Bible for prayer are: knowledge of God, salvation, forgiveness, anxiety, troubles, wisdom, guidance, Temptation, Sickness, decision, divine guidance, your leaders and you enemies. However, we should not test you God with prayer.

When we pray we should keep in mind that we are talking to the rule of the universe, who loves and wants to communicate with us. Jesus advised us to go somewhere private to prayer. Jesus also gave us a format in which to pray. It is the Lord's Prayer.

"Our Father in heaven, hallowed be your name, your kingdom come, your will be done on earth as it is in heaven. Give us today our daily bread. Forgive us our debts, as we also have forgiven our debtors. And lead us not into temptation, but deliver us from the evil one.

God wants us to be faithful in prayer. Before we pray, God wants us to believe in him and be right with others. He says that if you hold anything against anyone, forgive them. So that he can forgive us. When you believe and have faith in God he will listen. If we feel that you can't express your request the Holy Spirit will assist you in your prayer. The Holy Spirit will intercedes for your concerns or request to God. He tells us that a righteous man is more powerful and effective in his prayer and will have the ear of God. Extraordinary request may require fasting before they will be answered. God does not want us to stop praying because we have not been answered when we think we should. He wants us to be faithful in prayer and not give up. Jesus tells about the woman who was persistent and because she was persistence her prayers were answered. When there is a special illness; you can *call the elders* of the church to pray over that person and anoint him with oil in the name of the Lord. Anyone who has faith in Jesus and does what he was doing for God can ask in the name of Jesus Christ. The more you pray and have fellowship with the Father you will gain more faith in him. You will also love him as he loves you.

Scripture concerning prayer
1 Peter 5:7, Romans 12:12, Philippians 4:6, Mark 14:38, Colossians 4:2, 1 Thessalonians 5:16, Matthew 6: 6, Matthew 7:.7, Matthew 21:22, Matthew 11:24, James 5:13, 1 **Peter 3:12**, Matthew 15:44,**Matthew 4:7, Luke 18:1, 1 Thessalonians 5:5, Romans 8:26, Jude 1:20, James 5:13, Matthew 17**:

21, Romans 8: 26, Matthew 26: 41,John 9: 31, Matthew 17: 21, John 14:12, John15:15.

Heaven and Hell

We are composed of a body and a soul. When we die, we will leave our body and become spirits. Heaven and Hell are places where our spirits will go after this life on earth. If we follow God and his ways we go to Heaven. If we do not, we go to Hell. Jesus told us about Heaven through his parables which are record in Matthew. In his parables he states "The kingdom of heaven is like ….." He tells us about heaven using the following stories: Treasure in the field, precious pearl, sowing of seed, weeds, fishing net, unmerciful servant, workers in the vineyard, wedding banquet and the ten virgins. Many of these parables also tell how God determines who will go to heaven and who will go to hell. In order to go to heaven we must accept his salvation now and hold firm, so we will be ready for the unexpected coming of the Lord and his judgment. We must be ready because if we are not, we may miss it (The Parable of the Ten Virgins). Form these parables we can see that Heaven is such a treasure we will do anything to acquire it (treasure in a field and great pearl). Heaven is God kingdom with everlasting life. Heaven will expand large enough to hold all of Gods' family (mustard seed and yeast). Jesus came to earth to bring God's will and salvation plan for man. Those who believe and use the plan will receive their adoption into Gods' family. Gods' family lives in heaven. When anyone hears about God's kingdom and does not understand, the devil will come and snatch away the word of God from their hearts. Some receive the word joyfully and when trouble or persecution because of the word they forget it. Others worry about their earthly life, wealth and chose it over the hope of an eternal life. Those who hold to the promise will attain heaven. We need to accept god's' word simply like a child to enter heaven (Sowing of seed). The devil wants us to follow him instead of God. He sets his followers among Gods' followers. The two will be together until Jesus comes (Weeds). At the harvest of souls in the end times, all will be gathered and judged for their sins. He will be gracious and allow us to be forgiven in accordance with his salvation plan. However, he wants us to forgive others with our heart as we want to be forgiven (Unmerciful Servant). It does not matter when and how much work you have done. All those who believe and are saved will gain an eternal life in heaven (workers in the vineyard). The Good will separated from the bad. The good are adopted by God and live in heaven. They will receive their rewards and treasures. Angeles will gather the evil ones and send them to hell. After the judgment, there will be a new heaven and a new earth where God will live with his followers. This is explained in **Revelation Ch.21**. In this new heaven there will be no more death or mourning or crying or pain. Those that obtain salvation will be adopted by the father and will be citizens of Gods' kingdom. Jesus' resurrection showed us that we will have a new birth and a new body in heaven where our bodies will not perish spoil or fade. In heaven as followers of Jesus, we will have glorious bodies like him. Jesus told us that he was going away to prepare homes for us and we will live with him and the father.

Hell is a place for those that do not accept Gods' salvation plan and God judges them not worthy of heaven. It is a place where unbeliever, the vile, murderers, sexually immoral and those who practice magic arts, idolaters and liars. It is a place where even worms do not die and the fire in not quenched. It is dark and there will be torment, weeping and gnashing of teeth. Those that are there will be placed in the fiery lake of burning sulfur. This will be the second death.

Scriptures for Heaven and Hell

Mark 9: 43, Luke 16:23, Matthew 25:30, John 14:1, Matthew 25: 34, Mathew 13:19, Matthew 13:25, Matthew 13:31-33,, Matthew 13:37, Matthew 13:44, Matthew 13:47, Matthew 18:3, Matthew 18:32, Matthew 20:12, Matthew22:10, Matthew 25:8, Revelation 21:1, Revelation 21:4, Revelation 21:7.

New Heaven---- Read Revelation Ch.21.

God repeals some Hebrew ritual laws

The death of Christ for the remission of sins made the ritual sacrifices invalid. We have grace through faith in Christ for remission of our sins. As the Gospel was sent to the Gentiles and they did not know the ritual laws, there was no reason to bother them with these laws (sacrifice, circumcision, eating etc.). The adherence to God's will is now given to the hearts of man through the Holy Spirit. Following are some scriptures concerning this subject.

Scriptures concerning the laws

Galatians 3:23, Romans 7:6, Hebrews 10:5, Hebrews 10:16, Romans 14:17, Galatians 2:21, Acts 15:7, Acts 11:5, Acts 15: 28.

Prophecy

God has used prophecy throughout the Bible. He tells men what he is going to do in the future. Sometimes it is hundreds of years in the future. In fact, the entire Book of Revelations is future prophecy given to the Apostle John. God Prophets in the past have been so remarkable that their writings were put in the Old Testament. There are sixteen prophetic books telling about the life of the prophets and their prophecy in the Old Testament. We need to recognize that to be a prophecy of God; the prophecies had to be 100% correct. We should also remember that not all prophecies have taken place. Man's prophecies (many times guesses) do not meet this standard.

People, who need logic to believe in God, should look to the prophecies about Christ. Christ's life was foretold over 400 years before his birth. It tells he was to be of the genealogy of Abraham and David. He would be born of a virgin. He would be born in Bethlehem. He would be a light to the Gentiles. He would have a triumphal entry into Jerusalem. There are 33 prophecies (mostly in Isaiah Ch. 53) about his crucifixion. All this prophecies were completed as for told.

When you read the Bible and see the prophecies come about, you most certainly will see the hand of God in our universe. We see God's power, control and love for his creation.

See Prophecies List for examples of prophecies.

Church (Called out ones)

Jesus asked Peter who do you say that I am? He answered, "You are the Christ, the Son of the living God." Jesus replied, "Blessed are you, Simon son of Jonah, for this was not revealed to you by man, but by my Father in heaven. And I tell you that you are Peter, and on this rock I will build my church, and the gates of Hades will not overcome it." Some people in translating from the original text, feel that rock was referencing what peter had said, the fact that Christ was the Son of God. No matter how it is translated, we all know the church is built on the fact that Jesus is the Son of God and through him we may inherit the kingdom.

At Pentecost after the arrival of the Holy Spirit (Acts 2), Peter explained that these things they had seen were the fulfillment of what was spoken by the prophet Joel. He showed how Jesus proved that he was the Christ by miracles, wonders, and signs that God did through him in their presents. He then reminded them how the resurrection was for told by King David (Psalm 16-10) and God had fulfilled the resurrection that they had recently witnessed. Peter informed them that Jesus was exalted to the right hand of God. Jesus had informed them that when Jesus went to the father, the father would send the Holy Spirit to be with us. This promise was just completed by the pouring out the Holy Spirit as they had just seen.

Peter reminded them that they had crucified the Lord and Christ. Knowing what they had done, they asked what they could do. Peter told them if they repented and were baptized in the name of Jesus Christ for the remission of sins; that they would receive the gift of the Holy Spirit. Then those who gladly receive the word were baptizes, and about three thousand souls were added. This was the beginning of the Church.

After Pentecost, the Holy Spirit was with the baptized believers. The Holy Spirit sustains comforts and furnishes gifts to the believers. The Holy Spirit and faith in Christ are the foundation of the Church. Through the church Jesus' Great Commission is being accomplished. And Jesus has become a light to the Gentiles as he promised.

In the beginning of the Church, there was no special place for the Christians to worship. In the early church, most gatherings were in the homes of believer. As the number of believers grew larger meeting places were required. The places were later call churches because the "Called out ones" of Jesus would meet there for worship and fellowship.
.
The Church is composed of many believers of one body working together in its basic love and faith in Christ. They are united in worship and acceptance of Jesus as Lord. It gives a place for the teaching and practicing and teaching of the Gospel. The people aid each other with food, fellowship and prayers. They interacted with each other and learned more about God's will for them and how to treat their fellowmen. By living by example they drew others to Christ. The unity of Christians to one accord in Christ was very important. In The Epistles, the Apostles kept reminding the communities of believers that they needed to remain united (See Ephesians Ch. 4). This unity prevailed and consequently the body of Christ grew.

The church had growing pains while it was developing. Some believers were from the Jewish heritage and they wanted to continue with the same rituals as they had used in Israel. Through vision (Acts. 10:9) from God and the revelation of the Holy Spirits the ritual laws of circumcision and sacrifice were removed (See the section on God repeals his Hebrew ritual laws) from the worship. Jesus' sacrifice replaced the traditional temple sacrifice.

In some churches human philosophy crept in the worship services. The Apostles wrote several epistles to warn about false teachings to redirect the people back to Jesus' teachings. With the Holy Spirit in the believers and the letters from apostles the church stayed grounded in Christ.

As the apostles went from place to place starting new churches, they realized that there needed to leave the organization behind to further the Great Commission. Some items, which needed care, were: Worship, Teaching, Fellowship, Unity of believers and caring for each other. In I Timothy it tells how to accomplish some of these items.

The Jewish community, which did not believe, wanted to destroy the new sect of believers. They started to persecute the believers. Jesus selected a persecutor Saul and made him a believer. Saul (later named Paul) received the Holy Spirit and became an apostle of Jesus. He Spread the Gospel by starting many churches in the world of the gentiles.

Later the leaders of the Roman Empire saw a threat in

this growth of the Christians and started persecuting them. Even though there was dire persecution and laws against Christianity, it grew to one half of the population of Roman Empire.

The turning point for persecution was in 313 A.D. when Constantine was given the sign of the cross in the sky and heard the words "fight in this Sign and Conquer". He fought his battles and became victorious He then granted to Christians and all others, Full Liberty to follow whatever religion they may choose. He posted Christians in places of government offices and did a number of other things for the Church.

Today we need to be aware of the beginning of the Church and it problems. We still face many of the same problems and can use the experience of the early church to help us stay united in our one believe and faith the Christ.

Following scriptures describe how believers can stay united in one accord, worship and fellowship in the church.
Romans 12:5, Acts 2:42, Act 4:32, I Corinthians 1:10, Ephesians 4:4, I **Corinthians 12:12, 1 Corinthians 12:22, Acts 11:16, Colossians 1:18, John10:16, Acts. 20:28.**

Rewards
Many places in the Bible we are told that we will receive rewards. Jesus told us about rewards when he described the men who received talents and how they multiplied them so that the master was please and gave them charge of many things. The Bible also tells us to lay up treasure in heaven not hear on earth. As we cannot take anything

material things with us in heaven, the only thing we can take is our actions of righteousness and credit for the serving of God here on earth. Those are the treasures we can take to Heaven. If we perform acts to gain rewards here on earth, they will remain on earth. However, if we do them in secret, the Lord will reward us in Heaven. Rewards are given for small and large works. It can be as simple and furnishing someone a glass of water to bring many people to God. We need to recognize that God appreciates those who help him and he wants to reward them for their work.

Scriptures references to support these notes

Jeremiah 17:10, Revelations 22:12, Proverbs 11:18, Matthew 6:3, Matthew 9:41, Matthew 10:41, Matthew 16:27, Matthew 25:21, Luke 6:35, 1 Corinthians 3:8, Ephesians 6:7, Colossians 3:23.

Marriage

God knew that man needed a companion and life partner. He initiated this when he said "It is not good that man should be alone; I will make him a helper comparable to him" **(Genesis 2:18).** He then made woman to be with Adam. God set up marriage between a man and a woman when he said, "Therefore a man shall leave his father and mother and be joined to his wife and they shall become one flesh" **(Genesis 2:24).** Truly, God meant marriage to be a blessing and a fulfillment with a satisfying companionship.
The marriage commitment joins the partners into one unit, one flesh, and they live together in oneness. God recognizes this oneness and feels it is sacred No one

should interfere with the marriage commitment. Marriage is a special love between a man and wife. The couple begins abiding in each other's fervent love for one another. They honor one another and give affection to one other. They have Faith, hope, and love, in each other.

When they make decisions concerning important issues, they will consider the effects on one another. When a husband has to take a leadership role, he must consider the love and wellbeing of his wife. In so doing, they will make the best decision for the marriage.

In order for the marriage to succeed the man and wife must continue to love one another. They must recognize that love will maintain their commitment. Love holds each other in high regard and would not be self-serving, rude, envious, it does not provoke others, it is long suffering and is kind, it does not envy or have pride that interfere with the others.

In order to assure unity of the marriage, God assigned the man to be the leader. The wife is to be submissive to her husband. With this leadership comes responsibility. A man's leadership expresses care rather than control, responsibility rather than rule. The man is to love and honor his wife as he would love himself. He is to make her holy through Gods word. Wives add many wonderful qualities to the marriage and the family. The Bible tells of many wives that brought wisdom and strength to the marriage. Husbands should love their wives as their own bodies. He, who loves his wife, loves himself and the wife respects her husband. A wife of noble charter is worth far more than rubies. God wants man to enjoy life with his wife whom he loves all the days.

Due to immorality, each man should have a wife and each woman should have a husband. However, if you can maintain your morality you can remain single. Some people do not desire marriage as much as other life interests and remain single.

In marriage a man's body does not belong to him only it belongs to his wife. The wife's body also belongs to the husband. Do not deprive each others of your marital duty to each other except when there is mutual consent. Sex within this union brings a better relation and unity. Sex is holy and good in the marriage. Sex outside the marriage is destructive and God considers it sin. All through the Bible and life, we find that fornication causes life problems to those who do it. *(See the section on Sexual Immorality for more information.)*

God wants a man and a woman to be bound in marriage together as long as they are both alive. ("Therefore, what God has joined together, let not man separate." **Mark 10:6**) When a spouse dies the other is free to marry as long as they belong to the Lord.

God doesn't want man to separate from his wife. However, man has had many difficulties in their marriage relationships. God gives us many ways to have a successful marriage. However, man still struggles with his relationships, so God allowed divorce under certain circumstances. *(See the section on Divorce for more information.)*

Scriptures references to support this note

Geneses 2:20-24, Ephesians 5:33, I Corinthians 7:2-5, Exodus 20:14, Hebrews 13:4, Proverbs 3:14, Proverbs 31:10-11. I Peter 3:1-7, I Peter 3:7, Ephesians 5:22-33,, Psalm 128:3, I Corinthians 13:4-7, Ecclesiastes 9:9, I Corinthians 7:2-5, I Corinthians 7:10, I Corinthians 7:39,Proverbs 3:14, Proverbs 31:10-11,. Matthew 19:4-6. Hebrews 13-4, Colossians 3:-18-19

Husband and Wives Relationship

Love in marriage affords faith and hope in unity. A strong love furnishes a great regard for each other. Love, is not being self-serving, rude, envious, or have self-pride and you will not provoke your spouse. Your love for one another helps you overlook each other's faults.

God knew that man needed a companion and life partner. He initiated this when He said 'it is not good that man should be alone; I will make him a helper comparable to him.' He then made woman to be with him. God set up marriage between a man and a woman when he said, 'therefore a man shall leave his father and mother and be joined to his wife and they shall become one flesh'. Truly, God meant marriage to be a blessing and a fulfillment with a satisfying companionship.
God recognizes this unity and feels it is sacred. In marriage a man's body does not belong to him only, it belongs to his wife. The wife's body also belongs to the husband. Do not deprive each others of your marital duty to each other except when there is mutual consent. Sex within this union brings a better relation and unity. Sex is holy and good in the marriage. Sex outside the marriage is destructive and God considers it sin. All through the Bible and life, we find that sex outside the marriage causes problems. God wants us to be bound together in marriage as long as we live. That's

why he said 'Therefore, what God has joined together, let not man separate.'

When there is a disagreement spouses should talk it over. Both need to know each other's views and think over what is the best action for them. A united approach to your problems can assure a good marriage. When their differences cannot be resolved, they need a leader to resolve their differences. To assure a resolution, God assigned the man to be the leader. At this time a wife is to be submissive to her husband. With man's leadership comes responsibility. A man's leadership expresses care rather than control, responsibility rather than rule. When a husband has to take a leadership role, he must consider the love and wellbeing of his wife above his own needs. In so doing, they will make the best decision for the marriage. The man is to love and honor his wife as he would himself. He is to make her holy by assuring she understands Gods Word. Wives add many wonderful qualities to the marriage and the family. The Bible tells of many wives that brought wisdom and strength to the marriage. Husbands should love their wives as their own bodies. He, who loves his wife, loves himself and the wife respects her husband. A wife of noble character is worth far more than rubies. God wants man to enjoy life with his wife whom he loves all of his days.

Scriptures references to support these notes

Geneses 2:20-24,Ephesians 5:33, I Corinthians 7:2-5, Exodus 20:14, Hebrews 13:4, I Peter 3:1-7, I Peter 3:7, Ephesians 5:22-33,25, Psalm 128:3, , I Corinthians 13:4-7, .Ecclesiastes 9:9, I Corinthians 7:5, I Corinthians 7:10, I Corinthians 7:39,Proverbs3:14,

Proverbs 31:10-11,. Matthew 19:4-6. Hebrews 13-4, Colossians 3:-18-19

Divorce

Divorce is the breaking or dissolution of the marriage covenant. From the very beginning God did not want the marriage convent to be broken between a man and a woman because he was seeking godly offspring. He wanted a man and a woman to be bound together as long as they are both alive. If spouses separate from each other they must remain unmarried or else be reconciled.

In the marriage covenant, one believing spouse sanctifies and unbelieving spouse. If anyone is married to an unbelieving spouse who is willing to stay with them, they should not divorce them. There is always hope that the unbeliever will come to faith through the life of the believing spouse.

Because man has a hard heart and cannot completely remain pure, God has made some exceptions and allows a conditional divorce. When there is death of the spouse, the marriage is dissolved and the remaining spouse may marry again. Jesus was very clear that anyone who divorces his spouse, except for marital unfaithfulness it may make adulators of the persons involved. Unfaithfulness is a release from the marriage covenant. Another release of the marriage covenant is where the unbeliever leaves the believer and there is no chance of reconciliation, and then the believer is not bound in such circumstances.

Scriptures references to support these notes

Romans 7:2 Mark 10:2, I Corinthians 7:10, I Corinthians 7:27, Malachi 2:14, Matthew 5:31-32 Matthew 19:3, Luke 16:18, I Corinthians 7:15.

Guiding your children

Jesus said "Let the little children come to me, and do not hinder them, for the kingdom of heaven belongs to such as these". We know that our children are a blessing. Mothers realize this before their child is born. The father also realizes this blessing. We are told that we may have a long life when our children obey their parents. Your children are also a blessing for grandparents.

Now your guidance begins to assure that their child is brought up in a manner that is beneficial. At first it is difficult to communicate with the child so you start saying **No** to keep them from getting hurt. As time goes by, we learn to communicate with them and teach them how to love and live with others. When they start understand the difference between good and bad, it is time to tell them the reason why they need to do good. When you use your love and understanding to raise your children, they will respond to your love. You need to help them learn to use their free will in a positive way, where empathy, produces love and caring so they will use the golden rule. Remember what the Bible says "Train a child in the way he should go and when he is old he will not turn from it" If you do this, they will pass your lessons to their children.

In our lives we have had many problems which we don't want our children to experience. We need to teach them how to avoid these problems. As parents on earth we have the responsibility to instruct our children in the ways of the Lord and give them abilities to earn a living and have a successful life. We want them to have character, morals, ethics, determination and trustworthiness.

The disobedience to your teaching is usually caused by their selfish desires trying to overrule your teaching. The bible teaches that when this happens we should discipline them. Of course, all discipline is to be done with love. We are told not to embitter your children, or they will become discouraged. When the child turns against your teaching, the Bible tells to use the rod. It will not kill them but it will save their soul.

The child has responsibilities also. When they are to honor you in everything, this pleases the Lord. Their honor for you gives you a promises a long life.

Scriptures concerning guiding you child.

Matthew 19:14, Proverbs, 22:6, Colossians 3:20-21, Proverbs17:6, Ephesians 6:1-4, Proverbs 23:13-14, Proverbs **13:24.**

Christian Fellowship

Fellowship is where people gather together in a common interest to perform a task and experience being an associate. There have always been problems within fellowships because of the individual mindset of those involved. God recognized this problem when He set up the Israelite nation. He wanted them to have fellowship with Him and each other. He gave them commandments so they would know how to treat each other. He later sent Jesus with further clarification and instruction on governing their lives with each other.

Problems arose when the disciples started their fellowships to spread the Gospel. With the understanding of Jesus's teaching, the disciples and the writers of the New Testament told us how we should approach fellowship. They knew we were separate individuals with different skills. As a result, they told us how we could help one another to have a better fellowship. "If one part suffers, every part suffers with it; if one part is honored, every part rejoices with it. Paul the apostle told us this by explaining the use of parts of the body. Now you are the body of Christ, and each one of you is a part of it." Our fellowship needs us to love one another as God commands us to love.

The scriptures give us instruction that are helpful for us to keep our fellowship growing so it can accomplish spreading the Gospel.

Following are some of the instructions I have noted. Many of these instructions also apply to our everyday Christian life.

Be devoted to one another in brotherly love.
Use your gifts to serve others.
Consider how we may spur one another on toward love

and good deeds.
Honor one another above yourselves.
Live in harmony with one another.
Be sympathetic, love as brothers, and be compassionate and humble.
Practice hospitality and encourage one another.
Do good to all people, especially believers.
Share with God's people who are in need.
Build others up according to their needs.
Do what is right in the eyes of everybody.
Be quick to listen, slow to speak and slow to become angry.
Do not speak any unwholesome talk, slander or curse.
Do not judge one another, or you too will be judged.
Do not quarrel about words; it is of no value, and ruins listening.
Don't grumble against each other or repay anyone evil for evil.
Do not to put any stumbling block or obstacle in your brother's way.
Look not only to your interests, but also to the interests of others.
Do not be proud or conceited, but be willing to associate with people of low position.
Let us not give up meeting together.

Scriptures dealing with fellowship
1 Corinthians 12:19-24, Romans 12:9-17, Romans14:10-13, Philippians 2:4, James 10; 19-20, Ephesians 4:29, 2 Timothy 2:14-15, 1 Corinthians 4:3-5, Hebrews 10:22-25, Matthew 7:1-3, James 4:11-12, James 5:7-9, 1Peter 3:8, 1John 4;11-12, Peter, 4:10-11, Galatians 6;7-10, Ephesians 3:16.

Sexual Immorality

God's intends marriage to unite a man and women as one flesh. Sex within this union brings a better relation and unity to the spouses. (See the marriage section for more information.)
Any sex outside of marriage is fornication. The Bible is full of examples of how sexual immorality has had negative effects on individuals, marriages, and Kingdoms.

God wants the best for his creations, so his will is that we keep ourselves from fornication. He tells us not to be sexual immoral with his commandments of the Old Testament. He has also sent messages through Jesus and the Holy Spirit, which were recorded in the New Testament. It warns against Adultery, homosexual activities and general fornication.

Following are scriptures that relate to sexual immorality: I Thessalonians 4:3, Hebrews **13:4, Mark 7:21, Exodus 22:16, Exodus 22:19**, **Ephesians 5:5, Matthew 5:28, Matthew 19:9, I Corinthians 6:9, Revelations 21:8, Colossians 3:5, Leviticus 18:22, Leviticus chapter 18 lists many other relationships that are immoral) Leviticus 20:13, Romans 1:26, Genesis 19:5, Jude 1:7.**

God's Grace

God's Grace is an unmerited love and divine assistance given humans as manifested in the salvation of sinners and the bestowal of blessings. With God's grace we can have regeneration to sanctification.

God has given man grace since the beginning. When you look at the lives of Noah, Abraham, Joseph, Moses, King David and Solomon you can see the large amount of grace God gave through them. In his Grace, he performed miracles and gave them instructions to guide their lives. God, through his grace gave Solomon his request for wisdom and Israel became the premier nation of its time. When Solomon died, the leaders began believing in themselves rather than God. They felt they would be more successful without him. This thought was with them for some time and finally upset God, so he decided to show them that they needed him. He sent them in captivity for seventy years.

During the captivity, God set up a way for future generations to see His work and be reminded that He is a graceful God who cares for them, even though they don't merit it. He told about future events and how He would aid them in the future. He did this so when the prophecies were fulfilled men would understand his grace.

Many of the prophecies were about God sending his Son, so they could have forgiveness of sin, sanctification and salvation which lead to an eternal life. Now that we see that Jesus came and lived out his prophesized life, we are assured of God and his grace for us.

In his grace God did not stop there. He also told of many other events concerning the future so when they happened we are assured of God being in our lives. We know that these prophecies are from God because some prophets say that God told them exactly what to record so we would be assured it was from him. Zachariah is an example of this type of recording. God's prophets told of events that would happen from then to the end of time. Some of the Major Prophets were Isaiah, Jeremiah Ezekiel and Daniel. When you read their scriptures, you can see how God continues to give His grace so we can have an eternal life.

Many of these prophecies have been fulfilled and prove of God and his graceful assistance to man throughout the ages. We need to be aware of God's prophecies so when they occur we will recognize his handy work and place our faith in Him. The New Testament is full of Gods fulfilment of the prophecies concerning Jesus. This assures us of his grace in sending Jesus as our Messiah.

Prophecies are wonderful in proving God is in control and is with us at all times. The New Testament also tells more about the fulfilment of prophecy and adds to the future information concerning the future events. When you look and see God's handy work in our lives, we are assured of his existence, love and grace.

To aid your understanding, I have noted many prophecies (See Prophecy section). Those that have been fulfilled have the completion information. I urge you to look at the ones that have not been fulfilled so when they are fulfilled you will see God's glory in them. Additional information conserving some of the future prophecies is noted in my notes of end time prophecies.

God's greatest measure of grace was sending Jesus his messiah. This action went above and beyond previous graces for man. Jesus gave us a closer understanding of his father. He performed miracles to prove the power of

God. Jesus gave us an example of how we should live our life in God's truth and righteousness. God loves man, so in his grace he sent a plan of salvation to us through his son Jesus. As we are all sinners, we cannot earn our salvation. We need to recognize that it is only through God's grace that we will be found righteous.

Jesus instituted a new covenant between God and man which is called the Gospel. This covenant assures that all men who believe and put their faith in God and Jesus as their Lord are given the opportunity to have an eternal life. Jesus's sacrificial death atoned for man's sins and gave us a way to obtain forgiveness for our evil ways. Even though we all have sinned, with repentance we are justified with grace through the redemption that came by Christ Jesus. The gospel bears fruit and when people have heard its truth, they understand God's grace.

Within this covenant, He also sent the Holy Spirit to teach future generations how to learn his righteousness and be sanctified. With the Holy Spirit in our lives we can understand the truth of God and have his wisdom and understanding. God in his grace sent the gifts of the Holy Spirit in our lives. They enables us to help others so they can be reconcile to God and have eternal life

God continues to send his grace through Jesus and the Holy Spirit. You can see his actions in the New Testament. Through his grace, he enables his workers to perform miracles and testify about Jesus and his resurrection to spread the Gospel.

As individuals, we must remember God's grace is with us, even when we have trials. It restores us and makes us strong, firm and steadfast.

Scripture relating to God's grace are throughout the Bible. Following are some that came after Jesus brought the gospel. John 1:16-17, Romans 3:22-24, Romans 5:15, Acts 20:32, Romans 5:21, Romans 4:16, Ephesians 4:7-8, Colossians 1:5-6, Titus 2:11, 1 Peter 5:10, 2 Timothy 1:9, Hebrews 4:16, 2 Corinthians 9:8-9, Acts 14:3, Acts 4:33, Ephesians 2:8, Ephesians 1:7, Hebrews 4:16, James 4:6, 1 Peter 4:10 and Hebrews 4:16.

Giving (Tithing/use)

Most giving is taking a portion of your earnings and giving it to another for their use. The scriptures tell us how and why we should give. The two major areas of giving are; tithing for God's work and how we use our money.
Tithing is the giving one tenth of their first fruits. As culture changed from the barter system to a monetary system, it became one tenth of your money. God asked tithes of the Israelites in order to finance their religious government so it could aid the needs of its people and teach his righteousness to future generations. He wants you to give generously to him and do so without a grudging heart.
God recognizes your giving as an obedience of his command and knows that you are putting your faith in him. With your tithing he promises to pour out blessing. He will bless you in all your work and in everything you do. Jesus gave us further information when he came to earth as our redeemer. He told us about the poor widow and the Pharisee. The Pharisee gave out of his wealth and the widow gave out of her poverty, put in everything-all she had to live on. The gift of the widow

is greater in the eyes of God than the larger gift of the Pharisee. He also told us that "Give, and it will be given to you. A good measure, pressed down, shaken together and running over, will be poured into your lap. For with the measure you use, it will be measured to you." He wants each man to give what he has decided in his heart to give, not reluctantly or under compulsion, for God loves a cheerful giver. Sending tithes to aid God's followers will be accredited to your account. This is pleasing to God.

God has also sent us instructions on how we should manage our lives and use money. He wants us to keep our lives free from the love of money and be content with what we have because he said "Never will I leave you; never will I forsake you". He knows that where your treasure is, there your heart will be also and he wants your heart to be with him. He wants us to be righteous and be rich in good deeds and be generous and willing to share. In this way we will lay up treasure for ourselves as a firm foundation for the coming age.

He knows that desire for money can destroy our lives. He tells us we cannot serve two masters. We will hate one and love the other, or he will be devoted to the one and despise the other. You cannot serve both God and Money. This leads to being devoted to one and despising the other. We cannot serve both God and money. He wants us to store up our treasures in heaven rather than on earth. Jesus reinforced this when he talked to the rich man and ask him to sell everything so he could follow him. "Jesus looked at him and said, "How hard it is for the rich to enter the kingdom of God! Command them to do good, to be rich in good deeds, and to be generous and willing to share. In this way they will lay up treasure for themselves as a firm foundation for the coming age." Extra money should be used to help others rather than be stored up and not used. He wants us not to be greedy for money, but eager to serve. He wants us to share with our brothers and the poor and needy in our land. This giving should be done in secret. He will see this gift and will reward us. Use wisdom and restraint so you will not wear yourself out trying to gain wealth. If you have wealth, do not be arrogant and put hope in it, for it is uncertain. You need to put hope in God, who richly provides for us.

Scriptures concerning tithing Leviticus 27:30, Luke 6:38, 2 Corinthians 9:6-8, Deuteronomy 15:10-12, 2 **Corinthians 9:6-7**
Scriptures on the use of money
Luke 16:13, **Matthew 6:19-21, Proverbs 23:4, Hebrews 13:5, Mark 12:41-44, 1 Timothy 6:17-19, Luke 18:22-27.**

Communion

Why do Christians celebrate the communion? It is done to remind us what Jesus did in bring the Good News (Gospel) to men. At the last supper, he had communion with his disciples and asked them to do it in remembrance of him. Jesus said the bread represented his body given for you and the wine was the cup of the new covenant in his blood which is poured out for you. Jesus sacrificially gave his body and blood on the cross and then was resurrected to complete the implementation of the Gospel. Ever since the Last supper, Christians have been using communion for remembrance of Jesus and the new covenant.

God told us through the prophets Jerimiah and Isaiah that he would send his Messiah and a new covenant because his people had not kept his previous covenant. He also sent many prophecies about Christ so we would know that the new covenant was from him. When Jesus came he told us "I am the bread of life. He who comes to me will never go hungry, and he who believes in me will never be thirsty" (John 6:35). He also told us that that his blood was a covenant for the forgiveness of sin. Paul the apostle, told us: "While we were still sinners, Christ died for us. Since we have now been justified by his blood, how much more shall we be saved from God's wrath through him" (Romans 5:8).

God has always wanted us to remember what he has done for his chosen. It reminds us of what he has done down through the ages for his people. As we remember God's work for us, we grow closer to God.

The Bread and blood was use along with God's covenants. What does the bread and wine represent? The answers to this are found in the scriptures and past history of God's association with his people.

Blood has always been used in sacrifices to God for forgiveness. When Abraham gave his full commitment and was circumcised blood was given. During God's Passover blood was displayed and God protected his people. God instructed his people to always celebrate their Passover with blood sacrifices. He also told them to use blood sacrifices for the forgiveness of sin. He did this when he gave them the Law. In fact, the law requires that nearly everything be cleansed with blood and without the shedding of blood there is no forgiveness.

The other element of the communion is unleavened bread. It was used in the seven days that God used in the Passover. God instructed them to use unleavened bread for the Passover. He also said "Do not offer the blood of a sacrifice to me along with anything containing yeast.

God wanted them to remember what He had done in the Passover so He asked them to celebrate it once a year. He told them to "Obey these instructions as a lasting ordinance for you and your descendants."(Exodus 12:24) God's children followed these instructions for centuries. With Jesus bringing of the New Covenant He wants us to remember Jesus his Messiah. So now we remember Jesus in the same manner as he had disciples.do at the last supper.

Scriptures concerning communion

Mark 14:22-28, Luke 22:19-20, Matthew, 26:26-28, Exodus 12:13 -14, Exodus 12:13 -14, Matthew 26:28, John 6:58, Exodus 34:25, Exodus 12:17, John 6:56-37, Lk 22:19-20, Hebrews 9:22, Romans 5;8, and Luke 22:19-20.

<u>Christmas</u>

Christmas is a joyous celebration in remembrance of God sending his anointed son to earth as a man to give us his Good News of salvation and how we can obtain an eternal life. God wanted man to recognize his son when he sent him. To do this he sent prophecies to his people over 500 years before the birth of Jesus. They told about his birth, how we would recognize him as the Messiah by his teaching and miracles. He also told them how Jesus would institute the Good News with his sacrificial death and resurrection.

When people recognized that Jesus had come and what it meant for their eternal future they wanted to honor the remembrance of his birth. This is why Christians celebrate Jesus' birthday.

During Christmas celebrations, followers celebrate some of the events of the Birth. They remember how Mary and Joseph were betrothed. An angel appeared to Mary and told her she would be having a child sent by the Holy Spirit. As this also affected Joseph and angle was sent to him to explain what was going to happen. Mary and Joseph decided to follow God and raise this child.

The Roman government ordered people to go to their ancestors' town and register for a census.
Mary and Joseph went to Bethlehem for the census even though Mary was about to give birth to Jesus.

There was no place for them to stay. While they were there, the time came for the baby to be born, and she gave birth to Jesus. She wrapped him in cloths and placed him in a manger.

God felt that there should be two witnesses to collaborate the event. He sent angles to tell Shepard's about the birth and they went and found Jesus wrapped in cloths and lying in a manger just as he angles told them. He also directed Magi, from a foreign country, to follow a star that led them to witness the birth of the savior. They presented gifts of gold, incense and myrrh to Jesus.

On the eighth day Jesus was taken to the temple for circumcision. There were two faithful people (devout man Simon and a prophetess Anna) who were aware of the coming of Messiah and they acknowledged him and talked about his upcoming life. God had them witness the fact that He had sent his promised Messiah.

There were many prophecies concerning his birth. They are: The time period when Jesus would live, He would be born as a descendant of King David through a virgin in the city of Bethlehem. He foretold Mary and Joseph about the future birth of their son Jesus. It was foretold that Jesus was bring a New Covenant to man so there would be a new relationship with God and man which leads to an eternal life. *(See the prophecy section for the prophecies associated with Jesus.)*

Scriptures describing Jesus' birth are as follows.

The events of Jesus' Birth are told in **Mathew 1:18 –2: 11, Luke 1: 26-2: 20, Daniel 9:25, Isiah7:14, Isiah 11:1-3, Luke 1:26-37, Micah 5:2-5, Luke 2:1-20,. Matthew 2:1-5, Matthew 2:9-12, Luke 2:27-38, and Matthew 1:18-25.**

Easter

Easter is a Christian celebration of God's New Covenant with all men. "God sent a new promise to man through Jesus. It was a new way to assure man can have eternal life. It is a covenant called the Good News (Gospel). It offers man a way to have an eternal life with God. God wants to make us heirs to His kingdom. He promises that everyone in every nation, tribe, and tongue can have salvation and eternal life. Jesus implemented the Good News covenant by coming to earth, living the prophesied life and being sacrificed for our forgiveness and salvation. Then he was resurrected to prove we can be resurrected to his kingdom. Jesus' actions proved He was sent by God.

We are reminded how God gives us special dispensation or privileges with His unmerited love. It is through this love and grace we can be reconciled to Him. God wants us to believe and have faith in Him. I think God let us know about this Good News because he loves all men and wants them in his kingdom. When you look at his interactions with man down through the ages, you can see He wanted man to be part of his kingdom. He set up ways for us to get to know him and believe in him. Through it we learn his commandments to love Him and each other.

After building a relationship with his chosen people, God was now ready to implement his New Covenant. He wanted us to know that Jesus was his Messiah, so he sent prophecies some 500 to 600 years before he was born.

Some of these prophecies were: The exact time of Jesus' coming as the Messiah or anointed one; The Lord will give a sign by having a virgin give birth to a child and it is to be called Immanuel; Jesus the Messiah is a seed of King David; Jesus would be born in Bethlehem; Jesus (God's messenger) will bring a New Covenant; Jesus would live in Galilee; Jesus will be a prophet and put my word in his mouth; Gods messenger would teach using parables; He would perform miracles; Jesus would be a healer; Jesus' triumphal entry; A future king will present himself to Jerusalem while riding on a humble donkey; Jesus was betrayed by a friend for 30 pieces of silver; Jesus will be scourged; Messiah (Jesus) would be disbelieved and rejected by his people and Rulers; Jesus would be mocked and ridiculed. Jesus would be brought

as a lamb to slaughter; Jesus would be spat and struck; Jesus' hand and feet will be pierced; Jesus intercedes for sinners by bearing their sins; Jesus' life is a guilt offering for the sins of many interceding for the transgressions of many; Parting of Jesus's garments; Jesus' dyeing words; Jesus is put to suffer as the Lord makes his life a guilt offering for sin; Jesus is put to suffer as the Lord makes his life a guilt offering for sin; Jesus' side to be pierced; In 3 days Jesus was raised from the dead; Jesus is to be a light to the gentiles; Coming of the Holy Spirit.; Jesus is to be Gods' Messiah.
*(Scripture references to these prophecies and others can be found in the **Prophecies List** section of this book)*

Jesus, his begotten son, came and implemented the covenant as God had foretold. When Jesus brought this covenant, he also gave us a greater insight of God's will for man. He brought many other messages from God so we could know His Father. Jesus told us he only said what God told him to say. Jesus said "Don't you believe that I am in the Father, and that the Father is in me? The words I say to you are not just my own. Rather, it is the Father, living in me, who is doing his work. Believe me when I say that I am in the Father and the Father is in me; or at least believe on the evidence of the miracles themselves."

He also lived a life exemplifying God so we would know and understand His Father. Jesus taught us how to please God (Beatitudes). We can do this by: being poor in spirit, not being prideful, mourning for others, being gentle, enduring injury with patience and no resentment, living a righteous life, being compassionate to others and helping them, being pure in heart, maintain peace with others, and being righteous when you are persecuted. We need to confess with your mouth that Jesus is Lord of your life and believe in your heart that He is God's Son and he raised Him from the dead. For it is with your heart that you believe and are justified, and it is with your mouth that you confess and are saved.

However, in our remembrance of these events, we are reminded about Jesus' trials and tribulation while bring God's plan to us? Even though he was the Messiah, He grew up in a human family. Upon starting his ministry, he was baptized by John who foretold of his coming. At that time, God announce that Jesus was his son. Right after that, he had to go into the wilderness and be tempted by the devil for 40 days. The devil gave him three trails to lure him form God. Jesus resisted the devil and gave us examples of how we can resist the devil.

He also gathered his disciples and trained them in this new covenant. He performed miracles and healed people so they would know he was the Messiah. His miracles include healing sickness, driving out evil spirits, resurrecting people from the dead and calming storms. (*Examples are found in the **Miracles** section*).

However, during his ministry he had conflicts with the religious leaders. They felt that He was going to upset their religion and wanted to kill him. These conflicts grew over his 3 year ministry.

It became time to face His greatest trail, that of crucifixion. This was part of the implication of God's plan. (*See prophecies and crucifixion section in this book*). Jesus suffered greatly. The Jewish leaders mocked him, put a bag over his head and hit him. He was sent to the Roman governor Pilate who found no cause for a death sentence. Pilate decided to send him to King Heriod who could not find a cause for death. Heriod ridiculed and mocked him and returned to Pilate. Pilate found no reason for him to be put to death. The religious leaders insisted on him being crucified. Pilate wanted to stop a revolt and gave in to the crucifixion. It began with the guard ridiculed him and placed crown of thorns on his head. Then they took him out to be crucified. They nailed him to a cross where he suffered even more. At the end he said it is finished and bowed his head and gave up his spirit. (*More crucifixion detail is included in the* **Crucifixion** *section*)

In the old days, God wanted to make sure you were sorry you sinned. You had to give an animal sacrifice to God for forgiveness so you wouldn't do it again. In the new plan, Jesus was sacrificed for an atonement of your sins so you no longer have to sacrifice an animal. However, God wants to know that you will turn away from sin so He asks you to repent by learning to live in his will. When you ask for forgiveness and repent you are given a new start.

The next part of the plan was a glorious event of

resurrection. Jesus's resurrection demonstrated His ability to resurrect us for an eternal life. *(Further details can be found in the Resurrection section)* He also furnishes us the Holy Spirit and the Bible so we know him and recognize His love, power and ability to give us eternal life. This is the main part of the Easter celebration. **He has risen! He has risen indeed!**

The Easter scriptures are found in the following chapters Matthew **27-28, Mark 15-16, Luke 23-24 and John 19-20.**

Genealogy of Christ
.
Genealogy of Adam to Noah
Genesis 5, 1 Chronicles 1:1-4
Approx. 1656 years

Genealogy of Son of Noah (Shem) to Abraham
Genesis 10: 21- 11: 10-27
1 Chronicles 1: 8-34 Approx.427 yrs.

Genealogy of Abraham to Jacob   I Chronicles 1: 28-54

Genealogy of Jacob to David   Chronicles 2: 1-55

Genealogy of David to Jesus
Mother (In reverse order)   Luke 3: 23-38

Father   Matthew 1:1-18

End Times Prophecies

Prophecies are of interest to all believers because they know that God sends prophecies and then fulfills them.

This assures us of His greatness and holiness and his ability to be our Lord

End times Prophecies are scary because they tell us about the destruction of the world as we know it. They tell us about the war between God and his adversary, Satan, which is concluded here on earth. God also knows Satan will deceive many of His followers with miracles so he can use them in Satan's one world government. This government will be against God and His followers.

God places his faith in his people knowing they will not have to face the second death. He will protect his true believers by taking them away from the tribulation of one world government.

These prophecies deal with signs of approaching end times, Fourth world government, Tribulations under a world Government, Rapture of the saints, the Return of Jesus and his Millennium kingdom, , and the Armageddon war.

Prophecies are mysteries until they are fulfilled. When they are fulfilled, we know the power and the greatness of the One who gave it. The reason that God gives his prophecies he wants us to be looking for them and when it happens we see his power in their fulfillment

Many prophets, at various times, prophesied about The Messiah. During his life, Jesus fulfilled prophecies. Jesus' life was recorded in the gospels of the Bible. With this information, we can now review his life in accordance with the prophecies. In doing this, we see the fulfillment of them and know that he was sent by the Father in accordance with these prophecies. (See the **Prophecies** List Concerning Jesus)

At the time of Jesus, the Pharisees only recognized the prophecies of Jesus' reign (second coming). So they missed the full understanding and came to the conclusion that Jesus was not the Messiah. Their mistake demonstrates that we need to be continually searching the scriptures for a complete understanding of God's action in fulfillment of these prophecies

We must be aware of God's unfulfilled prophecies so when they are fulfilled, we will see God's Glory and have assurance of our eternal life with Him. We don't want to be like the Pharisees seeing only the parts we like. We need to be aware of all prophecies so we will see the fulfilment and not be deceived by Satan. We are told that all who stand firm in their faith will not have the second death.

Keep in mind that my notes may not include all the prophecies. You need to keep reading the scriptures so you will be prepared to go through tribulations and acquire an eternal life.

Signs of the End Times

Jesus told his disciples that in the future there would be many deceivers come after him. He asks us not to be deceived or be afraid of coming events. Some of the events prior to his return are; persecution of believers, wars, earthquakes, famines, pestilences and signs in the heavens. He told us that there would be many tribulations coming to earth near the time of his second coming. After these tribulations he would return to get his believers. Jesus told us that he would return to earth in the same manner he ascended to be with his father after his crucifixion.

These signs are found in **Matthew 24:4-35, Mark 13:5-31, and Luke 21:8-36**.

Luke21: 8 He replied: "Watch out that you are not deceived. For many will come in my name, claiming, 'I am he, and, 'The time is near.' Do not follow them. When you hear of wars and revolutions, do not be frightened. These things must happen first, but the end will not come right away." Then he said to them: "Nation will rise against nation, and kingdom against kingdom.
There will be great earthquakes, famines and pestilences in various places, and fearful events and great signs from heaven.

Matthew 24:24-31 For false Christs and false prophets will appear and perform great signs and miracles to deceive even the elect—if that were possible. See, I have told you ahead of time. "So if anyone tells you, 'There he is, out in the desert,' do not go out; or, 'Here he is, in the inner rooms,' do not believe it. For as lightning that comes from the east is visible even in the west, so will be the coming of the Son of Man. Wherever there is a carcass, there the vultures will gather "Immediately after the distress of those days "'the sun will be darkened, and the moon will not give its light; the stars will fall from the sky, and the heavenly bodies will be shaken.' "At that time the sign of the Son of Man will appear in the sky, and all the nations of the earth will mourn. They will see the Son of Man coming on the clouds of the sky, with power and great glory. And he will send his angels with a loud trumpet call, and they will gather his elect from the four winds, from one end of the heavens to the other.

Mark13:24-29 "But in those days, following that distress, "'the sun will be darkened, and the moon will not give its light; the stars will fall from the sky, and the heavenly bodies will be shaken.' "At that time men will see the Son of Man coming in clouds with great power and glory. And he will send his angels and gather his elect from the four winds, from the ends of the earth to the ends of the heavens. "Now learn this lesson from the fig tree: As soon as its twigs get tender and its leaves come out, you know that summer is near. Even so, when you see these things happening, you know that it is near, right at the door.

Jesus's End Time Prophecy

His prophecies of end times are found in **Matthew 24:1-51, Mark 13:1-30 and Luke 21:6-28.**

Matthew 24:1-35 Jesus left the temple and was walking away when his disciples came up to him to call his attention to its buildings. "Do you see all these things?" he asked. "I tell you the truth, not one stone here will be left on another; everyone will be thrown down." As Jesus was sitting on the Mount of Olives, the disciples came to him privately. "Tell us," they said, "when will this happen, and what will be the sign of your coming and of the end of the age?" Jesus answered: "Watch out that no one deceives you. For many will come in my name, claiming, 'I am the Christ' and will deceive many. You will hear of wars and rumors of wars, but see to it that you are not alarmed. Such things must happen, but the end is still to come. Nation will rise against nation, and kingdom against kingdom. There will be famines and earthquakes in various places. All these are the beginning of birth pains. "Then you will be handed over to be persecuted and put to death, and you will be hated by all nations because of me. At that time many will turn away from the faith and will betray and hate each other, and many false prophets will appear and deceive many people. Because of the increase of wickedness, the love of most will grow cold, but he who stands firm to the end will be saved. And <u>this gospel of the kingdom will be preached in the whole world</u> as a testimony to all nations, and then the end will come. "So when you see standing in the holy place <u>'the abomination that causes desolation,' spoken of through the prophet Daniel—let the reader understand— then let those who are in Judea flee to the mountains.</u> Let no one on the roof of his house go down to take anything out of the house. Let no one in the field go back to get his cloak. How dreadful it will be in those days for pregnant women and nursing mothers! Pray that your flight will not take place in winter or on the Sabbath. For then there will be great distress, unequaled from the beginning of the world until now—and never to be equaled again. If those days had not been cut short, no one would survive, but for the sake of the elect those days will be shortened. At that time if anyone says to you, 'look, here is the Christ!' or, 'There he is!' do not believe it. For false Christs and false prophets will appear and perform great signs and miracles to deceive even the elect—if that were possible. See, I have told you ahead of time. "So if anyone tells you, 'There he is, out in the desert,' do not go out; or, 'Here he is, in the inner rooms,' do not believe it. For as lightning that comes from the east is visible even in the west, so will be the coming of the Son of Man.

Wherever there is a carcass, there the vultures will gather. "Immediately after the distress of those days "'the sun will be darkened, and the moon will not give its light; the stars will fall from the sky, and the heavenly bodies will be shaken.' "At that time the sign of the Son of Man will appear in the sky, and all the nations of the earth will mourn. They will see the Son of Man coming on the clouds of the sky, with power and great glory. And he will send his angels with a loud trumpet call, and they will gather his elect from the four winds, from one end of the heavens to the other. "Now learn this lesson from the fig tree: As soon as its twigs get tender and its leaves come out, you know that summer is near. Even so, when you see all these things, you know that it is near, right at the door. I tell you the truth; this generation will certainly not pass away until all these things have happened. Heaven and earth will pass away, but my words will never pass away.

While reading this prophecy, you might think part of the prophecy has taken place. You can also see that not all these events (Gospel spread to the whole world, the universe being shaken, and the return of Christ did not happen in one family generation.) Jesus also said "These things must happen first, but the end will not come right away. Verses 15-20 seem to have been a partially fulfilled during the Jewish Revulsion where two million seven hundred thousand people were killed, and over one and half million were taken as captives and the Holy Temple was destroyed in 70 AD. It appears that there may have been an abomination that causes desolation also. The history of the events can be found in the history written by Flavius Josephus. According to his record, it happened within a family generation, as was noted in the prophecy. However, the generation that has the distress may be referring to the great tribulation rather than the destruction of the temple in 70 A.D. For a better understanding, I think you need to put this event into context. Percentage wise, for a peoples group, it would comply with this statement, especially when you see the horrific way they faced death (acute famine, the in-fighting, the cannibalism, the savagery, and crucifixions).

The fact that some events have not happened doesn't discredit the prophecy. Jesus also stated in **Luke 21:8** "These things must happen first, but the end will not come right away."

There is also some who believe this prophecy may have been written after the event. Recent proof has been established that the Book of Matthew was in existence before the event. This proves that the prophecy was made before its fulfillment.

Some of the other events were also prophesized in other books of the Bible. For more information you need to look at them. This will prepare you for understanding the fulfillment when it occurs and confirm your belief in God and his son Jesus.

If you are interested in the sequence of end time prophecies there are some indications found in scripture. However, there are many books about end times with different sequences of events. My investigation comes from the Book of Revelation.

Revelation 12:6 -9 The woman fled into the desert to a place prepared for her by God, where she might be taken care of for 1,260 days (*one half of the tribulation period*), and there was war in heaven. Michael and his angels fought against the dragon, and the dragon and his angels fought back. But he was not strong enough, and they lost their place in heaven. The great dragon was hurled down—that ancient serpent called the devil, or Satan, who leads the whole world astray. He was hurled to the earth, and his angels with him. Based on Ephesians the symbol of a woman is the church. The woman is in hiding (Raptured) during the time, times and one half of the tribulation. **Revelation 20:7** When the thousand years are over Satan will be released from his prison, and will go out to deceive the nations in the four corners of the earth —Gog and Magog—to gather them for battle. In number they are like the sand on the seashore.

The rapture happens prior to the war of God (Rev.12:6) and Satin where the devil is forced to the earth. The devil will be bound during the millennium. After his release he returned and got ready to fight God in the Battle of Armageddon. (Rev. 20:7)

These verses seem to indicate a possible sequence of some of the events is as follows: Satan's **government** comes and causes the **tribulation** where the **rapture** (Rev. 12:6) spares the Christians and Jesus comes to power. At the end of the **millennia**, Satan is release and a **war** begins between him and Michael the Archangel (Rev. 12:7-8). Satan is forced back to the earth and prepares for the war of **Armageddon** (Rev. 20:7-8).

Rapture

The Latin word rapture is not in the English Bibles. It was translated as "Caught up".

This is where people, who are in God's book of life, will be taken away from the earth. They are raptured so they will not have to face the hour of trail during the tribulation. They will be given imperishable bodies and be with Jesus. When Jesus returns to set up his kingdom, they will come with him and have imperishable bodies.

*For additional information see notes on **Rapture** section*

Tribulation

The tribulation is a time where Satan is given seven years to rule over the earth. He brings nations together to form a new kingdom. This kingdom in scripture is referred as the fourth beast or fourth kingdom. During this time Satan tries to set up a kingdom against God's. He deceives many in thinking he is in control and should be followed as a God. The first half (three and one half years) of his kingdom he gathers his people and uses various methods to peaceably convince people to follow his government. He does this by discrediting God and showing his power with miracles.

The second half he declares his Lordship over God by putting an end to peoples sacrifice and offering. On a wing of the temple he will set up an abomination that causes desolation.

He becomes more aggressive and wants to eliminate anyone that doesn't accept him. He then has people put his mark on their head or right hand. If they do not take the mark, they will not be able to buy or sell anything. Anyone who doesn't commit to his lordship is sentenced to death.

Those who stand firm in their faith in God and his son Jesus will die but will have their name in God's Book and have eternal life.
Those who commit to the rule of Satan will not have eternal life.

Further information is found the notes on the Tribulation section

Two Witnesses

During the tribulation there will be two witnesses sent by God. They will destroy enemies and be a witness to God. Eventually they will be killed and lie dead for three days. All the people of the world will witness their death. After the three days they will become alive and return to God.

Revelations 11:1-14 tells about this event. Now when they have finished their testimony, the beast that comes up from the Abyss will attack them, and overpower and kill them. Their bodies will lie in the street of the great city, which is figuratively called Sodom and Egypt, where also their Lord was crucified. For three and a half days men from every people, tribe, language and nation will gaze on their bodies and refuse them burial. The inhabitants of the earth will gloat over them and will celebrate by sending each other gifts, because these two prophets had tormented those who live on the earth. But after the three and a half days a breath of life from God entered them, and they stood on their feet, and terror struck those who saw them. Then they heard a loud voice from heaven saying to them, "Come up here." And they went up to heaven in a cloud, while their enemies looked on. At that very hour there was a severe earthquake and a tenth of the city collapsed. Seven thousand people were killed in the earthquake, and the survivors were terrified and gave glory to the God of heaven. The second woe has passed; the third woe is coming soon.

Revelation 11:1-14 I was given a reed like a measuring rod and was told, "Go and measure the temple of God and the altar, and count the worshipers there. But exclude the outer court; do not measure it, because it has been given to the Gentiles. They will trample on the holy city for 42 months. And I will give power to my two witnesses, and they will prophesy for 1,260 days, clothed in sackcloth." These are the two olive trees and the two lampstands that stand before the Lord of the earth. If anyone tries to harm them, fire comes from their mouths and devours their enemies. This is how anyone who wants to harm them must die. These men have power to shut up the sky so that it will not rain during the time they are prophesying; and they have power to turn the waters into blood and to strike the earth with every kind of plague as often as they want

Return of Jesus Christ

Jesus the messiah was prophesized down through the ages. As prophecies are general in nature some did not recognize him in his first coming. However, as we gained a better understanding of the prophecies, and saw he had fulfilled the ones for his first coming. Now we can see clearly, how they apply to his second coming. Jesus also told us he would return. He said that his father is the only one who knows when. Jesus also told us about his second coming and it is recorded in the Gospels. He will come during a time of stress and there will be signs in the heaven. Everyone will see him coming in the clouds. Coming with him, will be the resurrected dead who receive their salvation. Also returning with him, will be those who were raptured. They will also have imperishable bodies like that of the risen dead
Jesus establishes his kingdom to rule the earth. All the nations will be gathered before him, and he will separate the people one from another. He will reward each person according to what he has done. To those who by

persistence in doing good seek glory, honor and immortality, he will give eternal life. But for those who are self-seeking and who reject the truth and follow evil, there will be wrath and anger. He will rule them with an iron scepter. He will teach us his ways, so that we may walk in his path. Jesus will have a peaceful reign for one thousand years. During this time Satan will be put in chains for 1000 years (a millennium) so that he will not interfere with Jesus' rule. After this, Satan will start to cause problems and he and Michael the Archangel will have a war in the heavens. Satan will be destroyed.

Jesus will then reign forever and ever!

For additional more information see <u>Second coming of Christ section.</u>

Millennium

The Millennium is a thousand-year period of time when Christ will return and set up his kingdom and rule the entire world. It will last until Mans pride once again ruins the peace and Satan is released ending the Millennium.

Scriptures references to support these notes
Zechariah 14:4, Isaiah 2:3, Isaiah 11: 6, Isaiah 65:22, Isaiah 54:13, Zephaniah 3:9   Isaiah 61:19, Revelation 20:7, Revelation 20:1- 3.

Further information is found the notes on Millennium section

Armageddon War

This war is the final war fought on earth. It will cause suffering and death.

At the time of this war, the Jewish people will be living in peace. A large horde of Israel's previous enemies will gather and attack to destroy Israel. They will be confident that their great army will not have trouble in destroying Israel. However, God will protect his people by attacking their army with earthquakes, destroying the weapons of the attackers, plague, and bloodshed, torrents of rain, hailstones and burring sulfur. He will also send fire on land of Gog.
For a more descriptive account of the war see the notes on **Armageddon war section**

Signs of the second coming.

Jesus told his disciples that in the future there would be many deceivers come after him. He asks us not to be deceived or be afraid of coming events. Some of the events prior to his return are; persecution of believers, wars, earthquakes, famines, pestilences and signs in the heavens. He told us that there would be many tribulations coming to earth near the time of his second coming. After these tribulations he would return to get his believers. Jesus told us that he would return to earth in the same manner he ascended to be with his father after his crucifixion.

Luke21: 8 He replied: "Watch out that you are not deceived. For many will come in my name, claiming, 'I am he, and, 'The time is near.' Do not follow them. When you hear of wars and revolutions, do not be frightened. These things must happen first, but the end will not come right away." Then he said to them: "Nation will rise against nation, and kingdom against kingdom.
There will be great earthquakes, famines and pestilences in various places, and fearful events and great signs from heaven. . **Matthew 24:29** "Immediately after the distress of those days '"the sun will be darkened, and the moon will not give its light; the stars will fall from the sky, and the heavenly bodies will be shaken.' "At that time the sign of the Son of Man will appear in the sky, and all the nations of the earth will mourn. They will see the Son of Man coming on the clouds of the sky, with power and great glory. And he will send his angels with a loud trumpet call, and they will gather his elect from the four winds, from one end of the heavens to the other. See **Mark13:24** for additional description

The second coming of Christ

Prophecies concerning Jesus have been in the scriptures for centuries. They are confusing because Jesus comes to earth twice. He first came to implement God's Covenant for man's salvation. His second coming is for those that obtained their salvation and set up an eternal kingdom for them.
Jesus, prior to his death said he would be resurrected and later returns and set up his earthly kingdom. He told us no one knows about that day or hour, not even the angels in heaven, nor the Son, but only the Father. He will

come at an hour when you do not expect him. In the meantime, many will come in his name, claiming to be him and will deceive many, He wants us watch out so none deceived us. He wants to warn against this so we will remain faithful and be ready for his return. Before he returns, there will be signs in the sun, moon and stars. Nations will be in anguish and perplexity at the roaring and tossing of the sea. Men will faint from terror, apprehensive of what is coming on the world, for the heavenly bodies will be shaken. The sun will be darkened, and the moon will not give light. Suddenly, like the appearance of a thief, you will see Jesus coming in a cloud with power and his Father's glory with his angels. Everyone will see him just as they would see lightening in the east from the west. He will bring his saints, an army of angles. On his robe and on his thigh he has this name written: KING OF KINGS AND LORD OF LORDS.

He brings his followers from the dead who received salvation and have been resurrected with imperishable bodies and those who received imperishable bodies through the rapture.
He will set up his kingdom and strike down the nations and rule them with an iron scepter. An angle from heaven will announce "The kingdom of the world has become the kingdom of our Lord and of his Christ, and he will reign forever and ever" All the nations will be gathered before him, and he will separate the people one from another as a shepherd separates the sheep from the goats.

Jesus will rule for a millennium. During this millennium, there will be peace and he will reward each person according to what he has done. He will teach us his ways, so that we may walk in his path. To those who by persistence in doing good seek glory, honor and immortality, he will give eternal life.

At the end of the millennium, Satan will be released. He will then have a war with God in the heaven. He will lose this war and return to earth. He will try to deceive people again and then they will attack Jerusalem. This will anger God and he will destroy Satan.

Scriptures concerning Jesus's 2nd coming.
Mathew 24: 36, I Thessalonians 5:2, Hebrews 9:27, Mark 13:24-26, 1Thesaloinins 4:14-15, Matthew 24:27-31, Luke 21: 25, Matthew 16:27, Romans 2:6-8, Matthew25:31-32, Revelation 9:14, Revelation 11:15, Revelation 22:12 -14.

Rapture

The Latin word rapture is not in the English Bibles. It was replaced with the words "caught up". The Rapture is an event where believers will be taken up from the earth to meet Christ. Jesus described the event as follows: "Two men will be in the field; one will be taken and the other left. Two women will be grinding with a hand mill; one will be taken and the other left. Therefore, keep watch, because you do not know on what day your Lord will come."

Many people believed that this event is associated with the tribulation of end times. Bible scholars speculate as to exactly when it will happen. Some believe it will be at the beginning of the tribulation. Others believe that it will be in the middle or end of the tribulation.

In any case, it is when Jesus is getting ready to return to set up his earthly kingdom.

Dead believers will be resurrected imperishable to enjoy eternal life. After that, followers who are still alive will be caught up (Raptured) in the clouds and given imperishable bodies to live with Jesus forever. Everyone whose name is found written in the book of life will be delivered. This rapture is for the benefit and protection of believers from the hour of trial that is going to come upon the whole world. The believer will to be with Jesus when he returns for his millennia reign.

Scriptures references to support these notes

Matthew 24:40, I Thessalonians 4:16, Daniel 12:1, I Corinthians 15:50, Revelation 3:10, 1 Thessalonians 4:13-17, Revelation 3:10, Revelation 12:6.

Tribulation

Prophecies are mysteries until they are fulfilled and we have a full understanding of its fulfillment. The end time prophecies that bother Christians are those of Satan's world organization (Fourth beast/kingdom) and its tribulation period where Christian believers will be killed.
Daniel 9 prophecies concern a seventy-week period. Sixty nine of these weeks have taken place. The 70th week is said to be the time of the tribulation. In reviewing these prophecies and other accounts it was found that a week referred to seven years. The tribulation is seven years long and is divided into three and half years of world peace and three and on half years of extreme tribulation. During this

time a new kingdom will be established which is different than other kingdoms. It is described as having seven heads with ten crowns that has the power to rule the earth with the aid of Satan. When you see this kingdom, understand that the end is near and we must decide between God and Satan. It will have authority over all people and nations. It will be proud and will use blasphemy in order to exercise authority. Their leader and false prophets will appear and perform great signs and miracles. It will devour the whole earth using Satan's power. It will confirm a covenant with many for seven years. In the middle of the seven years he will put an end to peoples sacrifice and offering. And on a wing of the temple he will set up an abomination that causes desolation. This will start the second time, times and one half of the tribulation. Satan will give the beast (kingdom) power and authority to make war with all people and conquer them. It will last during the time of trial. This kingdom wants to be worshiped. It will be given power to bring forth a belief that all should worship. Anyone who will not worship will be killed. To insure this worship, they will force people to place a mark on their right hand or on their forehead. People that do not have this mark will not be able to buy or sell. This mark is the name or the number of its name (666). Those who do not want to follow the will of this kingdom will be killed.

We can be thankful God's followers who are in the book of life both dead and raptured will not face this tribulation. Those who have not made this decision will have to make their decision during the tribulation. Followers of God will be killed but their name will appear in God's book and they will receive eternal life with our Father and Jesus Christ. Those who chose life with Satan will live through this tribulation, but not have eternal life. At the end of the tribulation Jesus will come with his saint for his second coming. It is wonderful to know the God will conquer Satan and will bring with his lasting kingdom after this tribulation.

Scriptures regarding the tribulation
Matthew 24:9, Mark 13:19, Luke 21: 11, Daniel 7:7-8, Daniel 7:23-28 Daniel 8:19-25, Daniel 9:27. Daniel 12:7-8, Revelation 13:1-8, Revelation 13:11-18, Revelation 11:2-3, And Revelation 14:9

Woes to Christians ----Revelation 14:9, Revelation 14, John 12: 48.

Scriptures for hope in during this time.--Daniel 12:1, John 6:40, Revelation 3:10, Revelation 3:5, Daniel 12:11-12

Comments
In reviewing these prophecies, certain factors came to mind which gave me a different insight to these prophecies. As I am not a prophet, I cannot vouch for the correctness of my thoughts. If you are deeply concerned with these prophecies, I suggest you read them with an open mind and see if God will give you an understanding of the meaning of these prophecies.

My thoughts I had during my review are:
Daniel refers to the beast and coming governments in his vision in chapter 7. At this time, Nebuchadnezzar, who God had given power to rule the world, was dead. This would eliminate the Golden head noted in Daniel 2. This leaves 3 future national kingdoms to come forth. Those governments Persian, Greek and Roman have come and gone.

Later in Daniel 7, he discusses the fourth beast or kingdom. This is a new world power which is different than the previous kingdoms mentioned in Daniels 2. Looking at the surrounding prophecies, you see that nations are all mentioned. Even afterward, when Jesus returns, nations are mentioned. Daniel also mentions kingdoms that make up this new beast/ kingdom.

The fourth beast wants all men to follow and worship it. With the aid of Satan it will perform miracles to convince men to follow them. Then after they have done this, they will force people to their views. If you disagree, you will be killed or they will take away your ability to buy and sell. This seems to me that the beast is different because it is a war of men and their beliefs rather than a physical territory and earthly goods.

With all this in mind, I think we need to have hope and understanding of Christ's return which ends this tribulation. In the meantime, we need to abide in Christ, so we will be raptured and not face this test and trail.

Millennium

The Millennium is a thousand-year period of time when Christ will return and set up his kingdom and rule the entire world. It will last until Mans pride once again ruins the peace and Satan is released ending the Millennium.

Scriptures references to support these notes

Zechariah 14: 4, Isaiah 2: 3, Isaiah 11:6, Isaiah 65: 22, Isaiah 54:13, Zephaniah 3: 9. Isaiah 61:19, Revelation 20:7, Revelations 21:1.

Armageddon War

Earlier, God warned his people if they were disobedient or worshiped other gods, they would not live in the Promised Land. The Israelites started worshiping other gods and were disobedient to God's commands. As their father, He felt he had to discipline them so they would realize what they had done and return to Him. He sent them into exile for 70 years in Babylon so they would understand his lordship. When they still didn't respond, God increased their return time. Their return was delayed until 1948. God returned his people to their land in 1948 to 1967 as he promised. *(For an explanation of this, see the note on* **"God's exile of his Promised Land***")* He returned them and now he will protect them. He has planned this for some time. He sent prophecies over 2500 years ago, telling how he would protect his chosen people.

He wants his chosen people to live in peace in their own country. God knew that when he returned them, it would provoke enemies to devise an evil scheme to destroy his people. They will have one of the largest armies ever gathered.

Graciously, God will protect his people in such a way that all the nations will see his greatness, holiness and realize He is Lord. It is wonderful that God sends us prophecies and then assures that they are fulfilled so we will know Him and His love for all.

He sent prophesy concerning how he would assure the safety of his people from this attack. It describes the nations that will attack his people. The names go back to ancient times when the prophecy was recorded. So, we must look to see, who descendants are. The prophecy states that Gog, Meshech, Tubal, Persia, Cush Gomer Beth Togarmah and Put and many other nations attack Israel. Many of the names came from Noah's grandsons who settled north of Israel extending to southern Russia. This would be Gog, Meshech, Tubal, Gomer and Beth Togarmah. Persia is well known as Iran today. Some history indicates that Put is from Egypt and some say Cush (Kush) appears to be from the Sudan area. An exact placement of some of the counties may not be known until the time of the event. However, when we see the gathering of the noted countries above, we need to remember God's prophecy and his fulfillment actions. We are assured of God's greatness, holiness when we see this fulfilment and realize He is Lord.

God will have Gog, Beth Togarmah, Persia, Cush, Put, Gomer, and many other conspiring nations gather their whole armies into Israel. They will come as great horde, a mighty army, feeling that with their weapons, they will easily destroy unsuspecting peoples of Israel. They will be like a cloud covering the land. When Gog's great army attacks, this will anger God. In his zeal and fiery wrath there will be a great earthquake in the land and the mountains will be overturned. This will make all the people and animal on earth to tremble. God will issue judgment against the invading army. He will strike the invaders weapons and send plague and bloodshed and then pour down torrents of rain, hailstones and burring sulfur. Every man will be against his brother. The invading armies will fall in Israel's mountains. God gives Gog's army a burial place in Israel. God will also send fire against the land of Magog. God's in the ancient of days will and pronounced judgment in favor of his people and they will possessed the kingdom.

This shows us God's glory and the punishment he lays

on evil ones. God's actions prove his greatness and holiness so we will know He is Lord.

It also shows that God is with his people and he has completed their discipline for their prior sins. He wants his people to have their land and live peaceably. God says "I will no longer hide my face from them, for I will pour out my Spirit on the house of Israel declares the Sovereign LORD". God no longer wants his name profaned and the nations know he is Lord. His Holy name will be among his people.

Scriptures references to support these notes
Deuteronomy 30:17, Ezekiel 38:2, Ezekiel 38:5, Ezekiel 38:8, Ezekiel 38:15 , Ezekiel 38: 19, Ezekiel 38:21, Ezekiel 39:3, Ezekiel 39:6, Ezekiel 39:11, Ezekiel 39:23, Ezekiel 39:27, Ezekiel 39:29, Daniel 7:21,, Revelation16:16 Revelation16:21 Revelation20:7,

Judgment

Everyone will be judged as to his action he takes while living. The Bible has many warnings of judgment. Judgment is mentioned more than 300 times in the Bible. We are warned about the things that will bring about judgment. Some of the major ones are: murder, sexual immorality, impurity, debauchery, idolatry and witchcraft, hatred, discord, jealousy, rage, orgies. If we don't repent and ask for forgiveness and stop these things we will face judgment. All of these evil thoughts come from our hearts so we must monitor our thoughts to keep them out of our hearts.

There appears to be two major times that men will be judged. One is when Jesus returns in his glory at the beginning of the Millennium. The other is at the great white throne after the millennium before God and his Book of life.

Jesus' judgment comes at the end of tribulation when he returns in glory. All those that were killed due to their steadfast to Christ during the tribulation will be resurrected. Jesus then separates the people one from another as a shepherd separates the sheep from the goats. Those he shepherds will be given their inheritance in the kingdom and are not subject to the second death at the great throne judgment.

The second judgment is of the dead and those in Hades after the millennium at the Great white throne. There will be a resurrection of the good and the wicked. Those who are not in the book of life will die a second death when they are thrown in to the lake of fire. Those who are in the Book of Life will inherit the kingdom and will be with God and his sons.

Scriptures references to support these notes

Matthew 25:31, Revelations **20:4, Revelation 20:11, Galatians 5:19, Matthew 5:21, Matthew 12:36, John 5:55, Hebrews 9:27.**

Salvation

What must I do to be saved? God wants everyone to be with him. However, you must love and believe in him. You need to believe in Jesus and his resurrection. You are to be obedient to his will. God sees your love for him, when you are obedient. When you are not obedient you sin against him.

God understands and knows we have to go through a learning process thus he sent the new covenant where we can be forgiven and start anew by continuing in his will. When you believe and follow God and his son Jesus, God assures that you will have an everlasting life with him in heaven. When you ignore God's and his grace shown in the new covenant you will not have and eternal life with God and Jesus.

Following are scriptures concerning salvation. Romans 3:20, Romans 6:23, Romans 10: 9, Romans 10: 13, Ephesians 2: 8, Acts 16: 31, Romans 6:22, Revelations 19:6, John 4: 24, 1 John 4: 8.
More are found in the Gospel or Good new section

Fall of Jerusalem

After Josiah die (608BC) as a result of a battle with Egypt, his son Jehoahaz reigned for 3 months. Egypt then came to Judah and removed him and made his brother king of Judah. His brother was renamed Jehoiakim. Judah was now a vassal of Egypt. They were vassal for three years until Egypt was defeated at Carchemish by Babylon in 605BC. *(See 2 Kings 23:30-37, Chronicles 35:20-36:5)*

Nebuchadnezzar, the new king of Babylon then turned his attention on Judah. He besieged Jerusalem. Judah became a vassal to Babylonian. Nebuchadnezzar took some of the articles of the house of God. He also took some of the children of Israel, the king's descendants and the nobles. Daniel and his friends were part of those taken. This begins the servitude of Judah to Babylon. *(See 2 Kings 24:1-16, Chronicles 36:4-10, Daniel 1:1)*

After three years, Egypt and Babylon are still trying to control the lands. Jehoiakim feels that the time is right and he rebels against Babylon. Nebuchadnezzar is upset and comes against Jerusalem. He leads a siege of Jerusalem. Three months before the end of the siege, Jehoiakim's son Jehoiachin becomes king. The siege was ended when Nebuchadnezzar summoned Jehoiachin. He and his family were taken to Babylon in 597 BC. Babylon took all the treasures of the house of the Lord and the treasures of the king's house. He cut in pieces all the articles of gold, which Solomon had made in the temple of the Lord. He also carried into captivity all of the captain and mighty men of valor, ten thousand captives and craftsman. Only the poorest people were left. Nebuchadnezzar made Jehoiachin's uncle ruler. His name became Zedekiah. *(See 2 Kings 23-24:16, 2 Chronicles 36:4-10)*

Zedekiah reigned for nine years as a vassal of Babylon, and then Egypt became stronger. He decided it was a good time to rebel against Babylon. This angered Nebuchadnezzar. He brought his armies against Judah. They besieged Jerusalem. The siege lasted for 18 months (588-586BC). It was a terrible time of sickness and death. The King tried to escape, but he was captured later. Nebuchadnezzar made him watch the killing of his sons. Then he blinded the king. Zedekiah was taken to Babylon as a prisoner. All the treasures of the temple and the city were taken to Babylon. The House of the Lord and the kings and great men's houses were burned. The walls of the city and temple were torn down. *(See 2 Kings 25, 2 Chronicles 36:13-21)*

Isaiah (Isaiah 39:6) and Micah (Micah 4:10) predicted the captivity of Judah by Babylon 100 years before the event. The fall of Judah brought the ministries of Jeremiah, Ezekiel, and Daniel. Jeremiah predicted that it would last 70 years (Jeremiah 25:11).

The people returned after 70 years of captivity as Jeremiah had predicted. Their return is told in the books of Ezra, Nehemiah and Ester. There were three major returns. In 536BC.,Zerubbabel, with 42,360, 7337servents, 200 singers (Ezra 2: 64) returned to Judah., In 457B.C., Ezra Took 1754 males and their families.(Ezra 8:1) 444BC Nehemiah went back as governor, He took people with him. He later took account of those in Jerusalem. There were 42,360 and their servants (Nehemiah 7)

Israelites Captivity

The captivity started in 606B.C. A second group was taken on 597 B.C. The final group was taken and the temple was destroyed 586B.C.
Cyrus the king of Persia overthrew Babylon in 539 B.C. He allowed the Jews to return in 538B.C. The rebuilding of the temple began in 536B.C. The work was stopped in 534B.C. and resumed and the temple was finished in 520B.C.

Noah and the Flood
According to Bishop Usher.

The total time in the ark was 377days (based on the old calendar of 1 month = 30) days.

Embarking takes 7 days.   Genesis 7:4, 10

Rain lasts   40 days and 40 nights.   Genesis 7:4, 7:12
The water prevails for 150 days, Genesis 7:24

The water takes   150 days to subside   Genesis 8:3

After getting out of the arch it takes 70 days for the earth to dry. Genesis 8:4

Total   377 days

God told Noah and the family to enter the ark 7 days before he would bring the flood (Genesis 7:4.). God started the flood when Noah was 600, 2 months and 17 days old (Genesis 7:1). And it rained for 40 days and forty nights and the water covered the earth for 150 days (Genesis 7:24.). It took 150days for the water to recede and the Ark to stop on top of Mt. Ararat. (5 months after the start of the flood. Genesis 8:3-4). And it took another 70 days for the earth to dry. Noah tested for dry land using a raven and a dove. When the dove returned with an olive leaf Noah knew the earth was drying out. God informed him to come out of the arch when Noah was 601, 2 months and 27 days old (Genesis 8:14-16). This meant that from the day the rain started until God told him to come out it was 1 year and 10 days from the day rain came to getting out of the Ark (370 days) and 7days prior to rain making the entire time in the Ark 377days.

(Calculation Time is based on the Jewish calendar with 360 days). This event is thought to have occurred around 2348 BC. After the Flood Noah's sons went different directions to settle with their families. Shem's family probable went to Asia. Ham's family probably settled in Africa. Japhel's family probable settled in Europe

Tower of Babel The Tower has had many names in various cultures. It has been call The Tower of Jupiter Belus, Temple of the seven lights of the Earth, Tower of Tongues. It seems that it may have been located near the ruins of Babylon. It was 650 feet high, 8 stories, quarter of a mile square at the base. It is described by Nebuchadnezzar in the Borsippa inscription. It is estimated that this temple was built in 2300BC (See **Genesis 11:1-9**) After the Flood Noah's sons went different directions to settle with their families. Shem's family probable went to Asia. Ham's family probably settled in Africa. Japhel's family probable settled in Europe.

Tabernacle   God wanted the Israel people to have a place to worship while they the wilderness. God told them exactly how to build the tabernacle. This description is found in Exodus 25:31. It was a likeness of something that foreshadowed of heavenly things. Later when they built the temple, it follows some of the same principles. This structure and the temple were highly reverenced by the Israelites. The Tabernacle itself was 30 cubits or 45 ft. long, 10 cubits or 15 ft. wide and 10 cubits or 15 Ft high. Inside was a worship area where the most holy place or Holy of Holies where the Ark of the Covenant was kept. The Holy of Holies was in the west portion of the tabernacle and was a 15 Ft cube. The high priest would enter this area once a year for the atonement of the people. God would be present on the mercy seat of the ark. The Holy Place was the 30 feet on the east end of the tabernacle It contained the Table of Shewbread which was a symbol of gratitude to God for daily bread, on north side , the Candlestick on the south side; the Altar of Incense, just before the Veil. The veil was made of the finest linen blue, purple and scarlet, exquisitely embroidered with Cherubs. It separated the holy from the most holy. Outside this area was the Court. . The outer courts of the Tabernacle are 100 cubits or 150feet long, 50 Cubits or 75ft. wide and 5 cubits or 7.5ft. high. A Laver and an Altar of burnt offerings was in this court yard. The Laver was a great brass bowl to hold water, for the priest to wash their hands. The Altar for sacrifice of animals was 7.5 ft. Square and 4.5 ft. high. It was made of acacia boards covered with brass. It had a flame that never went out.

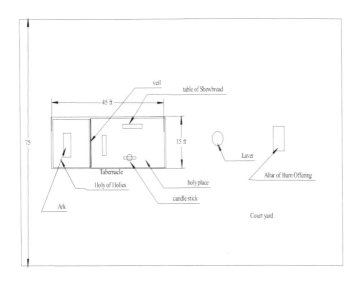

Sacred vessel of the sanctuary. The Ark was made of acacia wood two and a half cubits long, a cubit and a half wide, and a cubit and a half high. (A cubit is approximately 17 to 21 inches in length.) The wood was covered with pure gold overlay, both inside and out, and has a gold molding around it. Gold rings and put on each foot and another 2 rings are added on the sides so that the ark and be carried by putting poles through the rings. Poles are put in the rings where they stay when needed. The atonement cover is made of pure gold. It is two and a half cubits long and a cubit and a half wide. There are two cherubim made from gold. The cherubim are to have their wings spread upward, overshadowing the cover with them. The cherubim are to face each other, looking toward the cover. This cover is sometimes called the Mercy seat, where God is to meet with the high priest. Inside of the Ark are God Testimony (10 commandments) given to the people of Israel, a pot of manna and Aaron's rod.

Hebrew Calendar, Festivals and celebrations

Hebrew Calendar	Today's calendar	Israel's Festivals	Bible References
Abib (Nisan) 1st Month of calendar	March-April	Passover (Reminder of God's deliverance over death for his people)	Exodus 12:1
		Unleavened Bread (the beginning of the Exodus from Egypt.)	Exodus 12:31
		First Harvest (of 1st crop of the year	Leviticus 23:10
Zin (Iyyar)	April-May		

Sivan	May–June	Harvest (Pentecost or first fruits Joy and thanksgiving over the bountiful harvest)	Leviticus 23:9
Tammuz	June-July		
AB	July-August		
Elul	August-September		
Ethanaim (Tishri)	September-October	Trumpets (Rosh Hashanah) Day of Atonement (Yom Kippur) Shelters (Renewal to God and trust in his protection)	Numbers 29:1 Leviticus 23:26 Leviticus 23:24
Bul Marcheshvan)	October-November	First temple completed	1 Kings. 8:2
Kislev	November-December	Dedication (Hanukkah)	Nehemiah dedication to the rebuilding of Jerusalem
Teveth	December-January		
Shebat	January-February		
Adar	February-March	Purim (celebrate the saving of the Jews while in captivity in Babylon)	Esther 9:18

Hebrew Calendar

Hebrew months were alternately 30 and 29 days long. Their year was shorter than ours, (354 days). Therefore, about every 3 years an extra 29 day-month, Veadar, was added between Adar and Nisan. Jews had two Calendars one Civil and one Sacred.

**Names of Months (Hebrew and ours)   No. of Days.
Months of sacred year**

Abib (Nisan) Mar. Apr.30-1st. Mo.

Ziz (Iyyar) Apr. May29 -2nd Mo.

Sivan   May Jun.30 3rd Mo.

Tammuz   Jun.- Jul..29 4th Mo.

AB   Jul.-Aug.30 5th Mo.

Elul   Aug.-Sept.29 6th Mo.

Ethanaim (Tishri)Sept.-Oct. 30 7th mo.

Heshvan (Bul) Oct-Nov. 29 or 30th 8 mo.

Chislev (Kislev)Nov. – Dec.29 or 30 9th mo.

Tebeth   Dec. – Jan.29 10th Mo.

Shebat   Jan.-Feb.30,   11th mo.

Adar   Feb-Mar.29 or 30   12th Mo.

Twelve tribes of Israel
(Sons of Jacob) Judah, Reuben, Gad, Asher, Naphtali, Dan, Simeon, Levi, Issachar, Zebulun, Joseph, Benjamin. Levi and Joseph were not allotted land. Levi descendants became priest and lived in all the tribal lands. Joseph's land was given to his two children (Manasseh and Ephraim).

The greatest laws of God
(*The 10 Commandments*)

The detailed statements of the Laws are found in Exodus Chapter 20. Simply listed they are:

1. **You shall have no other gods before me.**

2. **You shall not make for yourself an idol and worship it.**

3. **You shall not misuse the name of the LORD your God**

4. **Remember the Sabbath day by keeping it holy**

5. **Honor your father and your mother**

6. **You shall not murder**

7. **You shall not commit adultery**

8. You shall not steal

9. You shall not give false testimony against your neighbor

10. You shall not covet your neighbor's

Jesus explained a summation of these commandments

Matthew 22:37-40
Jesus replied: "'Love the Lord your God with all your heart and with all your soul and with all your mind. This is the first and greatest commandment. And the second is like it: 'Love your neighbor as yourself. All the Law and the Prophets hang on these two commandments

God's 400 years of silence

After most of the people had returned to Judah and the city walls were repaired, God sent no messages to his people for 400 years. This silent period indicates that God was still upset with the disobedience of his people. The silence was broken when the Angel Gabriel told the priest Zacharias he would have a son John and later told of the birth of the Messiah. From that time on Jesus and the Holy Spirit communicated with man and God's teaching was recorded in the New Testament. Now we can review the messages from God and better understand him.

Monies and weights

Weights.
Talent   91 lbs.
Mina   18.2 oz.
Shekel   .364 oz.
Gerah   0.0182 oz.

New Testament Monies

Denarius   1 days wages
Copper coin   1/16 of a day's wages
Quadrans (penny) 1/64 of a day's wages
Mite   1/128 of a day's wages.

Measures of Length (Bible times)

Rod   9 ft.
Pace   3 ft.
Cubit   1.5 ft.
Span   9 inches
Hand-breath   3 inches
Finger   ¾ inch

Dry Measures
Homer   6.5 Bu.
Seah   2.1 Bu.
Ephah   65 Bu.
Omer   2.087 Qts.

Liquid Measures
Kor   60 Gal.
Bath   6 Gal.
Hin   1 Gal
Kab   2 Qts.
Log   1 pt.

1. Oldest men in Bible.
a. Methuselah 969
b. Jared 962
c. Noah 950
d. Adam 930
e. Seth 912
c. Cainan 910
d. Enos 905

2. Men who did not die
Enoch   Heb. 11:5
Elijah   2 Kings 2:11

Days of Creation

1st day	Heavens and earth
2nd day	Sky, sea and land
3rd day	plants, grass and trees
4th day	sun, moon and stars
5th day	fish and birds
6th day	Animals, insects, Adam and Eve.
7th day	God rested.

God, Man and Jerusalem

The Bible records the acts of God and man concerning Jerusalem. You can see God's love and man's desire to possess it.

One of the first times it is mentioned was when God had a high priest named Malchizedek who lived in Salem (Jerusalem). Abraham gave homage to God and Malchizedek in Jerusalem (Genesis 14:18-24). After he visited with Malchizedek, God gave him a vision and told him he would be with him and he would have a child for his inheritance. His descendants would be as many as the stars in the sky. He told him that his descendants should inherit the land (Genesis 15:1-7).

When Isaac grew up, God told Abraham to go to Mount Moriah (in Jerusalem) and demonstrate his faith by sacrificing his beloved son. As Abraham showed his faith, God stopped Abraham and Isaac was saved. God furnished a ram for his sacrifice (Genesis 22:2).

God told Abraham that his descendants would be stranger in a country and become slaves and mistreated for four hundred years (Genesis 15:13). This message was fulfilled by Joseph bringing them to Egypt (Genesis 45). During this time Salem (Jerusalem) was conquered by Jebusites. The Jebusites were able to hold ownership and they felt it could withstand an attack from anyone. When the Promised Land was given to the Israelites, they did not take Jerusalem.

When King David was gathering the Israelites and forming his kingdom, he decided to take Jerusalem. God allowed David to overcome the Jebusites (2 Samuel 5:7). God told King David, he was going to leave his tent (tabernacle) and have a home in Jerusalem. His son would build God's Temple. (2 Samuel 7:7-17). God told King David exactly where he wanted his temple in

Jerusalem (2 Samuel 24:18-25).

David continued to plan for God's temple but God told him that his son would build the temple. His succeeding son Solomon built the temple. God was pleased with the temple and appeared as a cloud filling it with his glory (1 Kings 8:10-15).

Israelites abandon God after Solomon's reign. God was angered and lost faith in his people. He then decided to discipline them. He had them removed from Jerusalem for 70 years. After that period he arranged for their return. When this new generation first returned they did not put importance in rebuilding God's temple. So God extended the time for them to regain ownership of Jerusalem (*See God's exile of his people section for further information and Bible references.*). During this exile, many people were killed in military battles to obtain Jerusalem. This conflict is caused by spiritual differences. The strange part of this is both recognize the same God of Abraham in different ways. God returned Jerusalem to his chosen people in accordance with his plan in 1967.

God tells us that Jerusalem's ownership will be resolved with the Armageddon war (See the section on the Armageddon war for more information). He also promises us a New Jerusalem where He and all men will live together in peace and joy. (Revelations 21:1-3).

Prophecies / Fulfillment

See the former things have taken place, and new things I declare before they spring into being I announce them to you.
Isaiah 42:9

Prophecies and their fulfillment tell us that there is a God that is controlling the events of mankind. Many of them are so far apart in time that you know it could not be done by man. It has to be done by someone who is eternal with power to make the prophecy and fulfill them over a period of time.

I gathered these prophecies and their fulfillment when I wanted to understand God's continued action with man. All of the prophecies are taken from God's word. Some of the fulfillments are also in his word. However, many of these fulfillments are found in man's history. Many great scholars have gone to the trouble of verifying these fulfillments. We need to thank them for proving God's love for man and his willing to teach us righteousness. I don't want to take credit for this information. I'm just furnishing what I have found. There are many books and internet sources, where you can find these and many more prophecies that verify their fulfillments. I hope that this list will aid you in helping other understand and believing in our God.

Prophecies concerning Jesus

1. The exact time of Jesus coming as the Messiah or anointed one. There were to be 69 week (483 year) of the 70 weeks prophesized by Daniel *(Daniel 9:24-25, 530 BC.)*
Fulfilled-Jesus came as prophesied and was anointed then was cut off of rule in the 69 week.. *(33 AD. Matthew 27, Mark 15, Luke 23, John19 and Jewish historians)*

2. The Lord will give a sign by having a virgin give birth to a child and it is to be called Immanuel. *(Isaiah 7:11-14, 686-650 BC.)*
Fulfilled: **Birth of Jesus,** *(0 AD., Matthew 1:23, Luke 1:26)*

3. Messiah would be from a woman. *(Genesis 3:15, 1446-1405 B.C.)*

Fulfilled: **Jesus was born of Mary** *(0 AD. 0 A.D.)*

4. Jesus the Messiah is a seed of King David. (*2 Samuel 7:12 Jeremiah 23:5, Psalms 89:3,110:1,132:11, Isaiah 11:1-11 686-650 B.C.)*
Fulfilled: **Jesus is a descendant of King David** (*Matt. 22:44, Mark 12:36, Luke 1:69, John 7:42, (Matthew 1:1, 22:44, Luke 1:69 John 7:42, Mark 12; 36, Romans 1:3, 0 AD.)*

5. Foretelling of the birth of Jesus to Mary *(Luke 1:26-37, Matthew 1:20, 1 BC).*
Fulfilled: Jesus the Christ was through Mary *(0 A.D. Matthew 2, Luke 2,)*

6. Jesus will be born of a virgin *(Isaiah 7:14, Matthew1:23 686-650 BC)*
Fulfilled: **Mary was a virgin and gave birth to Jesus.** *(Matthew1:22-25)*

7. Jesus will be born in Bethlehem, *(Micah 5:2, 425 BC.)*
Fulfilled: **Jesus was born in Bethlehem** (*Matthew 2:5-6 & John 7:42, 0 A.D., Matthew 2:1, Luke 2:4-6)*

8. Jesus (God's messenger) will bring a New Covenant, (*Malachi 3:1, 430 B.C.)*
11:10, Luke 7:27)
Fulfilled Jesus brought the New Covent by his action of his life (*Gospels verify the sending of the new covenant 30-33 AD.)*

9. A messenger will be sent ahead of Jesus to prepare his way. (*Malachi 3, 431 B.C, Isaiah 40).*
   Fulfilled: **John the Baptist prepared a way for Jesus** (*30 B.C., Matthew 11:10, Luke 7:27)*

10. Birth of John the Baptist is foretold to Zachariah in the temple, *(Luke 1:5-19, 1 B.C.)*
   Fulfilled: **John was born,** *1 B.C., Luke 1:57-63*

11. Jesus coming would cause a massacre of Bethlehem's children. *(Jeremiah 31:15, 627-580 B.C.*
   Fulfilled: **Herod had the children of Bethlehem killed.** *(1 A.D., Matthew 2-17-18).*

12. Jesus would go to Egypt *(Hosea 11:1, 760-720 B.C.)*
   Fulfilled: **Jesus' family goes to Egypt** *(1 AD., Matthew 2:13-15)*

13. Jesus would live in Galilee *(Isaiah 9:1, 686--650 BC.)*
   Fulfilled: **Jesus came from Galilee to begin his ministry***(1-30 AD, Matthew 4:15, Mark 1, Luke 2& john 4)*

14. Jesus will live in Nazareth *(Isaiah 11:1, 686--650 BC.)*
   Fulfilled: **Jesus lived in Nazareth** *(1-30 AD., Matthew 2:23,)*

15. Jesus will be a prophet and put my word in his mouth. *(Deuteronomy 18:15-18, 1446-1405 B.C.)*
   Fulfilled. **He also said that his words came from the father. They were leaders, delivered from death as infants, performed miracles they were intermediaries between God and Man.** *(30 A.D., Matthew 13:57)*

16. Gods messenger would teach using parables *(Psalm 78:2, Hoses 12:10 Proverbs 1:6 Ezekiel 20:49; Isaiah 6:9-10, 760 B.C. Psalms was edited 200 B.C. 686-650 BC,)*
   Fulfilled: **Jesus, Solomon, Ezekiel and Isaiah spoke in parables.** *(30-33 AD., Matthew 13:10-15, Mark 3:23and 4:11, Luke 8:10 John 12:39-40)*

17. He would perform miracles *(Isaiah 35:5, 686-650 BC)*
   Fulfilled: **Jesus performed miracles of healing, weather, and driving our spirits.** *See Miracles section for more information.* **Many miracles recorded the Matthew, Mark, Luke and John** *(30-33 AD)*

18. Jesus would be a healer *(Isaiah 53:4, 686--650 BC.)*
   Fulfilled: **There were many healings in ministry** *(30-33 AD., Matthew 8:17)*

19. A messenger will prepare for Jesus coming as the messiah John the Baptist announces him *(Isaiah 40:3-5, Malachi 3:1, 4:5, 686-650 BC & 425 BC.)*
   Fulfilled: **John the Baptist announced Jesus coming** *(30AD., Matt.3:1-10,11:10-14,Mark 1:2-8,Luke 3:3-6,7:27, John 1:19-26)*

20. Jesus triumphal entry. A future king will present himself to Jerusalem while riding on a humble donkey *(Zephaniah 9:9, Isaiah 62:11, Psalm 118.26, 200BC. 520 BC. 683-650 BC.)*
   Fulfilled: **Jesus rode a donkey into Jerusalem on his triumphant entry** *(33 AD., Mark 11:7, and John 12:13-18 Matthew 21:5, Luke 19:35-36)*

21. A friend will be against him *(Psalm 41:9, Psalms*

was edited <u>200BC</u>. Luke 22:54 Luke 22:1-6) (John 13:18)
   <u>**Fulfilled**</u>: **Judas betrays Jesus** *(<u>33 AD</u>., John 4/:2),*

22. **Disciples forsake Jesus** *(Zechariah 13:8, 2 Samuel 17:2& Mark 14:27, <u>931 B.C. 520 B.C. & 32AD</u>)*
   <u>**Fulfilled**</u>: **Disciples left him when he was taken prisoner by the Jewish leaders** *(<u>33 AD</u>., Matthew 26:15 Mark14:15, 14:66-72; Luke 22:55-62; John 18:16-18, 25-27)*

23. **His Disciple Judas will forsake Jesus**, *Psalms 41:9,<u>200B.C.)</u>*
   <u>*Fulfilled*</u>: **Judas brought soldiers and official to point out Jesus. All forsook him and fled** *(<u>33 A. C.</u>, John 18:2, Luke 22:1-6)*

24. **Jesus foretells he will be deserted by his followers and Peter will deny him three time during the night** *(Mathew 26:31 Mark 14:27, <u>32A.D.</u>)*
   <u>*Fulfilled*</u>: **Judas betrayed Jesus and his other disciples left him when he was taken prisoner by the Jewish leaders.** *(<u>34 AD</u>.,)*

25. **Jesus was betrayed by friend for 30 pieces of silver and it would be given to the Potter** *(Zephaniah 11:12, Psalm 41:9, <u>520 BC</u>.)*
   <u>**Fulfilled**</u>: **Judas received 30 Pc of silver and later this money purchased land from a potter** *(<u>33 AD</u>., Matthew 26:14-15-10, Matt.27:9-10, John 13:18-19, Luke 22:47-48)*

26 **Jesus predict Peter's Denial** *(Matthew. 26:31-35, Mark 14:27-31, Luke 22:31-34*
   (Hours before the event.)
   <u>**Fulfilled:**</u> **Peter disowns Jesus** *(hours later. Matthew 26:69-75, Mark 14:66-72, John18:16-18)*

27. He will be despised and rejected by men (*Isa 53:10, 686-650 B.C.*)
Fulfilled: He was despised and rejected by the religious leaders and men at the crucifixion and at his trials (*33 AD. Matthew 27, Mark 15 Luke 23, John 19*)

28 Jesus' sorrows and sufferings (*Isaiah 53, Psalm 22, 686-650 BC*)
Fulfilled: **Jesus crucifixion** (*33 AD. Matthew 27, Mark 15 Luke 23, John 19*)

29. Jesus did not open his mouth to defend himself. (*Isaiah 53-7*)
Fulfilled: During his trails with Pilate and Herod. (Luke 23:9, Mark 14:61)

30. Jesus was assigned a grave with the wicked and with the rich (*Isaiah 53:9, 686-650 B.C.*)
Fulfilled: **He was placed in a rich man's tomb where the wicked would lie.** (*Mark 15:46, Mathew 27:60, John 19:4 1 (33 A.D.,)*

31. Jesus will be scourged (*Isaiah 50:4-11, 686--650 BC.*)
Fulfilled: **Soldiers scourged Jesus** (*33 AD., Matthew 27:28*)

32. Events of the crucifixion (*Psalm 22:1- and, 69:1-36, Isaiah 53(Psalms was edited 200BC.Isiah 686-650B.C.*)
Fulfilled **Jesus was crucified** (*33 A.D., John 19:17-37, Luke 23, 26-34, Mark 15:21-41 Matthew 27:32-44*)

33. Crucifixion foretold by Jesus (*Matthew 26:2-5, Mark 8:31, 9:31, 10:32-33, (33A.D.)*
Fulfilled **Jesus was crucified as foretold** (*33 A.D.,*

Matthew 27, Mark 15 Luke 23, and John 19)

34 Messiah (Jesus) would be disbelieved and rejected by his people and Rulers. *(Psalms 69:4, Isaiah 29:13 Isaiah 6:10, 53:3, Psalms was edited 200BC. Isaiah 686-650 BC.*
 Fulfilled: **Jesus was disbelieved and rejected by Jewish and Roman leaders (***30-33 AD**. Matthew 15:8, 21:42, Mark 7:6, 12:10 Luke 20:17 John 1:11, 7:5, 12:37-40*

35. Jesus predicted his own death *(Matthew 20:17-19, Mark 10:32-34, Luke 9:22)(33 A.D.)*
 Fulfilled: **Jesus was killed by crucifixion.**.*(33 A.D., Matthew 27:33-44, Mark 15:22-32, Luke 23:33-43, John 19:17-24)*

36. Jesus would not open mouth when oppressed *(Isaiah 53:7, 686-650 BC.)*
 Fulfilled: **He answered him not a word** *(33 AD., Matthew 27:14, Mark 15:4-5)*

37. Jesus would be mocked and ridiculed. *(Psalm 22:7-8, Psalms was edited 200BC.*
 Fulfilled: **Jesus was mocked while he was on the cross** *(33 AD., Luke 23:35-37)*

38. Jesus will be brought as a lamb to slaughter *(Isaiah 53:7, 686--650 BC.)*
 Fulfilled: **The Lamb of God who takes away the sin of the world** *(33 AD., John 1:29)*

39 A smitten Shepherd *(Zech. 13:7, 520 BC.)*
Fulfilled: **Jesus as shepherd for man was smitten** *(33 AD., Matthew 26:31, Mark 14:27,)*

40. Jesus would be spat and struck *(Isaiah 50:6, 686-*

650 BC)
***Fulfilled*:** **The priests stuck and spit on him, while he was on trial.** *(33 AD., Mathew 26:67)*

41. Messiah would be crucified with transgressors *(Isaiah 53:12 Luke 22:37, 686-650 BC,)*
Fulfilled: **Two transgress or sinners were crucified with him** (33 AD., Matthew 27:38, Luke 23:33)

42 Jesus hand and feet will be pierced *(Psalms 22; 16, Zechariah 12:10, Psalms was edited 200BC.)*
***Fulfilled*:** **Jesus asks Thomas to verify piercing** *(33 AD., John20:27)*

43. Gall and vinegar offered *(Psalm 69:21, Psalms was edited 200BC.)*
***Fulfilled*:** **At Jesus crucifixion he was offered Gall and vinegar** *(33 AD., Matthew 27:34, John 19:29,)*

44. Jesus intercedes for sinners by bearing their sins *(Isaiah 53:12, 686--650 BC.)*
Fulfilled **Jesus bore the sins for all men when he was sacrificed on the cross** *(Matthew26:26, Luke 24:36, Acts 5:31)*

45. Jesus' life is a guilt offering for the sins of many interceding for the transgressions of many. *(Isaiah 53:10-11, 586B.C)*
***Fulfilled*:** **Jesus was scarified for the sin of others.**(*33 AD., Acts 2:38, 5:31, 10:43, Romans 3:5, 4:25, 5:6 1 Corinthians 15:3 Hebrews 2:17, 9:15, 1Peter 2:24,)*

46. Parting of Jesus garments *(Psalm 22:18, Psalms*

was edited 200BC.)
   ***Fulfilled*: Soldier casted lots for Jesus clothing** *(33 AD., John 19:24, Matthew 27:35)*

47. Jesus' dyeing words *(Psalms 22:1, 31:5, Psalms was edited 200BC.)*
   ***Fulfilled:* "My God, my God, why have you forsaken me?"**(*33 AD., Matthew 27:46, And Mark15:34, Luke 23:46)*

48. He commends his spirit *(Psalm 31:5, Psalms was edited 200BC.)*
   ***Fulfilled:* Jesus commending his spirit** *(33 AD., Luke 23: 46)*

49. Jesus is put to suffer as the Lord makes his life a guilt offering for sin *(Isaiah 53:5-11, Zechariah 12:10-13:1, 520 B.C., 686--650 BC.)*
   ***Fulfilled:* Sacrificial Death on the cross for forgiveness** *(33 AD., Luke 23:33, Romans 8:3, 5:9-11, Hebrews 13:11-12)*

50. No broken bones as Jesus was a sacrifice *(Psalm22:17, 34:20, Numbers 9:12, Exodus 12:46, Psalms was edited 200BC, 686-650 BC.)*
   ***Fulfilled:* Jesus legs were not broken** *(33 AD., John 19:33-36)*

51. Jesus side to be pierced *(Zephaniah 12:10-14, psalm 22:16, Psalms was edited 200BC.)*
   ***Fulfilled:* Soldier pierced his side** *(33 AD., John 19:36)*

52. Jesus buried with rich *(Isaiah 53:9, 686-650 BC.)*
   ***Fulfilled:* Joseph gave his tomb to Jesus** *(33 AD., Matthew 27:57)*

53. Judas's 30 Pc silver purchase land *(Zephaniah 11:13, 520 BC.)*
   Fulfilled: **Potter field purchased** *(33 AD., Matthew 27:3-10)*

54. Jesus foretells his resurrection in 3 days *(Matthew 20:17-19, Mark 8:31, 10:32-34, 34 A.D.)*
   Fulfilled **Jesus was resurrected in 3 days***(33 A.D., Mathew 28:1-8, Mark 16:1-8, Luke 24:1-10,46)*

55. Jesus appearance would be disfigured in his crucifixion and some would recognize him *(Isaiah 52:14, 586 B. C)*
   Fulfilled: **When people saw him right after the resurrection they did not recognize him until he spoke** *(33A.D. Luke 24:16, John 20:14)*

56. In 3 days Jesus was raised from the dead *(Hosea 6:2, Psalms, 16:10-11, Psalms was edited 200BC.)*
   Fulfilled: **Resurrected on the third day** *(33 AD., Luke 24:46)*

57. Jesus would be resurrected from the dead *(Psalm 16:10, 49:15, Psalms was edited 200BC.*
   Fulfilled: **Jesus was resurrected and appeared to many** *(33 AD., Matthew 28:2-7, Mark: 16:6, Luke 24:6, Acts 2:22-32)*

58. Resurrection of Jesus and later man *(Psalm 68:18, Isaiah 25:6-9, 26:1, Daniel2:12 19, Psalms was edited 200BC.)*
   Fulfilled: **Jesus raised from dead in new body***(33 AD., Mathew 28:1-8, Mark 16:1-8, Luke 24:1-10,45)*

59. Jesus will be heir to King David's throne *(Isaiah 9:6-7, 931 B.C.)*

Fulfilled: Jesus was born in the linage of King David and when he returns he will take David's throne *(when he returns Luke 1:32-33)*

60. Jesus is to be a light to the gentiles *(Isaiah 49:6/42:1, 686-650 BC)*
  Fulfilled: **Jesus became a light to gentiles and passed it on through the apostles.** *(33 AD. To present, Acts 28:28)*

61. Jesus' rejection would be followed by the destruction of Jerusalem and great tribulation *(Daniel 9:27, 11:31, 12:1-11,, 530 BC, Zechariah 13:7-9 520B.c.. (70A.D.., Matthew 24:15, Mark 13:14 Luke 21:20)*
  Fulfilled: **History, Rome destroyed Jerusalem and temple**

62. Coming of the Holy Spirit. *(Jeremiah 31:33, John 14:26, Jeremiah 627-586 B.C. and 32A.D.)*
  Fulfilled: **The holy Spirit came to the believers and believer still acknowledge it.** *(33 A.D. , Acts 2)*

63. Jesus brought justice to all nations through the Gospel. *(Isaiah 42:1-4, 686--650 BC.)*
  Fulfilled: **Jesus brought justice to all nations** *(33 AD., Matthew 12:18)*

64. Jesus Deity *(Zechariah 12:8, Psalm 2:7, 640-630 B.C.)*
  Fulfilled: **Jesus returned to his father to rule** *(33 AD., Matthew, Mark Luke and John. And Jesus declares his deity Matthew 3:16-17)*

65. Jesus is a light to the gentiles *(Isaiah 42:1-6, 49:6, 686-650 BC)*
  Fulfilled: **Jesus' Good news was taken to nations. He became a light to gentiles.** *(34 AD to present, Luke*

2:32, Matthew 12:18-21)
 Fulfilled After Jesus returned to his father, his teaching were spread to the world by his disciples *(33A.D. till today)*

66. Jesus sits at right hand of the father *(Psalm 110:1, Psalms was edited 200BC.)*
 Fulfilled: **Jesus in heaven with God** *(33 AD., Mark 16:19, Acts 3:20-21)*

67. Jesus is to be Gods' Messiah *(Isaiah 42:1-4, 686-650 BC)*
 Fulfilled: **Jesus life** *(33 AD., It was Proven in the Gospels as they describe his life. Matt. 12:12-15.Mark 12:36)*

68. Jesus came as Gods' cornerstone for a foundation of his kingdom *(Isaiah 28:16, Psalm 118:22-24, 686-650 BC)*
 Fulfilled: **Jesus's life was the foundation for the new covenant** *(33 A.D., Matthew 21:42, Mark12:10)*

69. The Lord God will rise up a prophet like himself from among your own and we must listen for God will tell him what to say. *(Deuteronomy. 18:18-22, 1446-1405 B.C.)*
 Fulfilled: **Jesus was the prophet God sent** *(33 A.D., Matthew 3:17, 12:18, John 3:34)*

70. Before Jesus returns to earth the Gospel will be preached to the entire world *(Matthew 24:14 33A. D.)*
 Fulfilled: **Today the Gospel is preached all over the world.** *(21 Century, future)*
71. The coming of Christ to earth *(Deuteronomy 18:15 12400 B.C.)*

***Fulfilled*:** Jesus came to man to tell God's new promise of salvation *(0 A.D, Luke 24:25-27, Acts 26:22-23)*

72. Jesus predicts his Death and resurrection *(Matthew16-21&17-22, Mark 8-31, Luke 9-22 & 26-6 (32 A.D.).*
     ***Fulfilled*:** History and proclaimed by Eye witnesses
(33 to 70 A.D.)(Luke 24 7-9, John 2:22, Luke 24:44. Acts 3-13, Acts 2-23)

73. Jesus foretold he would be in the heart of the earth for 3 days. *(Matthew 12:40)*

Fulfilled: *(33 A.D.)Mathew 27:64, 28:6-7*

Prophecies concerning the Jewish Nation

1. To your descendants I will give the land from the river of Egypt to the Euphrates. *(Gen 12:7 &15:18-21, 1950 B.C)*
     Fulfilled: The land was distributed to the Israelites *(1430 B.C., Joshua 13 thru 19)*

2. Abraham's descendants would be enslaved for 400 years. When they leave they will take the owners possessions *(Genesis.15:13, 1900 B.C.)*
     Fulfilled: They exodus from Egypt. *(1500 BC, Exodus 12:31-32)*

3. The Israelites would have a home land in Canna *(Genesis15:18, 1405 B.C.)*
     ***Fulfilled*:** Moses and Joshua lead the people to the promised land of Canna *(1390 B.C, Joshua 1:2)*

4. Birth of Isaac *(Genesis 18:1-15, 2100B.C)*
   Fulfilled: **Isaac 1st born of Abraham arrived.**(*2100 B.C., Genesis 21:2*)

5. Joseph received a dream that his brothers serve him *(Genesis 37, approx. 1693 B.C.)*
   Fulfilled: **Joseph brothers go to live in Egypt where Joseph was head of pharaohs court.**(*1708 B.C. Genesis 45*)

6. Nations blessings vs. curses. God will give blessings when you Obey God and keep all his commandments. If you do not he will curse *(Deuteronomy 28 and later Kings 9:4-7, 1400 BC.)*
   Fulfilled: **Blessings where given and curses were issued in accordance with the behavior to God's covenant.** *(From 1400B.C. to present, Described many time in the books of Kings & Chronicles)*

7. God tells Solomon that the kingdom will be divided after his reign but Judah would remain.(*1 Kings 11:11-13, 1000 B.C.)*
   Fulfilled: **The Kingdom was split and Judah was separated**. *(This was recorded in the end of 1st Kings and 2nd. kings, (605 B.C., Described many times in the books of Kings & Chronicles)*

8. God will send prophet *(Deuteronomy 18:18, 1405 BC.)*
   Fulfilled: **Many were sent including Jesus** *(1004-425BC., Judges and the various prophets were recorded in scripture.)*

9. Moses is told by God that he is to go up to Mount

Nebo where he will die. *(Deuteronomy. 32:48-51, 1400 B.C.)*
   Fulfilled: Moses died on Mount Nebo *(1400 B.C., Det. 34:7)*

10. Your enemy will lay siege to your cities and cause suffering to the point of eating your children. *(Deuteronomy 28:53, 1400 BC.)*
   Fulfilled: **Sieges were put on Jerusalem by Babylonians and Rome to conquer Jerusalem and they were forced to eat the fruit of their whom** *(605 B.C. - 70 A.D., Kings, Chronicles, Jeremiah and Ezekiel)*

11. The Jewish nation will be exiled and taken with your king to a nation unknown to you and your ancestors. *(Deuteronomy 28:36, 1400 BC.*
   Fulfilled: **The nation was taken by Babylonians for 70 years.** *(605 B.C. 538 B.C. Daniel and Ezekiel write about their experience in their captivity.)*

12. The Chosen People will return from Babylon to Jerusalem after 70 years *(Jeremiah 29:10, 586 B. C.)*
   Fulfilled: **Cyrus allowed them to return** *(450 B.C, Ezra 1:2-3)*

13. King David will have a son to rule his kingdom and build a house for the lord. *(2 Samuel 7:12, 931 B.C.)*
   Fulfilled: **Solomon reigns as told and built the temple of God** *(King Solomon reigned and built the temple in 1004 BC., 2 Chomical 2 through 5)*

14. Jews will be scattered among other nations. *(Deuteronomy 28:64, 1400 BC.)*
   Fulfilled: **This was done by Assyria capturing**

Israel, the Babylonians concurring Judah, Greek invasion of Judah, and Rome with they destroyed the nation in 70AD. *(The Jews did not have a home land from 721 BC to 1948 A.D. Many Jews are still in many countries, world history)*

15. Babylonian captivity *(Deuteronomy 28:36-41, 1400 BC.)*
   ***Fulfilled*: History Babylon came three times and took people in captivity** *(606B.C. 597 BC. & 539 B.C., 2 Kings & 2 Chronicles)*

16. Romans (eagle army) will come against you *(Deuteronomy 28:49-53, 1400 BC.)*
   ***Fulfilled*: Romans lead by Pompey captured the Jewish home land.** *(63 B.C., World history Historian Cassius Dio said villages in Israel were destroyed and Josephus indicated that the Roman army's destruction was very complete.)*

17. Captivity of Jews would last 70 Years and Babylon will be punished *(Jeremiah 25:11, 627 -580 BC)*
   Fulfilled*: some Jew started captivity 609BC Cyrus released Jews in 539BC. Babylon was punished when the Persian defeated them.(609-539 B.C. , Ezra 1:1, Chron. 36:22)*

18. Dispersion of Jews *(Deuteronomy 28:64, 1400 BC, Zechariah 10:9, 520BC*
   Fulfilled*: History The Jews did not have a home land from 70 AD to 1948AD.(721 B.C. to 1948AD, World history)*

19. All of Israel's treasure and some of its people will be in captivity in Babylon *(Isaiah 39:6, 686-650 BC)*

Fulfilled: Treasures and people taken to Babylon *(605-856 B.C., 2 Chronicles 36:17)*

20. The Northern kingdom of Israel will be destroyed and put in captivity *(Amos 5-27, 760 B.C.)*
Fulfilled: **Assyria conquered Israel and deported its people.** *(721 B.C., 2 Kings Chapter 17 explains why and when)*

21. The 2nd Temple would be destroyed and not one stone would be left standing on top of another *(Matthew 24:1-2 Luke 19:44, Mark 13:2, 34 A.D.*
Fulfilled: **The Romans cane and tore down the Temple** *(70 A.D. Josephus an historian said the destruction was so complete that even the foundations were dug up.)*

22. King Cyrus is to defeat Babylon and free Israelites to rebuild their temple 150 years before the event *(Isaiah 44:28 to 45:13, Jeremiah 29, 686--650 BC.*
Fulfilled: **He allowed Israel to return Home to build their temple** *(530 B.C., Ezra 1:1, and 2 Chronicles 36:22)*

23. The Jewish people will be scattered throughout the world. *(Deuteronomy 28:63-64, 1400 BC*
Fulfilled: **Israel's people were scattered by Assyria, and Babylonians, and the balance we scattered later by the Romans**.*(721 B.C. -70 A.D. , Historical events)*

24. Jews will not be a large population among the other nations. *(Deuteronomy 28:62, 1400 BC.)*
Fulfilled: **Since the destruction of Jerusalem the Jews were scattered and became part of other cultures. Thus today their number in the New Israel**

are not one of the larger populations.*(the Jews were so separated that they did not become a large part of the other nations. 721 BC to 1948 A.D. World history.)*

25. Unceasing persecutions *(Deuteronomy 28:33-57, 1400 BC).*
Fulfilled: **There will be persecution of the Jews down through the ages.** *(1400B.C. to present, World history has recorded the problems of the Jewish people down through the ages.)*

26. King Zedekiah and his officials will be handed over the king of Babylon because the king did not honor God. Then they would destroy Jerusalem. *(Jeremiah 38:23, Approximately 590 B.C)*
Fulfilled: **The Babylonians came and captured King Zedekiah killed his family and took him captive to Babylon and destroyed Jerusalem** *(586 B.C., 2 Kings 25 &World history)*

27. God's temple will be destroyed *(Jeremiah 7:14, 590 B.C.)*
Fulfilled: **Jerusalem and the temple were destroyed** *(586 B.C. Jeremiah 52, 2 Kings 25 and world history)*

28. Gods' chosen people will be brought back to their land from many countries. *(Ezekiel 11:16-17, Leviticus 26, 1446 B.C.)*
Fulfilled: **Through all the wars the Israelites have survived as a people.** *(Continuous, there are still Jews all around the world today)*

29. Jerusalem and its people will be destroyed. *(Luke 19:42, 21:24, 33 A.D.)*
Fulfilled: **The Romans came and destroyed the**

city people in it. *(70 A.D. and 135 A.D., Josephus a Jewish historian stated that 1.1 million Jews died and hundreds of thousands were forced out of the country.)*

30. The Jewish second Temple would be destroyed by the ruler *Romans (Daniel 9:26, 530 BC.)*
   Fulfilled: **The temple was destroyed by Romans,** *(70 AD, Roman history.)*

Prophecies for others
1. All nations would be blessed because of Abraham's obedience *(Genesis 22:18, 1446-1405 B.C.)*

   Fulfilled: **Jesus was a descendent of Abraham and he was a blessing to all nations by bringing the Gospel**. *(Present, Matthew 1:1, 4:23, 9:35)*

2. Announced the destruction of Sodom *(Genesis 18:16-33, Approx. 1870 B.C.)*
   Fulfilled: **Sodom was destroyed** *(Approximately 1870 B.C., Genesis 19:24)*

3. God will bring an end to Nineveh (Assyrians) while their soldiers are drunk.*(Nahum1:8-10,3:11, Zephaniah 2:13-15, 663 B.C.)*
   Fulfilled: **Babylonians, Chaldeans and Medians destroyed Nineveh** *(612 B.C., Historian Diodorud Siculus states that the soldiers were furnished while they were drunk.)*

4. It was also prophesized Nineveh would be damaged by fire and the soldiers would be devoured by the sword *(Nahum 3:15, Zephaniah 2:13-15, Zechariah 9:3-4, 663 B.C.*
   Fulfilled: **Babylonians, Chaldeans and Medians**

destroyed Nineveh. *(612 B.C., History & Archaeologists found the site and it had layers of ash covering the ruins).*

5. **The Assyrians soldiers would flee from the Nineveh battle and the Assyrians would not heal.** *(Nathan 3:17-19, 664 B.C.)*
  Fulfilled: **Assyrian army fled from the battle. The Assyrian nation has never recovered.** *(612 B.C. Historical records)*

6. **The City of Tyre will be destroyed and never be rebuilt** *(Ezekiel 26, 590-570 B.C)*
  Fulfilled **Alexander the Great conquered Tyre** *(332 B.C., History confirms the fact.)*

7. **Edom would be destroyed by many nations because of their continuous wars with Israel.** *(Ezekiel 25:14, , Jeremiah 49:7-22, 590-570 B.C.)*
  Fulfilled **Babylon warred against them, Alexander the great defeated them in 332 B.C. and Hasmonaean subdued and destroyed the Edomite's** *(2nd century B.C., as rescored in history*

8. **Egypt will be destroyed and will never ruler over other nations** *(Ezekiel 29:15, 590-570 B.C.*
  Fulfilled **After Jews left Egypt, Egypt has not ruled any other nation.** *(559 B.C., History has shown the event happened and it has never became a major nation since.)*

9. **The countries of Edom, Moab and Ammon, Tyre and Sidon must give in to the Babylonians or they will be punished by God** *(Jeremiah 27:3-6, 586 B.C)*
  Fulfilled **All these nations are no longer in existence. They have been destroyed. They were**

invaded by the Egyptians, Babylonians Persians. Historical events of wars in the area including Alexander the Great *(340 B.C., History)*

10. Ammon will be destroyed. *(Ezekiel 25:7-11, 570 B.C)*
__Fulfilled__ The last mention of Ammon was when the fought against Judah (Maccabee). They are no longer exist *(160 B.C, History)*

11. Moab will be destroyed *(Ezekiel 25:10-11, 570 B.C)*
__Fulfilled__: Moab was destroyed *(in 330 B.C. and there is no record of them today.)*

12. Tyre will have many nations against it to the point that it would be a bare rock *(Ezekiel 26:3-5, 570 B.C.)*
__Fulfilled__ It was attacked by many countries, and Alexander the Great was the last. It was baron from then on. *(340 B.C., history)*

13. God told Egypt that he would bring armies against them and they would go into captivity for a while and they would never rule over other nations *(Ezekiel 29:8-15, 570* **B.C**)
__Fulfilled:__ Their country was ruled by the Babylonians, Assyrians, Persians and Greeks. Since then Egypt has never ruled over other peoples. *(340 B.C., History)*

14. Existence and fall of Babylon *(Isaiah 13-14, 686-650 BC)*
__Fulfilled:__ God gave power to Babylon then he took it away. *(606-538 B.C. an historic events. Jews were put in captivity by Babylon 606BC, Babylon was defeated by Persia 536BC. Also describe in 2*

Chronicles.)

15. The Medes will destroy Babylon . *(Jeremiah 51:11, 686 BC)*
   Fulfilled: **Meds and Persians lead by Cyrus defeated the Babylonians** *(538 B.C., History states that Cyrus is the Persian king that conquered Babylon.*

16. God would open the gates of Babylon for Cyrus and his attacking army *(.Isaiah 45:1, 590-570 B.C.)*
   Fulfilled **Cyrus diverted the flow of the Euphrates River into a large lake basin. Cyrus then march hi army across the river bed into the City.** *(538 B.C. , History states that Cyrus was the Persian king that conquered Babylon.)*

17. There will be 4 world kingdoms then the Messiah (Jesus) will come. Babylonian (Head of Gold), Persian (silver) Greek (Bronze), Roman (Iron) *(Daniel 7, 530 BC)*
   Fulfilled: **Babylon existed and was destroyed. Persia rained next and were conquered by Greek Alexander the great and his kingdom was separated into four parts then the Romans conquered the known world Jesus was born in the 4 kingdom** *(605 B.C.to 476 A.D., World history 534BC. to Christ Babylonian empire 606-536BC.,Persiand Empire 536-332BC., Roman Empire 146BC.-400AD)*

18. Tyre's stones, timber and soil would be thrown into the sea. *Ezekiel 26:12, 590-570 B.C.)*
   Fulfilled:. **Alexander's forces took rubble from Tyre's mainland and tossed it stones, timber and soils into the sea.** *(333-332B.C., History tells about Alexander's forces built a bridge to attack Tyre and it is*

still there today.)

19. After Gods' people have completed their captivity in Babylon He will punish Babylonians and their land will be desolate forever. *(Jeremiah 25:12 , 586 B.C)*
 Fulfilled: The Babylon Empire was crushed by the Meds, Persians and Greeks. The City is still desolate today. *(520-300 B.C. History)*

20 People will honor God with lips but their hearts are far from him. *(Isaiah29:13, 686--650 BC.)*
 Fulfilled: Some references to the Pharisees were an example. Today you can see some people become false teacher for their own benefit. *(33 A.D., Mark 7:6)*

21. God tell us how he will bring blessing and cursing on nations in relation to how they interact with him. *(Jeremiah 18:7-10, 586 B.C.)*,
 Fulfilled: God seems to be doing this when you look at history *(Down through history, Kings, Chronicles, Jeremiah and Ezekiel)*

22. God will hand over the Countries of Edom, Moab and Ammon, Tyre and Sidon to the Babylonians. *(Jeremiah 27:3-7, Approx. 593 B.C)*
 Fulfilled: All of these countries were destroyed and no longer exist. *(520 B.C., History)*
23. God foretells about the implementation of the New Covenant of the Gospel *(Jeremiah 31: 33-34, 586 B.C.)*

24. Paul had a vision that their ship voyage is going to be disastrous and bring loss to their ship. *(Acts 27:10, 27:21-24, Approx. 65 A.D.)*
 Fulfilled: The ship was wrecked and all survives as he told them.*(Approx. 65 A.D month later., Acts*

27:27)

Future Prophecies

1. Signs of End Times (Matthew 24:1-51, mark 13:1-37, Luke21:5-36, <u>33A.D.</u>

2. At End Times many will go here and there and they will be increase in knowledge *(Daniel 12:4, <u>530 BC.</u>)* ***We can all see how this is occurring.*** *(In process)*

3. Jesus in the future he will rule as an eternal King *(Isaiah 9:1-2: 6- 7, Jeremiah 23: 5, <u>686--650 BC.</u>)*

4. Signs of the second coming of Christ *(Luke 21:8, Matthew 24:29, <u>1 century AD</u>*

5. Then you will be handed over to be persecuted and put to death, and you will be hated by all nations because of me *(Matthew 24:9, <u>1st century AD.</u>)*

6 Time of tribulation *(Matthew 24:9 Mark 13:19, Luke 21:11 & Daniels l9:27, <u>1 century AD)</u>*

7. Child is born and the government will be on his shoulders. He will be called Wonderful counselor, Mighty God, Everlasting Father, Prince of Peace.*(Isaiah 9:6, <u>740-680 B.C.</u>, This is expected to be in the second coming of the Jesus*

8. Second coming of Christ *(Zechariah 14:4, Matthew 24:29-31, 24:36-39, Mark 13:24-26, Luke 21:25-27, Acts 1:11, 1 Thessalonians 4:16-17, <u>1st century</u>*

9. Christ the Messiah will have an increase of

government and peace will have no end. H will reign on David's throne and with righteousness forever.(Christ the Messiah will have an increase of government and peace will have no end. H will reign on David's throne and with righteousness forever. *(740-680 B.C.) This is expected to be in the second coming of the Jesus*

10 They will see the Son of Man coming on the clouds of the sky, with power and great glory *(Matthew 24:31, 1st century AD).*

11 Armageddon is the final war. Israel will be attacked by a large army composed of many countries. These people will come from the land of Gog chief prince of Meshach and Tubal (Black Sea area and Turkey), Persia (Iran), Cush and Put (Ethiopians and Egyptians and Canaan) Gomer (Son of Japheth settled in indo European area), Beth Togarmah (Far north of turkey) will gather and come against Israel with and evil scheme. At that time God will be angered and will create a great earth quake and all will fear his presents. He will bring plague and bloodshed, torrents of rain, hailstones and burning sulfur on the army. When he does this the nations will know he is the Lord (Genesis 10 describes the families mentioned in the prophecies and where they were located. *(Ezekiel 38 & 39, Joel 2:38 and 1 Corinthians 1, 600 B.C.)*

12. There will be false Messiahs *(Matthew 24:23-25, 33 A.D.)*

13. Scoffers will come *(2 Peter 3:3, 1 century A.D.)*

14. False Christ's and false prophets will appear and perform great signs and miracles to deceive even the elect—if that were possible. *(Matthew 24:11-24 33 AD,)*

15. Tribulation *(Matthew 24:9-24, 33 AD.)*

16. Rapture *(Matthew 24:40, 1 Thessalonians 4, 1st Century A.D Daniel 12:1-2,600 B.C.)*

17. Spirit of the lord will come upon sons and daughters and prophesy, Old men will dream dreams and young men will see visions. *(Joel 2:28, 32; 3:13 acts 2:16-21, 9th century B.C.*

18. End of the Age *(Matthew 24:4-35, Luke 21:8, 33 A.D.)*

19. Millennium (**The thousand years rule of Jesus Christ--** *Zechariah 14:4, Isaiah 2:3, Isaiah 11:6, Isaiah 65:22, Isaiah 54:13 Zephaniah 3:9 Isaiah 61:19 Revelation 20:1-7 , 21:1, century AD)*

20. Man's judgment *(Matthew 13:41-42, John 5:25-29, Romans 2:5-16, 2 Corinthians 5:10 Revelations 20:11-15, 1 century AD)*

21. There will be a new Heaven and earth. *(2 Peter 3:13, Revelation 21:1-3, 1 century AD)*

22. God will return with the raised Jews and live in Jerusalem *(Ezekiel 37:12-14, 590-570 B.C.)*

23. The sun will be darkened and the stars will fall from the sky and the heavens will be shaken and the son of Man will be coming on a cloud in power and glory. *Mark 13:24-26, 33 AD.)*

24. Jesus causes division between family members due to their belief in him *(Mica 7:6, 700 B.C., You can see there is a division between believer and non-believers., Luke 12:53, Mark10:38, Matt 10:34)*

25. Gods' people, who have their name in the book of life, will be delivered. *(Daniel 12:1-3, 530 BC.)*

26. The length of the most terrible distressful time will be 1290 days. Those that honor the Lord will be blessed after 1335 days. *(Daniel 12:11-12, 530 BC.)*

27. God's two witnesses come during the tribulation with Gods testimony. They will eventually be killed and then resurrected. *(Revelations 11:4-12), 1AD.*

Miracles

These miracles are placed in this Appendix to help the reader understand how God has helped nations, communities and individuals down through the centuries. Miracles give an understanding of God's love and desire for us, so we will believe in him. Of course it doesn't list all the miracles, because God is continuing to perform miracles to help us.

My list is a simple index, so you can find some miracles for mentoring others. The listed items were derived from the Bible and various other sources. We need to thank many people who have witnessed Gods miracles and recorded these events so future generations will see the greatness of our God. We also need to thank those who evaluate these events and give explanations concerning them. If you want to know about miracles you can find them just as I found them. You can read the Bible, search other books and use the internet for better understanding.

Note: Dates of miracles are the date recorded rather than date occurred.

Major Miracles performed by God prior to Christ Birth

1.   **Creation of earth and man** (Genesis 1, 4000 B.C.)

2.   **Great Flood with Noah** (Genesis 7, 2400B.C)

3.   **Destruction of the Tower of Babel** (Genesis 11, 2247 B.C.)

4.   **God selects Abram as father of his people** (Genesis 12, 1921B.C.)

5.   **Destruction of Sodom and Gomorrah** (Genesis 19, 1898 B.C)

6.   **Birth of Isaac late if life of Abraham and Sarah** (Genesis 21, 1868B.C.)

7.   **Abraham's family is moved to Egypt through Joseph** (Genesis 39, 1706 B.C.)

8.   **God turns Mosses staff into a snake and then turns it back into his staff.** (Genesis 4, 1494 B.C.)

9. God turns Moses hand into leprous and then makes it well again (Genesis 5, 1495 B.DC.)

10   God delivers the Israelites for Egypt with 10 Plagues, including the "Pass Over. (It is also known as the signs and Wonders. Exodus 7, 1491 B.C)

11   God parts the Red Sea to protect his people (Exodus 14:26, 1491 B.C.)

12   God destroys the Egyptians as they try to cross the Red Sea. (Exodus 14, 1491 B.C.)

13   God furnished sweet water to the Israel when they were at Mariah (Exodus 15:22, 1491-1451 B.C)

14   Moses drawing water from a rock (Numbers 20:8, 1491-1451 B.C)

15. God furnished Manna and quails to the Israelites while they were in the wilderness (Exodus 16, 1491-1451 B.C.)

16   God cared for 600,000 people above the age of 20 by furnishing food, water   and protected them and their clothing for 40 years. (Numbers, 1491-1451 B.C.)

17. God furnished water from rock for the people (Exodus 17, 1491-1451 B.C.)

18. Israel was guided in the wilderness by supernatural cloud (Exodus, 1500 B. C.)

19. Chosen people's clothes did not wear out. (Deuteronomy 8:4, 1491-1450 B.C.)

20. Korah and his rebels swallowed by earth. (Exodus 6, 1500 B. C.)

21. God wrote the 10 commandments in stone with his finger (Exodus 20, 1485 B.C.)

22. God appears to Moses on Mount Sinai. The people see the thundering the lightning flashes, the sound of the trumpet and the mountain smoking. God furnishes the 10 commandments (Exodus 20, 1485 B.C.)

23. God fills the Tabernacle with His Glory (Exodus 40:34, 1475 B.C.)

24. People were healed from snake bites in wilderness (Numbers 21 4-9, 1476 B.C)

25. Men treated God with contempt and God had them swallowed up in the ground with an earthquake (Numbers 16:28-32, 1477 B.C.)

26. Aaron's staff budded and produced almonds choosing his people to become the priest of Israel. (Numbers 17:1-10, 1478 B.C.)

27. Miraculous crossing of the Jordan (Joshua 3, 1451 B.C)

28. God calls Moses at the miraculously burning bush (Exodus 3, 1426B.C)

29. Destroying the walls of Jericho (Joshua 6, 1452 B.C)

30. Shamgar killed 600 Philistines with an ox Goad. (Judges 3:31, 1370 B.C)

31. After eight year of being in the hands of the king of Aram Naharaim. The Israelites wanted to return to God. He empowered Othniel and they were freed them from their captivity and they had forty years of peace. (Judges 3:12-11, 14 century B.C)

32 While the Israelites wee under Eglon King of Moab, they cried out to God and he chose Ehud lead the Israelites in killing ten thousand Moabites. This gave them eighty years of peace. (Judges 3:12-30, 14 century B.C.)

33. Deborah was told by God to free his people from the Canaanites. God gave her a plan of attack that gave the advantage to Gods people. God routed the enemy and their chariots. (Judges 4, 12 century B.C.)

34. Israel is saved during its early years by God sending Judges and miracles to help them.(Book of Judges, 1260 B.C)

35. Israel is saved during its early years by God sending Judges and miracles to help them. (Judges 6, 1258 B.C.)

36. God shows Gideon he is with him by causing his fleece of will to be filled with dew and no other dew around the fleece (Judges 6, 1259 B.C.)

37. Gideon defeated 135,000 Midianites with 300 soldiers. (Judges 6-8, 1260 B.C.)

38. God gave power to his Judge Jephthah to aid

his people against the Ammonites. He subdued twenty towns and brought peace back to his people. (Judges 11:32-33, 11 century B.C.)

39. God had Elijah fed by ravens (I Kings17:3-7, 1150 B.C)

40. God proved he was stronger than Baal. He did miracles with Elijah that Baal and Asherah could not. He made fire come down from heaven and start a sacrifice to God. (1 Kings 18:20-39, 1151 B.C)

41. God aided David to defeat Goliath (I Samuel 17, 1100 B.C.)

42. Elijah had the jars of Flour and Oil that repeatedly refill themselves to support him and a widow where he was staying. (I Kings 17:14, 1150 B.C.)

43. God brings a widows dead son to life when Elijah asks him (I Kings 17:17-23, 1151 B.C)

44. Elijah call down fire from heaven that consumes 100 soldiers.(II Kings1:6-18, 1152 B.C)

45. Miraculous Birth of Samson and his strength (Judges 13, 1160 B.C)

46. Samson the Nazirite killed a lion with his bares hands. He killed 1000 Philistines with a donkey's jawbone tore of an Iron Gate. After losing his strength, God gave him strength again when his enemies wanted to make fun of him now that he was blind. He pushes on the temple pillars and the temple

collapsed and killed 3000 of Israel's enemies. (Judges 13-16, 1000BC)

47. Elijah taken to heaven in a fiery chariot (II Kings 4, 1110 B.C)

48. God does miracles for Elisha (Widow's oil, Shulamite's son, Deadly Stew Healing of Naming, Floating Ax Head, Gods' Chariots and Horses, Syria's Army Blinded.(2 Kings 4 & 5, 1100 B.C.)

49. God does miracles for Elijah (Miracle of Drought, Miracle of Food, Miracle of resurrection of the Gentile son, Fire on Mount Carmel, and Rain. I Kings 17 & 18, 1100 B.C)

50. God cursed the Philistines by giving them tumors because they stole the Ark of the Covenant. (1 Samuel, 1100 B.C.)

51. God confused the Philistines when they came to attach Israel. (1 Samuel 7, 1100 B.C.)

52. God caused a drought in Israel for few years and the sent rain when Elijah prayed for rain. (1 Kings 18:42, 1025 B.C.

53. David kills Goliath with the aid of God. (1 Kings 18:42, 1100 BC)

54. Elijah taken in to Heaven in a whirlwind (2 Kings 2-12, 1000BC)

55. Destruction of Assyria by God (Isaiah 10, 700B.C.)

56. **Hezekiah's death postponed and suns shadow reversed** (Isaiah 38 & II Kings 20:8-11, 700B.C.)

57. **God keeps Jerusalem safe by killing 185,000 Assyrians soldiers** (Isaiah 37:33-38, 586B.C)

58. **Jonah and the whale** (great fish), (Jonah 1, 612 B.C)

59. **God also prepared the way for Jesus and assured that all his prophecies concerning Jesus came true**. (See Jesus section on his prophesies and the miracles of completion, 600 B.C. - 0 B.C.)

60. **Shadrach, Meshach and Abend-Nego and an angle survive the fiery furnace** (Daniel 3, 587 B.C.)

61. **King Nebuchadnezzar was made sick and acted like and animal until he acknowledge that Heaven rules.**(Daniel 4, 530 B.C)

62. **Daniel saved in the Lion Den** (Daniel 5, 539 B.C)

63. **Supernatural placement of handwriting on the wall** (Daniel 5, 539 B.C.)

64. **Jesus' first miracle turning water into wine** (John 2:1-11, 30-33 A.D)

65. **Providing fish so they would be fishers of men** (Luke 5:1-1, 30-33 A.D)

66. **Another bring of fish.** (John 21:6, 30-33 A.D)

67. **The Leper is cleansed** (Matthew 8:2. Mark 1:40, Luke 5 12, 30-33 A.D.)

68. **The Centurion's Servant is healed** (Matthew 8: 5 Luke 7:1-10, 30-33 A.D)

69. **Peters mother-in Law is healed** (Matt 8:14, Mark 1:29, Luke 4:38, 30-33 A.D

70. **Demoniac spirits driven out of a man** (Mark 1:21-25, Luke 4:31-37, 30-33 A.D.)

71. **Jesus drives out an evil spirit** (Mark 1:21-26, Luke 4:31-37, 30-33 A.D.)

72. **Jesus heals many in** Capernaum (Mark 1:29-32, Matthew 8:14-16, Luke 4:38-41, 30-33 A.D.)

73. **The stormy Sea is stilled** (Matthew 8: 23, Mark 4:35, Luke 8:22, 30-33 A.D.)

74. **Demons are cast into swine.** (Matthew 8:28, Mark 5; 1, Luke 8:26, 30-33 A.D)

75. **Paralytic is forgiven and healed** (Matthew 9:2-8 1, Mark 2:3-12, Luke 5:17-26, 30-33 A.D.)

76. **Daughter's life is restored.** (Matthew 9:18, Mark 5; 21, Luke 8:41, 30-33 A.D)

77. **Sight is restored for Two blind men** (Matthew 9: 27-31, 30-33 A.D.)

78. **Jesus sends his apostles to heal many** (Matthew 10:7-8, Mark 3:13-15, 30-33 A.D.)

79. Jesus removes a demon from a Syrophoenician woman's daughter (Mark 7:26-30, 30-33 A.D)

80. Man with Dropsy is healed (Luke 14:1, 30-33 A.D)

81. The cleansing of Ten Lepers (Luke 17: 11, 30-33 A.D.)

82. Christ heals from a distance. It was a royal official's son. (John 4: 46-54, 30-33 A.D.)

83. Christ heals a crippled man (John 5: 5, 30-33 A.D.)

84. Raising Lazarus for the dead (John 11:1-44, 30-33 A.D)

85. Withering fig tree (Matt. 21:17, Mark 11:12, 30-33 A.D.)

86. Jesus healed many other people. (Matthew 4:23, 9:35, John 2:23, 30-33 A.D.)

87. Healing of the cut off ear (priests captain) (Luke 22:50, 30-33 A.D)

88. Roman officers son healed (John 4:46, 30-33 A.D)

89. A cripple healed at pool (John 5:1, 30-33 A.D.)

90. A leper is healed (Matthew 8:14, Mark 1:29 Luke 4:38, 30-33 A.D)

91. **A leper healed** (Matthew 8:2, Mark 1:40, 30-33 A.D)

92. **Man healed when let down through roof so Jesus could help him.** (Matthew 9:2, Mark 2:3 Luke 5:17, 30-33 A.D.)

93. **A shriveled hand Healed.** (Mark 3:1, Luke 6:6, Matt. 12:9, 30-33 A.D.)

94. **Healing of a Centurion servant** (Matthew 8:5, Luke 7:1, 30-33 A.D)

95. **Two blind men** (Matt. 9:27, 30-33 A.D.)

96. **Deaf and mute man healed** (Mark 7:31, 30-33 A.D.)

97. **Dead daughter raised to life** (Matthew 9:18, Luke 8:4, Matt. 9:18, 30-33 A.D.)

98. **Blind man healed in Jerusalem** (John 9, 30-33 A.D)

99. **Blind healed in Bethsaida** (Mark 8:22, 30-33 A.D.)

100. **A women who was bent over for 18 years is healed** (Luke 13:10, 30-33 A.D.)

101. **Women with hemorrhage healed** (Matt. 9:20, Luke 8:43, Mark 5; 25, 30-33 A.D)

102. **Dropsy healed** (Luke 17:11, 30-33 A.D.)

103. Multiple healings by Jesus (Matthew 4:24, 15:30, 30-33 A.D)

104. Blind beggar healed (Bartimaeus) (Matthew 20:29, Mark 10; 46 Luke 18:35, 30-33 A.D.)

105. Fig tree withered (Matthew 21:18-22, mark11:12-20, 30-33 A.D.)

106. Healing Malchus' of ear which was cut off by Peter (Luke 22:50, 30-33 A.D.)

107. Furnished fish when men could not catch any (Luke 5:1, John 21:6, 30-33 A.D.)

108. Jesus calm a storm (Matthew 8:23, Mark 4:35, Luke 8:22, 30-33 A.D)

109. Food appeared to feed 5000 people. (Matthew 14:13, Mark 6:34, Luke9:11, John 6:1, 30-33 A.D)

110. Jesus walked on water (Matthew. 14:22, Mark 6:45, John 6:19, 30-33 A.D)

111. 4000 people feed when food appeared (Matt. 15:32, Mark 8:1, 30-33 A.D.)

112. Two Blind men healed (Matthew 9:27, 30-33 A.D.)

113. Blind healed (sin caused? -No) (John 9: 1, 30-33 A.D.)

114. Christ raises Lazarus his friend (John 11: 1, 30-33 A.D)

115. Healing of withered hand (Matt. 12:9, Mark 3:1, 30-33 A.D)

116. Healing of Blind and Dumb (Matthew 12:22, Luke 11:14, 30-33 A.D.)

117 Speech is restored (Matthew 9: 32, 30-33 A.D.)

118. A Canaanite woman demoniac daughter healed (Matthew 15:21-28, Mark 7:24:30, 30-33 A.D.)

120. Getting tax money out of water (Matthew 17:24-27, 30-33 A.D)

121. Jesus heals a gentile Woman (Matthew 15: 21, Mark7:24, 30-33 A.D.)

122. Jesus ascended to heaven (Acts 1:9, 30-33 A.D.)

123. The Transfiguration (Matt: 17:8 Mark 9:2, 30-33 A.D)

124. Two Blind men healed (Matthew20: 29 Mark 10:46, Luke 18:35, 30-33 A.D.)

125. Blind man healed (Mark 6: 22, 30-33 A.D)

126. Blind Man at Bethsaida (Mark8: 22, 30-33 A.D)

127. Blind Bartimaeus healed. (Matt. 20:29, Mark 10:46, Luke 18:35, 30-33 A.D)

128. Syrophoenician-Phoenician's Daughter (Matthew 15:21-28, Mark 7:24-30, 30-33 A.D.)

129. Deaf and Dumb Man Healed (Matthew 17:14-21, Mark 9:14-29, Luke 9:37-41, 30-33 A.D.)

130. Deaf and Dumb Man Healed (Mark 7:31, 30-33 A.D

131. A widow's son is raised from the dead (Luke 7: 11, 30-33 A.D)

132. Demoniac Son healed (Matthew 17: 14 Mark 9:14, Luke 9:37, 30-33 A.D)

133. Blind and Dumb Demoniac (Matthew 12:22, Luke11:14, 30-33 A.D)

134. Demoniacs removed from two men. (Matthew 8:28, Mark 5:1-20, Luke 8:26-39, 30-33 A.D.)

135. Woman with 18 year Infirmity (Luke 13:10, 30-33 A.D.)

136. A mute man had a Demoniac remove so he could speak (Matthew 9:32, 30-33 A.D.)

137. Women with Hemorrhage healed.(Matt. 9:20 Mark 5:25, Luke 8:43, 30-33 A.D)

138. Blind Bartimaeus healed (Mathew 20:29, Mark 10:46, Luke 18:35, 30-33 A.D)

138. Prison gates opened of its own accord (Acts 12:10, 33-70 A.D.)

139. The Resurrection of Christ (Matthew 28, Mark

16, Luke 24, John 20, 33 AD)

140. Physical Appearance of the Holy Spirit at Pentecost. Acts 2:3, 33 A.D)

141. Many wonders and signs were done by Apostles. (Acts. 2:43, 5:12, 33-70 A.D)

142. Healing of a lame man at the temple (Acts 3:7, 33-70 A.D.)

143. Earth shook as a result of prayer (Acts: 4:31, 33-70 A.D.

144. Ananias and Sapphira killed due to lying (Acts5:5, 33-70 A.D)

145. Multitudes healed by Peter's shadow (Acts 5:15, 33-70 A.D)

146. Prison doors opened (Acts 5:19, 33-70 A.D.)

147. Stephen wrought wonders and signs (Acts 6:8, 33-70 A.D)

148. Philip did miracles (Acts 8:6, 7, 13, 33-70 A.D)

149. Saul (Paul) was converted by voice from heaven (Acts 9:3-9, 33-70 A.D.)

150. Peter healed Aeneas (Acts 9:32, 33-70 A.D)

151. Peter raised Dorcas from the dead (Acts 9:40, 33-70 A.D)

152. Prison gate opened (Acts 12:10, 33-70 A.D)

153. Paul did signs and wonders in I conium (Acts 14:3, 33-70 A.D)

155. Paul healed cripple (Acts 14:8-18, 33-70 A.D.)

156. Paul did multiple miracles (Acts 19:11, 33-70 A.D)

157. Paul raised a man form the dead (Acts 20:8-12, 33-70 A.D)

158. Wonders and signs done by the Apostles. (Acts 2:43, 33-70 A.D.)

159. More miracles, wonders and signs by the Apostles. (Acts 5:12, 33-70 A.D.)

160. Multitudes from surrounding cities were healed by Peters' shadow. (Acts 5:15, 33-70 A.D)

161. Prison doors were opened by an angel (Acts 5:19, 33-70 A.D.)

162. Ananias gives Paul back his sight (Acts 9:17, 33-70 A.D)

163. Peter raises Tabitha from the dead (Acts 9:36-40, 33-70 A.D.)

164. Cornelius was converted by the appearance of an Angel and the confirmation of Peter and the Holy Spirit (Acts 10:3, 44-47, 33-70 A.D)

165. Paul performed miracles in Ephesus (Acts 19:11, 33-70 A.D)

166. Peter was released by an angel form Heriot's prison (Acts 12:5-11, 33-70 A.D)

167. Herod was struck down and eaten by worms (Acts 12:23, 33-70 A.D)

168. In Lystra a man with crippled feet and lame from birth was healed (Acts 14:8-11, 33-70 A.D.)

169. Paul was stoned and did not die (Acts 14-19, 33-70 A.D.)

170. Paul and Silas were changed in a prison and an earthquake opened the prison doors (Acts. 16:25-27, 33-70 A.D)

171. In Ephesus God did extraordinary miracles through Paul (Acts 19:11-12, 33-70 A.D.)

172. Paul raised man from dead. (Acts 20:8-12, 30-70 A.D)

173. Paul and fellow passengers survived a ship wreck as they were told by an angle. (Acts 27:10, 27:22-23, 30-70 A.D.)

174. God protected Paul from a viper bite (Acts 28:3-6, 30-70 A.D.)

175. Paul healed Publius father who was suffering from fever and dysentery. After that the rest of the sick on the island came and were cured (Acts 28:7-9, 30-70 A.D)

Books of the Bible

The Bible, as we know it, was not gathered into one book until the early Christians decided they needed it to spread the word to all the gentiles. They gathered the Old Testament, which told about God's dealing with his chosen people and his prophecies about the coming of Jesus. Then they added the word of the witnesses of Christ life and his teachings (Gospels). They also added other lessons that they learned from the Holy Spirit (Epistles.)

Forty inspired men, over a period of sixteen hundred years, wrote the Bible. It covers four thousand years of History, prophecies and events concerning God's guidance. There are sixty-six books; thirty-nine in the Old Testament and twenty-seven in the New Testament There are one thousand, one hundred eighty-nine chapters in the Bible.

Following are some of the Bible verses that explain the scriptures: **2 Timothy 3: 16** All Scripture is God-breathed and is useful for teaching, rebuking, correcting and training in righteousness, so that the man of God may be thoroughly equipped for every good work. **2 Peter 1:21** For prophecy never had its origin in the will of man, but men spoke from God as they were carried along by the Holy Spirit **I Thessalonians 2: 13** And we also thank God continually because, when you received the word of God, which you heard from us, you accepted it not as the word of men, but as it actually is, the word of God, which is at work in you who believe. **Romans 15:4** For everything that was written in the past was written to teach us, so that through endurance and the encouragement of the Scriptures we might have hope. **II Timothy 3: 15** and how from infancy you have known the holy Scriptures, which are able to make you wise for salvation through faith in Christ Jesus. All Scripture is God-breathed and is useful for teaching, rebuking, correcting and training in righteousness, so that the man of God may be thoroughly equipped for every good work.

The Bible is the inspired word of God. However, it is 66 Books that were written by many individuals, which reflected their times and writing styles. Some of the styles are poetry, narratives, parables, letters, prophecy, laws, psalms, proverbs and idioms.

The books of the Bible are often referred to in the following categories of **the Law** (Genesis, Exodus, Leviticus, Numbers, Deuteronomy)**, History** (Joshua Judges Ruth 1 and 2 Samuel, 1and 2 Kings, 1and 2 Chronicles, Ezra, Nehemiah, Ester), **Poetry** (Job, Psalms Proverbs, Ecclesiastes, Song of Solomon), **Major prophets** (Isaiah, Jeremiah, Lamentation, Ezekiel, Daniel), **Minor Prophets** (Hosea, Joel, Amos, Obadiah, Jonah, Micah, Nahum, Habakkuk, Zephaniah, Haggai, Zechariah, Malachi), **Biography (The Gospels)** Mathew, Mark, Luke, John and Acts, **Epistles**-Letters(Romans,1 and 2 Corinthians, Galatians, Ephesians, Philippians , Colossians, 1 and 2 Thessalonians,1 and 2 Timothy, Titus, Philemon, Hebrews, James 1 and 2 Peter,1,2 and 3 John, and Jude), **Prophecy**(Revelation)..

The books of Bible were originally written in Hebrew, Aramaic, and Greek. Later it was translated in to English. As with any translation, it is determined by the understanding of the translator. Some of these translations are difficult to understand with the constant changing use of languages.

When trying to understand a passage it may help to look at several translations. Some of the translations (such as King James and the New International Version) tried to translate it word for word. Others such as the Living Bible and the Philips translation work more with phrases and their meaning. The comparison of these and other translation is valuable to your understanding. If you are still having trouble, a commentary or a Bible handbook may be helpful.

Whenever you read the Bible and want to understand its meanings, you should do the following:

1. Pray for the assistance in giving you wisdom, discernment & understanding.
2. Understand the background (History and Cultural) of the book and its author.
3. Find out the time and circumstances in which it was written.
4. Determine what the subject of the book and chapter.
5. Understand Context of the book and chapter you are reading to determine the meaning. It is always a good idea to read some before and after a verse to understand its context of that particular verse.
6. Be aware of the use of words. A word may have many meanings
7. Look at the author and his time and situation, then put yourself in his circumstances and try to understand his message for his point of view. As the Bible is inspired by God, you should also see what God is trying to express through the author.
8. When there is difficulty in understanding, use other

translation and commentaries.
9. See how it applies to us today.
10. Evaluate the passage as it relates to your life, in relation to God's will for you.

Apocrypha   These are the book that concerned the Bible and its history. However, when the Bible was delineated they were not felt to be worthy enough to be placed in the Bible. They were 1 Esdras, 2 Esdras, Tossbit, Judith, Additions to Esther, Wisdom of Solomon, Ecclesiasticus, Baruch, A letter of Jeremiah, The Song of the Three, Daniel and Susanna, Daniel, Bel and the Snake, Prayers of Manasseh, 1 Maccabees and 2 Maccabees

Septuagint The Septuagint translation contains the standard 39 books of the Old Testament canon, as well as certain apocryphal books. The term "Apocrypha" was coined by the fifth-century biblical scholar, Jerome, and generally refers to the set of ancient Jewish writings written during the period between the last book in the Jewish scriptures, Malachi, and the arrival of Jesus Christ. The apocryphal books include Judith, Tobit, Baruch, Sirach (or Ecclesiasticus), the Wisdom of Solomon, First and Second Maccabees, the two Books of Esdras, additions to the Book of Esther, additions to the Book of Daniel, and the Prayer of Manasseh Septuagint (sometimes abbreviated LXX) is the name given to the Greek translation of the Jewish Scriptures. The Septuagint has its origin in Alexandria, Egypt and was translated between 300-200 BC. Widely used among Hellenistic Jews, this Greek translation was produced because many Jews spread throughout the empire were beginning to lose their Hebrew language. The process of translating the Hebrew to Greek also gave many non-

Jews a glimpse into Judaism. According to an ancient document called the Letter of Aristae's, it is believed that 70 to 72 Jewish scholars were commissioned during the reign of Ptolemy Philadelphus to carry out the task of translation. The term "Septuagint" means seventy in Latin, and the text is so named to the credit of these 70 scholars.

The following information is furnished to assist your understand of the books of the Bible.

Times, People and when Old Testament books were written.

Dates are not exact due to lack of calendars and event recording based on people's lives. Estimates were made concerning people's lives and the events associated with them. There are two different view of the length of time noted in the bible and the B. C. Calendar. One states that there were 3569 years and the other 2384 years between Adam and Abraham. The dates for Abraham to Exodus vary from 645 B.C. to 430 B.C. Many people use rounded off dates. They say that Adam was 4000 B.C., Flood was 2400 B.C., Abraham was about 2000 B.C., Exodus was 1400 B.C., David was 1013 B.C; Judah captured by Babylon was 600 B.C.

Calendar time was changed from the time of Rome, to the birth of Christ. However, Dionysius Exiguus, when making the calendar made a mistake. He made the birth of Jesus on Roman calendar of 753 and it should have been 749.

Dates B.C.	Persons or events
Undetermined Past.	Adam
2348	Noah and the Flood
2133 to 1876	Abraham, Isaac, Jacob & Joseph
1876 to 1446	Living with Egyptians
1446 to 1406	Moses in wilderness
1406 to 1050	Conquest & Judges in Promised Land Joshua, Deborah, Gideon, Jephthah Samson
1050 to 931	**Samuel, Saul, David & Solomon United Kingdom** 931 to 875 Kingdom divided to South and North Kings Rehoboam vs. Jeroboam I.
875 to 790	Jehoshaphan-Ahab, Uzziah & Jeroboam II, Assyrian domination, Fall of Samaria
640 to 597 Ezekiel's	Josiah –Judah alone, Daniel &
754-650	Assyrian
625 to 539	Babylonian Supremacy
539-331	Medo-Persian rule
586 to 515`	Jeremiah (Fall of Jerusalem), Restoration of temple Zerubbabel, Haggai, Zechariah

458	Ezra's Return to Jerusalem
444	Malachi Nehemiah's return
1st.Century AD	Formation of the Church
70 A.D.	Destruction of Jerusalem and temple

Books of the Bible-written

Torah or 1ˢᵗ 4 books of the Bible
    Genesis
    Exodus
    Leviticus
    NumbersMoses   (1446 BC to 1405 BC)

Deuteronomy   Moses   1400BC
Joshua   Joshua   1405BC and 1390BC
JudgesUnknown Most likely Samuel   1043BC-1004BC
1& 2 Samuel   Samuel and his associates   931 BC
1 & 2 Kings   Tradition is Jeremiah and Associate
                      722 BC-586BC

1 & 2 Chroniclestradition suggest Ezra 450BC-400BC
Ezra   Ezra   450BC

Nehemiah   Nehemiah & assoc.   425BC to 400 BC

Ester   known   483BC-383BC

Job   Unknown events   1900Bc to 1800BC

PsalmVarious (Moses, David, Asaph, 400BC (approx.) Korah, Solomon, Herman, Ethan)
Edited 200 BC

Proverbs   King Solomon,   Agur, Lemuel, & others.
                    930BC-700BC

Isaiah	Isaiah	740BC-680BC
Jeremiah	Jeremiah	627BC-586BC
Lamentations	Jeremiah	586BC
Ezekiel	Ezekiel	590BC-570BC
Daniel	Daniel	530BC
Hosea	Hosea	760BC-720BC
Joel	Joel	9th Century BC
Amos	Amos	60BC
Obadiah		9th Century BC
Jonah	Unknown	prior to 612BC
Micah		739BC-686BC
Nahum		663BC-612BC
Habakkuk,		prior to 605BC
Zephaniah		640BC-630BC
Haggai		520BC
Zechariah		520BC
Malachi		432BC-425BC
Matthew		50 AD– 60 AD

Mark	Mark (Friend of Peter)	57AD
Luke	Luke (Assoc. of Paul)	60BAD-70AD
John	John the apostle	60SD-70AD
Acts	Luke	62AD
Romans	Paul	57AD
1 Corinthians	Paul	55AD
2 Corinthians	Paul	55AD
Galatians	Paul	57AD-58 AD
Ephesians	Paul	60AD-62 AD
Philippians	Paul	60AD-62AD
Colossians	Paul	60AD-61AD
1 Thessalonians	Paul	51AD
2 Thessalonians	Paul	51AD-52AD
1 Timothy	Paul	62AD-64AD
2 Timothy	Paul	66Ad-67AD
Titus	Paul	63AD-66AD
Philemon	Paul	60AD

Hebrews	Paul or associates	65AD
James	(Jesus brother)	30AD-40AD
1Peter	Peter	60AD
2 Peter	Peter	Late 60's AD
1 John	John the apostle	Prior to 90AD
2 John	John the apostle	after 90AD
3 John	John the apostle	after 90AD
Jude	James (Jesus brother)	70AD-90AD
Revelation	John the apostle	95AD

The Old Testament was inspired by God and written by Gods' chosen people. Their language was Hebrew. It is composed of messages from God and the history of his chosen people. It covers 6000 years of history. There are 39 books, which compose the Old Testament. They are:

The Torah 5Books
Genesis, Exodus, Leviticus, Numbers, Deuteronomy

Historical 12 Books
Joshua, Judges, Ruth, I & II Samuel, I&II Kings, I&II Chronicles, Ezra, Nehemiah, Ester

Poetic 5 Books
Job, Psalm, Proverbs, Ecclesiastes, Song of Solomon

Prophets 17 Books
Isaiah, Jeremiah, Lamentations, Ezekiel, Daniel,
 Hosea, Joel, Amos Obadiah, Jonah, Micah, Nahum,
Habakkuk, Zephaniah, Haggai, Zechariah, Malachi

The entire Old Testament was translated to Greek. There were 72 elders from each of the 12 Israel tribes who translated the Old Testament to Greek language. The translation was called the Septuagint. This translation was accomplished between 200 and 300BC. This was done because the people of Israel were scattered in various areas of the then known world. . This is important to us because the Old Testament prophesied Christ and his life. These prophecies were validated in the New Testament. Thus, no one can say that these prophecies were added after the fact.

Bible Books
(*Descriptions*)

The following information came from some study Bibles that had notes similar to these notes. It is placed here to furnish a simple outline understand and the times and place of their writing. I would suggest that your look at your study Bible for a more complete understanding.

The books are arranged the same as in the Bible. For a Page number for a specific Book, see the index.

Book of GENESIS   Creation of the universe & Founding of the Hebrew Nation

Author: It is believed that Moses is the author. He gathered the history of old and placed it in this book Genesis tells us that God is an eternal being who has power to create all things. God created our universe, which includes the Stars, Light, Oceans, Lands, Plants, Animals, and Man. This book tells us about the origin of the universe, our earth, plants, animals and human beings. It also tells us about the beginning relationship between God and man. It tells about the extraordinary efforts God made to have a relationship with man. Even with this effort, man rebelled against him. Man disappoints God to the point that he wants to start over. So he has a great flood and destroys most of mankind. In his love for his creation he saves Noah and starts over to build a relationship with man. Genesis tells us about the history of Gods and his people. It tells about his attempt work for the redemption between him and man. God set apart, a group of people (Abraham's family) for his reconciliation with man. It tells the history of God's work among his people. It is a history of the many things he did to provide for his chosen people proving he loves them. God's work was done so that man would return his love and through their relationship he could be reconciled to all men.

In the beginning God wanted man to live a righteous life with him. However, God gave man a free will and man used his pride, lust and covertness to do unrighteous works.
God sees man's unrighteousness and tries to teach us to be righteous. He tries to do this through discipline. The book describes these attempts.

1 Adam and Eve eats the forbidden fruit.

2. Cain Killing Able.

3. All the people except Noah became depraved. God told Noah build an Ark,
to save him and regenerate the earth. He then flooded the earth destroying the unrighteous.

4. Again man's pride became strong and he tried to build a tower to heaven. God was upset and changed the language between the people so they could not talk to each other and complete the tower.

5. God saw the sexual unrighteous of man in the cities of Sodom and Gomorrah. He destroyed these Cities and their inhabitants.

God decided he needed to restart with one man and work with that man to build a righteous people. The book then tells the story of this man and his descendants and their success and failure on the road to this nation.

1 He chose Abraham to be the father of this nation.

2. God tell Abraham he will make his descendants a great nation. However, he does not have children until late in life. Later, he has a child, named Isaac, God asks him to sacrifice him. God sees he is loyal and stops the sacrifice.

3. Isaac marries Rebekah and they have two sons Esau and Jacob.

4. Jacob through deception acquires the family blessing of Isaac.

5. Esau' descendants became the Edomite's.

6. Jacob later was named Israel. His descendants became the nation of Israel. Jacob had 12 sons. His favorite son was Joseph. Joseph's brothers were jealous and sold him to be a slave in Egypt.

7. God helps Joseph interpret dreams. One day he interprets and important dream about a future famine for the King of Egypt. Joseph becomes second in command of Egypt to handle the upcoming famine. Due to a famine in the land, Jacob's family is moved to Egypt and is reconciled with Joseph.

8. The Israelites (Jacob's descendants) live in Egypt for

400 years and multiply in number.

Outline of Genesis

Chapter 1-3 Creation and man in the Garden of Eden

Chapter 4   Beginning and trial of the first borrn (Cain and Abel

Chapter 5   History of man before the flood

Chapters 6-9 The flood and Noah

Chapters 10   The nations of the sons of Noah after the flood

Chapter 11   The scattering of people due to the tower of Babel.

Chapter 12-25 The story of Abraham

Chapter 26-19   The story of Isaac and Jacob

Chapter 36   The line of Esau

Chapter 37-50   Story of Joseph and his family in Egypt

Book of EXODUS   The Covenant with the Hebrew Nation

It is believed that Moses was the Author. The Book was probably written during the forty-year wilderness journey between 1445 B.C. and 1405 B.C.

Exodus is the story of God rescuing his people from the oppression they had in Egypt. It tells of the many miracles he used to free them from Egypt. On their way to the Promised Land God kept trying to condition his people to his way. However, they still did not put their faith in him so he did not let that generation in to the Promised Land. These struggles and God's covenants are recorded in Exodus.

The book can be divided into 3 areas

Chapters 1-18 are the history of Moses' life and the Israelites deliverance from Egypt..

Chapters 19-24 God makes a covenant the Israelites.

Chapters 25-40 God establishes proper worship for the Israelites.
Plagues that freed the Israelites were against the Gods of Egypt.

Following is further information concerning the historical events.

Israel's children multiplied greatly in Egypt. They became oppressed with severe affliction. The Egyptians gave and order that at birth all Israel's male children should be killed by throwing them in the river. .

Moses' family set him adrift in a basket saved him. He was found and raised with the Pharaoh's daughter. He later saw the mistreatment of his people. In anger of some mistreatment, he killed an Egyptian man. The Pharaoh was upset with Moses and wanted to kill him.

Moses left Egypt.

While in exile, Moses was approach by God in the burning bush. Moses felt unqualified, but took the task of leadership of his people.

Moses returned to Egypt. God wanted to fulfill his promise to make a great nation of Abraham's descendants. He used Moses to gather his people and communicate with the Egyptians. God showed Pharaoh his power through Moses and his rod. He asked the Pharaoh to let his people go! The Pharaoh refused and God convinced the Egyptians to release his people with the use of Ten Plagues. God kept his people safe during these plagues. The Plagues were as follows:

1. Blood in all the waters of Egypt.
2. Frogs were sent all over the Land.
3. Lice on man and beast.
4. Swarms of flies on the people and the land.
5. Disease on the Egyptians animals.
6. Boils on Man and Beast.
7. Rained hail and fire on men and animals the land of Egypt.
8. Locusts were sent and they covered the earth. And they eat everything that was left to eat.
9. Darkness for three days.
10. Death of the entire first born of Egypt.

During the 10th plague, God spared Abraham's nation with the use of a Passover sacrament. This event is still celebrated by the Hebrews today.

The Pharaoh finally agreed to let God's people go. The people left taking animals and possessions. .

Pharaoh wanted to kill God's people so he followed them. At the Red Sea, God saved them by parting it and making a dry path to the other side. He destroyed the Egyptians, who were trying to kill his people, by letting the sea fall on them and drowned them.

God furnished his people with food, water and statues (10 commandments was given) while going to the promise land.

God made a covenant with his people. "If you will indeed obey my voice and keep my covenant, then you shall be a special treasure to me above all people; for all the earth is mine. And you shall be to me a kingdom of priests and a holy nation. These are the words which you shall speak to the children of Israel."

God made provision for approaching him. He didn't want them to worship anything but him. You shall not make for yourselves Gods of silver or gods of gold. An altar of earth you shall make for me (God) and you shall sacrifice on it your burnt offering and your peace offerings, your sheep and your oxen.

God started giving statues for the people to live as a nation. This included such things as: Rights of person, property and conduct: Feasts, Conquest regulations; Religious regulation; Tabernacle worship and artifacts. He also set up ceremonial worship.

While Moses is in the mountains, the people broke the covenant. They build a golden calf. This violates the 1st. & 2nd commandment. God was angered and wanted to destroy them. Moses asks God not to destroy them.

Moses went down and destroyed the Golden Calf and informed the people of their great sin. God made a new covenant with his people. He would drive out the people in the land, which he had promised to Abraham and they were to take it as he directed.

The people prepare the Tabernacle for worship. God then fills the Tabernacle with His Glory. The cloud of the Lord was above the tabernacle by day, and fire was over it by night, in the sight of all the house of Israel, throughout all their journeys.

Book of LEVITICUS   Laws of the Hebrew Nation

It is believed that Moses wrote Leviticus. The book was written about 1405 BC.
Some people describe the book as the Priest Manual.

Leviticus is instruction of worship to God. It deals with worship, service and obedience to God. It discussed laws of sacrifice, inaugural service at the sanctuary, laws of impurity, Day of Atonement ritual and sanctification.

Included are the Laws of the Priest, laws of Israel purity, Laws of Atonement, Sanctification for the people, Sanctification for the priesthood, laws of sanctification in Worship and Sanctification in Canaan.

The book describes the sacrificial system. . Chapter1-7 sets the laws of sacrifice. Chapter 8-10 is the installation of the priesthood. . Chapters 11-15 are the laws of ritual purity and impurity. Chapters 16 concern the Day of Atonement. Chapter 17 tells how to kill for food. Chapters18-20 is the laws of Holiness. Chapters 21 and

22 tell about the disqualification of priests and sacrifices. The festival calendar is in Chapter 23. Chapter 24 has some regulations. Chapter 25 discusses the sabbatical and jubilee years. Chapter 26tell of a curse if the law is disobeyed or a blessing it is kept.

Book of NUMBERS   Journey to the Promised Land

It is believed that Moses wrote this book. It takes place 1444 to 1405 BC.
Another name for this book is" In the Wilderness". This is because it describes the events of the 40year wandering in the wilderness. The Numbers name came from the fact that it begins with the first numbering of the men of Israel and ends with the numbering of the men forty years later at the plains of Moab. The first census was the people that left Egypt that God would not let into the Promised Land because of their disobedience. The second census was the new generation which became adult's while he Israelites were in the wilderness. The second group was the ones that would go to the Promise Land.

Chapter 1-25 tell about the first generation that failed to take the Promised Land.
Chapters 26-36 are the history of the second generation. It describes the preparation to take the land and the appointment of Joshua as their leader. It gave instruction on how to successfully take the Promised Land.

Following is a brief description of the book.

After the first numbering, the people were asked to go to the Promised Land. They sent out spies to see the strength of the enemy. They went and saw that the enemy was very strong. Upon the report of the spies, the People of Israel rebelled against God and wished they were still in Egypt or left in the wilderness to die rather than be killed by the enemy. Joshua and Caleb spoke to the people and said that they should have faith in God. But this didn't change the mind of the people.

God was very upset with his people. Moses intercedes for the people and God does not destroy them. However, Because of lack of faith, God decides that that generation would not be allowed to go the Promised Land and would die in the wilderness. The spies, that discouraged the people, die immediately. As Joshua and Caleb had faith in God spared their live in the wilderness. The Children of the ones who left Egypt were allowed to go to the Promised Land. During the 40 years they made a sojourn to Sinai and wondered in the wilderness. During this time, the people learn to prepare for battle and the Levites carried the sanctuary. Moses was not allowed to go to the Promised Land because he misrepresented God, in the eyes of the people of Israel when they needed water at Meribah. God allowed Moses to see the Promised Land just before they were to enter the land. As Moses was not allowed in the Promise Land God had Moses Anoint Joshua to take the people to the Promise land.
The book also outline the following; organization of Israel, priests and the Sanctification of Israel. . It tells about the failure of the people during this period. The people were given laws on how to organize the promised lands and how to do offerings

God's religious values lie in the reinforcement of the conviction that God manifest himself in history and he demands obedience to his will. This thought helps us to understand the thinking of the people who lived during the events of the Old Testament.

Book of DEUTERONOMY   Laws of the Hebrew Nation

The Old Testament attributes this book and the rest of the Pentateuch to Moses. It is sometimes referred to as the Second Law. The book was written at the end of the 40 years in the desert. It was written approximately 1405 BC. The book is a religion-philosophical guideline. It instructs the new generation of Israelites about the previous laws that were given to their parents and how they had to live up to the laws and Gods' covenants.

An outline of the book is as follows.
Chapter 1-4 discusses the history of God's covenants
Chapter 5-26 Are the Laws of the covenant
Chapter 27-30 describes the sealing of the covenant.
Chapter 31-34 places the leaders of the covenant.

The book has three sermons that Moses used to review and expand the covenant between God and his people. The sermons tell what God has done, what he expects and what he will do for the people in the Promised Land. It expands the law. It gives new commands regarding blessing, love, study, Ceremonial laws, Civil laws, Family laws. God makes Covenants with the people concerning the laws being used in the Promised Land. The new people who were to go to the Promised Land ratified the original covenant of the 10 commandments. The people ratified the Canaan covenant and the Palestinian Covenant.

The Song of Moses is found here.

All the people who are to enter the Promised Land ratify god's covenants. Moses blessed the tribes of Israel. He then went up to Mt. Nebo and the Lord showed his all the land. Moses died and was buried in the valley of Moab. Joshua is given the leadership of Israel.

Book of JOSHUA
The Conquest of Canaan

God promised Israel's people a land of their own. Until the events of this book they had none. Joshua tell how the promise was fulfilled   It is the story of Israel's conquest of Canaan and the Allocation of the land among the Israel tribes.
As Moses was not allowed to enter the Promised Land because he misrepresented God when they wanted water, Joshua led the people in to the Promised Land.
It is believed that Joshua wrote the book. It includes events from 1405 B.C.to1390 B.C. It is a narrative about events from the wondering in the wilderness through the settling on the Promised Land. It discusses the military action needed to obtain the land, the settlement of the tribes in their area, the setting up of cities and the sanctuaries.

It describes how the people of Israel go from the wilderness to the Promised Land. This is the fulfillment of the promised homeland. It takes them seven Years to conquer the land of the Canaanites, Amorites and other smaller kingdoms. This includes the famous story of the falling of the wall at Jericho. God demonstrated awesome power assisting soldiers to take the Promise land. He altered the course of the heavenly bodies.(Sun

stood still over Gibeon and moon in the valley of Aijalon). It also tells of the settlement and division of the land by 12 original tribes. 6 cities of refuge were to be set up and 48 cities as inheritance of the Levitical priests. Alters of worship were set up and there was a renewal of the Gods' Covenant
God tells them he will be with them for the conquering of the land, if they continue to follow him and destroy the people of the land. However they do not follow God's instructions they made covenant relationships and intermarried with the local people.. God later tried to aid the settlement by using the Judges.

Book of JUDGES   First 300 years of the Land

The exact author is not known. It was written 1004 B.C. (During Samuel's time.). It is felt that Samuel or someone close to him wrote the book. The events covered in Judges took place from 1380 BC. to 1045 BC.. The Israelites did not complete their order from God to take all the land and destroy it inhabitance. As a result they had problems with the people who lived in the country before them. Judges is a book concerning the history of how God attempted to help his people by sending a special person or judge to help them in troubled times. God used Judges to help the Israelites after Joshua died until the time of the Israel monarchy by appointing inspired leaders to defend them
The Book describes the final conquest of the Promised Land, the Judges and their saving acts, the movement of Dan's tribe to the North and the war with the Benjamin tribe.
Some of these areas still had gentiles living in the land God said if they lived by his covenant, he would continue to give them the rest of the land. .

However, the Israelites began to change and forgot their covenant with God. They lost their faith and thus their ability to take their land. They did not drive out their enemies. Their enemies have different morals than that of their God and this immorality starts working on the people. God is disappointed but he wants to help them. He picks out people (Judges) who support his wishes for the Israelites and makes them leaders. God helps these Judges deliver Israel for its enemies and a new relation with God. However, the People of Israel continue in a cycle of deterioration, deliverance and depravity. God brings new Judges to aid them in time of trouble. The people did what they thought was right. However, the immoral ideals of their enemies, which lived in their country, distorted their thoughts, actions and faith. It was "evil in the sight of the Lord" This caused God to call on many of these Judges.

The Judges were: Othniel, Ehud, Shamgar, Deborah and Barak, Gideon, Abimelech, Tola, Jair Jepthah, Ibzan, Elon, Abodon, and Samson. In most cases God raised the judges to be a military leader to defend the people of Israel.

With the continued failure to restore faith in God, the people turn to idolatry and personal immorality. The people start living like the Canaanites.

The advances of neighboring people and their inability to secure the land cause them to want a national government with a king to defend the various part of the land.

Book of RUTH   Beginning of the messianic Family of

David and the Kinsman Redeemer

It is not know who wrote this book. The events took place during the time of the Judges. Ruth is a story of a woman who gave love and devotion to her Israelite family and took God as her God. As a result she later remarried an Israel man and she became the Great grandmother of Jesus

A Hebrew named Elimelech and his wife Naomi left the Bethlehem due to a famine and went to Moabite. Elimelech died and left his wife along with two sons. The sons grew up and married. Ruth and Orpah were the daughters in law. The two sons died. This left the three women alone. Naomi told Ruth and Orpah to return to their kinsman because she could not protect them. Orpah Stayed in that land. Ruth wanted to go to Judah with Naomi to be with her God and people. She so eloquently stated she desire to return with Naomi that she said:" Your people shall be my people and your God my God". They returned to the city of Bethlehem. Ruth went into the field to glean them for food. She gleaned in the fields of one of Naomi's husband relatives. His name was Boaz. He saw her and knew of her loyalty to Naomi. So he protected her from the men of the field and provided for her. Naomi tries to provide security for Ruth by asking Boas to exercise his right as kinsman. He states he is not the nearest kinsman. Naomi sends Ruth to Boaz's threshing floor. Ruth lies down at Boaz's feet after he goes to sleep. He awakes during the night and finds Ruth. He asks why she is there. She says that she is his maidservant. He gives her some barley and sends her away. He then decides she is a virtuous woman. Boaz then deals with the near kinsmen to acquire Naomi's land and Ruth. Ruth marries Boaz and their child is the Grandfather of King David

Book of I SAMUEL Organization and Birth of the Kingdom

It is believed that the Author was Samuel. The events of the book are from his birth (1105 B.C.) until the first king Saul is killed (1015 B.C.). The books of I Samuel and II Samuel were originally one Book Samuel was the last of the Judges and later he was called a prophet. When the people wanted a monarchy Samuel was against it. Later when God decided he would accept it, he told Samuel to anoint Saul. It is a story of King that strayed away from God's covenants and how God would choose another to rule because of Saul's not continuing in Gods' will.

This book describes the history of the decline of the Judges to the end of the first king of Israel.

Samuel was called by God to replace Eli the priest as representative of God. The philistines oppress Israel and kill Eli and his sons. They also take the arch of the covenant. Samuel functions as the last of the Judges and becomes a prophet. Samuel ministry leads to a reform and restoration of the people of Israel. During the time that the philistines had the Ark, God gave their gods and people in the town sickness. The philistines sent the Ark form city to city with the same results. They returned the Arc with a trespass offering. With the return of the Ark, Israel returned to the lord. Samuel approaches God and he gave them victory over the philistines with confusing them. There was peace than and Samuel was Judge of the county. When Samuel was old he appointed his sons a Judges. However, they didn't follow the righteousness of Samuel and the people wanted a king instead of the son's judges. Samuel relayed the words of the lord concerning what kings would do to them. They still wanted a king. God choose Saul to be king. Samuel anoints Saul and he becomes King of Israel. At first Saul is a success as king. But he becomes sinful and selfish and disobedient. God reject Saul as King and anoints David. David comes to prominence when he defeats Goliath the Giant. David goes and lives with Saul in the palace. He becomes friends with Jonathan the king's son.

The people want to follow David. Saul is angry and tries to kill David by throwing a spear at him. David flees and gathers a small army. Saul pursues David. David refuses to kill Saul even though he has many opportunities. David and Saul both fought the enemies of Israel. However, the Philistines have a battle and Saul doesn't want to be killed by the Philistines and he kills himself by falling on his Sword.

Book of II SAMUEL   Reign of David.

Second Samuel is a continuation of the first Samuel. The author is believed to be Samuel or at his direction (Nathan and Gad). The time of this book is the rule of David from 1011 B.C. to 1004 B.C. rule in Heron and 1004B.C. to 971 B.C. in Judah.

After the death of Saul, David became the king of Judah. He was a successful king for 7 years. He then became king or Israel. The kingdom was moved to Jerusalem. David reigns for 33 years in Jerusalem. David triumphs over his enemies, including the philistines. However, as with all men he has failures. They are revealed with his adultery and having the women's husband killed.. David arranged his death by sending him in to battle and deserting him. The enemy then killed him. David is made aware of his sins and repents. He then has problem in his house during the rest of his reign. Through the trails of time David continues to be a good king over Israel. The book describes David's triumphant events and his trials. Gods promises David that after his death he will set up his seed (Jesus) after him, who will come from his body, and God will establish his kingdom.

Book of I KINGS Division of the Kingdom **Book of II KINGS** History of the divided Kingdom.

The author is not mentioned but many believe it to be mostly written by Jeremiah and his contemporary. The time of I Kings is 971 B.C. to. 851 B.C.

Originally I Kings and II Kings was one Book that was divided later. It is a continuation of the book of Samuel. A general outline of the book is as follows.

Chapter 1-11 The monarchy under David and Solomon
Chapters 12- through II Kings Chapter 17, The division and rule of the two kingdoms.

I Kings Chapter 18-25 After the fall of Israel it tells about Judah

It begins with the appointment of Solomon as King. It describes the Kingship of Solomon. Solomon was noted for his great wisdom, which he asked and received from God. With this wisdom he set up a great government and the temple and many other great edifices. He dedicated the new Temple to God. He wrote Proverbs, Ecclesiastes, and Song of Solomon. He became well known all over the world for his wisdom and greatness he brought to Israel. However as with all great men, pride became a problem and he relied on his own judgment rather than letting God's wisdom rule. He acquired many idolatrous wives and concubines. It is said that he had 700 wives and 300 concubines. The influence of his women led him away from God. Eventually this led to the destruction of Israel.

Israel was then divided into two kingdoms. 10 of the original tribes were the Northern kingdom called Israel. The tribes of Judah and Benjamin formed the Southern Kingdom called Judah.
The Northern Kingdom lasted over 200 years and was destroyed by Assyria in 721 B.C. There were 19 King during this period. They worshiped the Golden Calf or Baal during their reign.

The Southern Kingdom lasted approximately 300 years and was destroyed by Babylon around 600 B.C. They had 20 kings during its reign. God was worship by some of the kings. God blessed their kingdom. Other kings would worship Baal and other Canaanite religions. However, Idolatry became the style of the county. This became the destruction of Israel. At the end of the kingdom, most of the Israelites were in captivity in Assyria and Babylon

God continued to try to revive his worship in the country during this time. He sent the following prophets to the Northern Kingdom: Elijah, Elisa, Amos, and Hosea. He sent the following Prophets to the Southern Kingdom:

Obadiah, Joel, Isaiah, Micah, Nahum, Zephaniah, Jeremiah, and Habakkuk.

Book of I CHRONICALES Reign of David
Book of II CHRONICALSE History of the Southern Kingdom

The authorship is not stated, but most scalars believe, it was written by Ezra and Nehemiah. I Chronicles and II Chronicles was originally one Book. The I Chronicles Book discusses the genealogy from Adam to King David. The time of this book without the genealogy is during King David reign. (1004 B. C. to 971 B.C.) . II Chronicles Deals with the beginning of King Solomon's reign (971 B.C.), and the reign of the Southern Kingdom (605 B.C.). It includes the destruction Jerusalem and Solomon temple, and the taking of the people to Babylon. After the 70 years of captivity God has Persians defeats the Babylonians. King Cyrus of Persia releases the Israelites from bondage.

Kings are books the describe Israel's political history. Chronicles is a divine description of the same time period. However, it doesn't describe the Northern Kingdom after the separation of the kingdoms, because God was not part of it, even though he tried to revive it through the prophets. Prior to the separation and the idolatry or the Northern Kingdom, God sent the following prophets to the Northern Kingdom: Elijah, Elisha, Amos, and Hosea. God wanted to hold David's kingdom, Judah, as long as he could. He sent the following Prophets to the Southern Kingdom: Obadiah, Joel, Isaiah, Micah, Nahum, Zephaniah, Jeremiah, and Habakkuk.

The book can be outlined as follows.
Chapter 1   Genealogical list of descendants form Adam to Isaac.
Chapters 2-9   List of Israelite tribes
People of Jerusalem and Gabion; Levitical functions
Chapters 10   Death of Saul
Chapters 11-29   The Story of David   II Chronicles 1-9
 The story of Solomon and the Kings of Judah.
Chapters 10-36   Babylonian Captivity.

After the Genealogies, I Chronicles discussed the death of Saul and the anointing of David as King. David's military victories making Israel a great nation He sets up and organizes the country. He prepares for the building of a temple of God, even though God will not allow him to build it. It tells about the last days of David.

II Chronicles tell about Solomon's glorious Kingdom. He built the temple for the house of God. This was time of Israel's greatest accomplishments. Her wealth and prestige was world-renowned. It describes the visit of the Queen of Sheba and Solomon's wealth. It describes the death of Solomon and the division of the country into the Northern and Southern Kingdoms.

After the division of the Kingdoms All the kings of the North worshiped the Gods of the Golden Calf. God then left them to their ruin, and they were no longer discussed in this book. The Southern Kingdom was also idolatry worshiping. However, they would sometimes return to God. He gave them blessings when they did. However, idolatry prevailed even with the prophets trying to persuade them to return to God. They were finally sent to Babylon, as was prophesied by the prophets.

Book of EZRA Return from Captivity

The author of Ezra is believed to be Ezra. The time of the book is from 538 B.C. to 473 B.C. Ezra was a scribe and a priest for the people in captivity in Babylon. Persia conquers Babylon. The King of Persia sees the Glory of God and allows the Israelites to return to build their temple. The books of Ezra, Ester and Nehemiah are the main source of information concerning Israel's history concerning the return from Babylonian exile.

The return to Jerusalem was accomplished in three groups. Ezra went with the second group by the decree of King Darius. Ezra wrote his book to record the events of the return to Jerusalem.
God told his people that they would be in exile for 70 years. The return was done in three different events. The first was when Cyrus King of Persia, recognized God. He made a proclamation throughout his kingdom that the Israelites would return and build a house of God at Jerusalem. Gifts were given by the people of Israel and Persia to build the temple. At this time, some of the people returned to build the temple. Some of the people enjoyed being in Babylon and did not return then. The book of Ester tells about the people who stayed in Babylon. Zerubbabel returned in the first group. He and his brethren built a new alter to the lord and the religious feasts before beginning work on the temple. In the second year after the return word was started the building of the temple and a religious rebirth. There is trouble with people in the land and they try to have the building stopped. The work on the

temple was interfered. It took 20 years before it was completed. However the Persian Kings allowed the continuing of the Temple.

After the temple is completed, more people return to Israel. Artaxerxes, a new king, wrote a letter allowing people to return to Israel with Ezra. Ezra worked on the reformation of the people.

Book of NEHEMIAH   Rebuilding Jerusalem

The author of Nehemiah is Nehemiah. The time of the Book is the same time as Ezra. 464 B.C. to 423 B.C. Nehemiah was the Persia king Artaxerxes' cupbearer. Ester is King Artaxerxes' Stepmother. She was probable a Good friend of Nehemiah.
Nehemiah hears about the walls of Jerusalem were broken down and the gates were burnt with fire. This distressed him greatly. He intercedes with God and then the King. The King made him the civil governor with his authority and gave him a letter of passage to Judah. He led the third and final group to Jerusalem and finds the wall in disrepair. He gathers the people to rebuild the wall. There is great opposition to the rebuilding of the wall by the Gentiles. The people gather and rebuild the wall in 52 days. The people, who were resisting the building of the wall, now knew that God helped because of the immense task and the speed in which it was done. Nehemiah and Ezra join forces to restore the people to God. They set up the organization of Jerusalem and the worship system. The people renewed the covenant with God. The people became obedient to Gods covenant. They settle the country, brought back the practices of the people of God.

Book of ESTHER   Jews deliverance from extermination.

The author of the book is not known. It was a person who had access to Persian custom and knowledge of Israel's books. The time of the book was during the period when the people were returning in stages to Judah. The events of the book took place between 483B.C. and 473B.C. This period of time was between, the first group of people led by Zerubbabel and the second led by Ezra. This book is read in the synagogues on the festival of Purim.

Ahasuerus was the king of Persia. He had a great feast and requested his wife Queen Vashti to come to him so he could show her beauty. She refused and would not let the princess go to the feast. This angered the king and he send a declaration to his kingdom the all wives should obey the husbands. He removed her from the throne. He decided to replace her. He had all the young virgins taken to a place so he could select a new queen. Esther was one of the virgins brought to the king's palace. She became friend with the man in charge and he aided her. Esther was selected as a replacement to Queen.
There were plots against the King. Mordecai who was ester's guardian learned of the plots. He told Esther and she revealed it to the King. The King stops the plot. He publicly honors Mordecai. Haman, who doesn't like Mordecai, is forced to honor him. He does not like honoring a Jew. Haman plots to kill Mordecai along with all the Jews. Haman tells the king that there are certain people who are scattered throughout the kingdom which do not keep the laws of the King. He convinced the king to let him destroy the Jews. This plot is revealed to Ester. She knows that she is risking her life,

but decides to reveal it to the king.
Ester has a feast and tells the king what Haman is planning. She also reveals that she is a Jew. This upsets the King and he leaves. When he returns he finds Haman on the couch with Ester. He is upset and has Haman hung because of his deception and plan to kill Mordecai. The King then sends a decree to allow the Jews to protect themselves against Haman's people. However, some of Haman's people still want to kill the Jews. The Jew defeats them in battles and the Jews are again safe in Babylon.
God's hand of providing for his people and their protection are seen in the Book of Ester.

Book of JOB   Problem of Suffering

The author of Job is unknown. However it is believe it first became writing about the time of Moses. It appears that it happened during the time of Abraham. Most of the book is written in poetry.

Job was a man of God and God gave him many blessings. The devil goes before God. God asks devil what he thinks about Job. The devil says that Job only likes God because God protected him. He states that if God took away his protection and blessing that Job would curse God. God allowed the devil to take all he had but not his person. The Devil killed his children and many of his animals. This destroyed Job, but he kept blessing God. The devil tells God that Job will change if his person is attacked. God allows it except for his life. The devil struck Job with painful boils from the sole of his foot to the crown of his head. His wife asks him to curse God and die. Job continues to thank God. Job's

Friends come to see him. They debate about Job's situation and it relation to God. Job complains about God's punishing him and allowing bad things to happen to him. One of his friends tells him that he needs submit to God's process of purifying his life through trials and the greatness of God. God comes and questions Job. God talks to Job out of a whirlwind on the ignorance, impotence, helplessness and infinitesimal smallness of man compared to God, asking question after question that cause Job to become silent. Job confess lack of understand and repents of his thoughts against how God works. God then restored Job's losses and gave him twice as much as he had before.

One question that arises out of Job is how God can allow suffering. Job learns we are born for trouble and it is a reality of life. God allows suffering to happen to a person who is innocent. He learns God is superior to man. When God allows suffering there must be a good reason. Job recognizes the majesty and sovereignty of Gods and repents and no longer demands an answer as to why we have sorrow and pain. God is sovereign and worthy of worship over all creation in whatever he chooses to do.

Book of PSALMS   National Hymn Book of Israel

Psalms is a collection of songs of praise of the lord. It is composed of five books of songs. At the end of each book is a doxology. The authors or editors was believe to be King David and Korah, Asaph and anonymous others. The basic contents were Songs of worship, hymns of national interest and anthems of praise. The time of compilation was from 1020B.C. to 430B.C. The subjects of the Psalms are worship, prayer, sorrow, confession, lament, thanksgiving, celebration, and praise.

Psalms was divided in to five sections. David wrote Book 1(1-41) was written and the subjects were mains songs of worship. David and Korah wrote Book 2(42-74). The subject of these psalms was hymns of national interest. Asaph wrote Book 3 (73-89) and the subjects were that of national interest. The author of book 4(90-106) is unknown. Its subject was anthems of praise. David and others authors wrote the Book 5 (107-150) It was also anthems of Praise. There are many prophetic items also found in the Psalms. Many of these psalms were used in the temple for special events.

Book of PROVERBS   Wisdom of Solomon

Proverbs is a book about wisdom. Solomon furnished most of the proverbs. He is credited with 800 of the proverbs. As he asked God for wisdom, it is fitting that he should pass it on in this book. There were other authors and it is felt that wisdoms may have been collected for other sources and put into the book. Solomon wrote Proverbs 1 –10. They deal with Poetic sayings and proverbial saying of Solomon. Hezekiah added Solomon's proverbial sayings in 25-29. Agur added 30 proverbial sayings. King Lemuel added 31.

The purpose of the book was to give instruction on how to deal with everyday life and its problems. It dealt with subjects concerning God, family problems, neighbors, and national associations. Solomon wrote it in poetry, questions, and small stories. . It is a book where you can look for wisdom for your everyday use.

Book of ECCLESIASTES   Vanity of Earthly Life

It appears the Solomon wrote this book. It was written around 935 B.C. Solomon wrote this book in his later years when he was expressing his regret for his self-indulgence, earthly life and idolatry.

The book discussed vanity from a personal experiences and observing others. It shows that one's life is changed when they diligently search for wisdom, various life pursuits, and pleasures of life, eternity, hard work, popularity, wealth, oppression, and authority. All of these searches are not rewarding. It advises to enjoy life and live joyfully with your wife, do well, from your youth and fear God and keep his commandments for God will bring every work into judgment. It shows how man cannot find the answers of life through his efforts. It tells that if we fear God and obey his commands we will have the proper perspective on all that we do in life.

Book of SONG OF SOLOMON Glorification of Wedded Love

The author is not mentioned but it has many things that would be common to Solomon. This leads, most in stating that it was Solomon who wrote the Book. The book seems to have been written around 965 B.C. The book is presented in a poetry format. Many people feel that the book could be a book of love between anthology book between God and Israel and some think it is Christ and the Church. This is though because Israel is regarded as the bride of Yahweh and the Church is the bride of Christ. However, a more earthly view would be that it was a poem about Solomon and one of his brides. In any case, it is a celebration of a passionate love between lovers. The sexuality of a marriage is in God's plan. It represents the unity or oneness of the marriage. Whether it is of a man and woman or God and his creation it is sanctioned and celebrated by God.

The book is a love story between the King and Shulamite. It deals with the courtship, wedding and struggling in love and their ever-growing love.
The king, his lover and the daughters of Jerusalem tell the story. Each tells their portion of the story in great description analogies. The descriptions are done in a very elaborate method to emphasize and show the strong feeling between the King and his lover. This book is read in synagogues during the holiday of Passover, reelecting the season of spring.

Book of ISAIAH   The Messianic (Jesus) Prophet

The author on this book is Isaiah. Some believe others may have added to the Book. However, the people in the New Testament who quote this book always say that it was Isaiah who said it. Isaiah was a prophet who lived the Southern Kingdom. His ministry occurred from 745B.C. to 695 B.C. Isaiah was called the Messianic Prophet because his writing reflected the belief that Israel would one day be a blessing form God to all nations. He prophesied during the last years on the northern kingdom and ministered to Judah. He warned Judah of Babylon. God called him to his ministry in a vision. It is felt the he was a member of the royal family of Judah. He foretold details concerning the coming messiah's life. Isaiah sees visions and delivers prophecies against Israel and Judah and other nations. The subjects of some of the prophecies are: Judgment of Judah, Destruction of Israel by Assyria, Destruction of

Assyria, against Egypt, Babylon, Arabia, and Jerusalem. He also Prophecies: restoration of the Messiah's Kingdom, thanksgiving in the Messiahs Kingdom, Messiahs birth, the coming King, Judgments of the tribulation. Behold the coming King.

Isaiah's ministry was commissioned by a vision from God. In his commissioning a voice asked whom shall I send and who will go for us? The Isaiah made a wonderful commitment statement. Here am I! Send Me.

During his ministry some of the Kings of Judah turned to God and were blessed. However, the kingdom continued toward idolatry, and went to Babylon as he prophesied.

The King of Assyria challenges God and states he will take Jerusalem. The King of Judah goes to Isaiah. God tell him not to worry. Angels of the Lord went out and killed 185,000 in the Assyrian camp. When the King of Assyria heard this he left Judah.

Later Isaiah gives comforting prophecies concerning: Israel's deliverance, Israel's restoration, Destruction of Babylon.

He also prophesies about the Messiah and Israel Glorious Future. Many events of Jesus life are prophesized. Thus proving, that God was in control of event here on earth and that Jesus was sent to us by God. One of the main thoughts of the book is to remain loyal to God, repent and hope for Gods blessings

Book of JEREMIAH A last effort to save Jerusalem

Jeremiah wrote this book. It was written and destroyed and rewritten. His ministry was from 627 B.C. to 580 B.C. Other prophets of his time were Zephaniah, Habakkuk, Daniel and Ezekiel. They persecuted Jeremiah during his ministry and would not return to the true God. The book has poetic oracles of judgment, sermons in prose, biographical narrative, and poetic oracles against foreign nations. The book also has several accounts of prophecy.

Jeremiah is a prophet from the time of the last godly king to the exile of Judah to Babylon.
Some of his prophecies were given as sermons to the people. The subjects of the Prophecies were Judah's sinning, Judah to be judged, Judah's breach of God's covenant, its conflicts within and without. He also prophesied about other nations and what would happen to them.
Jeremiah had the difficult task of warning the people to turn away from idolatry and moral degeneracy and return to Gods will. He kept trying to tell the people that the only way to keep from losing their land was to return to God. He prophesied about the fall of Jerusalem and that they would be taken away to Babylon for 70 years if they did not return to God. He believed that Babylon was as instrument of divine judgments upon Judah for her sins. As they would not repent, God allowed Babylon to take Judah in to captivity. His hope was in God who loves with an everlasting love. He envisioned a restoration of Israel, after the 70 years. He had great word of hope and encouragement. God tell him to tell about the future restoration of Jerusalem and the coming of the Messiah and the Holy Spirit. (Ch38)

When Jerusalem fell, he fled to Egypt to avoid the Babylon captivity.

Book of LAMENTATIONS Jeremiah's funeral weeping over the desolation of Jerusalem

Jeremiah is the author of this book. He wrote the book during and just after the destruction of Jerusalem. Nebuchadnezzar laid siege to Jerusalem in 588 B.C. to 586 B. C. The Book is written in poetry form with each paragraph starting with a letter of the Hebrew alphabet. It was arranged in alphabetical order.

Jeremiah tells about his sorrows for the city, the desolation of the temple and the cause of the destruction. He tells of the anger of God and his agony over the city. He says prayers for mercy. He confesses his faith and confidence in God. He describes the Siege, its cause and the consequences. He reviews the need for restoration, need for repentance of Sin and request for its restoration. With all this sorrow and disappointment we need to understand that not was all lost. Gods discipline was being accomplished but, he would continue with his promise to keep his people.

Book of EZEKIEL They shall know that I am God

Ezekiel's name meant "God Strengthens." He wrote the book between 592 B.C. and 570 B.C. He was priest and a prophet. Jeremiah stayed in Jerusalem while Ezekiel and Daniel were taken in captivity to Babylon. He was also commission in a vision by God. He lived and taught in the country while Daniel lived in the City. Most of his work was done during the 70 years of Babylonian captivity. Ezekiel was taken to Babylon in the second group. He prophesied in Babylon about the destruction of Jerusalem. They did not believe him until the fall of Jerusalem. Later he had visions that prophesied the restoration of Jerusalem and her events in the far future.

His message was similar to that of Jeremiah. His message was one of judgment and hope for the exiles. He used odd acts and visionary experiences to deliver his message. He symbolically acted out his messages by lying on his side and tunneling through the city wall. He gave the signs, messages and visions of the judgment, which Judah would incur because of their lack of repentance. He tells of sins of the people have brought this judgment to them and the restoration of Israel. He describes the idolatry act of the Judah's rulers and the priest. He foretold the coming disastrous events as he sees them in visions. He prophesies against the Gentiles in the area (Ammon Moab, Edom Philistia Tyre Sidon and Egypt).

He then uses other visions to proclaim the restoration of Israel and the blessings, which will come to her. He describes a new and restored temple with the return of the Glory of God to the Temple. He also describes the duties of the priest, the land of the temple priest, and the land around the City. Many of these visions are thought to be prophecies about the end time and the New Jerusalem. He had vision of the future, which was the same as John had in the Book of Revelation (Cherubim, Gog and Magog, Eating the Book, New Jerusalem, and the River of water of life.). God wanted the people to know he was God so He told Ezekiel in many of his visions "They Shall Know that I am God"

Book of DANIEL The Prophet at Babylon

Daniel was the author of the book. It was written during the Babylon Captivity (605 B. C. and 536 B.C. The book can be divided into two sections. Chapters 1-6 are a collection of stories about Daniel and his friends. The second section would be apocalyptic vision prediction the course of world history.

Daniel was related to the royalty of Judah. He was taken into captivity in 605 B.C.
The Babylon King noted the wisdom of Daniels and his three friends. He had them instructed at the best schools in Babylon. Daniel and his friends were faithful to God. Their first test was when they wanted to eat food in accordance with God's will for them. They eat their food rather than that which the king furnished and they were healthier than those who ate the king's delicacies. When presented to the King, Daniel and his friends seemed to be more knowledgeable then others in the Kingdom.   The four of them stayed in the service of Nebuchadnezzar.

God give a dream to the King Nebuchadnezzar. The King didn't tell what the dream was about and threatened to kill his wise men if they didn't interpret the dream. This would have meant the death of all the wise men, which included Daniel and his friends. Daniel prayed and God reveals the dream. Daniel goes to the King and tells him that God revealed the dream. The King now saw the mighty power of God. He said" Truly your God is the God of Gods, the Lord of kings, and revealer of secrets, since you could reveal this secret. The King became a believer of God and his greatness.

This action made the king realize the good qualities of Daniel and his relation to God. Daniel was made ruler over the Babylon providence and chief administrator over the wise men.

King had his image made of gold. He asked that everyone bow and worship it. Daniel's friends would not bow due to their loyalty to God. As a result they were put into a furnace. God sent an angle to protect them. The furnace did not hurt them. This further showed the power of God to the people and the King. This is the famous story of Shadrach, Meshach, and Abed-Nego.

Daniel's faith was proven when Darius is King. The Governors of the court wanted to get rid of Daniel so they suggested that whoever petitions any god or man for thirty days, except the King shall be cast into the den of lions. Daniel worship God in prayer and the Governors told the King and Daniel was put into the Lion's den to be killed. God protected Daniel. The King realized that he had done wrong. The King then decreed all men must tremble and fear before the God of Daniel.

Daniel was given many visions into the future. They were the great image, image of Gold, great tree, handwriting on the wall, four beast, Ram and Male Goat, Seventy weeks, Israel's future, revelation of the sixty-nine weeks (messiah coming), the seventieth week, The great time to trouble was in the seventieth week.
Many of the visions have related to the time of Christ and his second coming. Daniel also prophesied about the rise and fall of the gentile countries for many years in the future. His prophesies also told of that the followers

of God would receive his kingdom with eternal life.

Book of HOSEA   Apostasy of Israel

Hosea wrote this book. He is considered a Minor Prophet. He lived in the northern kingdom, which fell to Assyria prior to the captivity of the southern kingdom. The ministry was approximately 40 years (from 755 B.C. to 710 B.C.). He was called to prophesy during the later years of the Northern kingdom. He warned against having reliance on military and political strength over God's strength.

God was upset and the spiritual adulteress of Israel. He wanted the people to know how he loved them, but let them know how he felt about their trespasses against him. To do this, he selected his prophet Hosea and had him put himself in a similar situation. He had him marry a harlot and have children. Hosea married Gomer and they had two boys and a girl. God had Hosea name the children with special names. Jezreel was named for God to avenge the bloodshed of Jezreel on the house of Jehu and end the kingdom of house of Israel. Lo-Ruhamah was named to show that God would no longer have mercy on Israel. Lo-Ammi was named because the people were not God's and he would not be their God. Gomer becomes and adulteress and runs away from her husband who still is faithful to her. Hosea later finds Gomer in a slave market and he purchased her. He then tells her that she shall have no men. She and Israel shall no longer betray their lovers.

He then describes the adultery of Israel, her refusal to repent, Gods judgment and the restoration of Israel to God. God promises to heal their backsliding and he will

love them greatly and he will again bless Israel.
His love for Gomer shows us about Gods love. It is loyal, it never fails, and it is faithful and it is forgiving.

Book of JOEL   Prediction of the Holy Spirit Age and Day of the Lord

Joel son of Pethuel was the author of this book. He is considered a Minor Prophet. His book was written during the reign of Joash in the Southern Kingdom around 835 B. C. At this time, the enemies of the Southern Kingdom were Phoenicia, Philistia, Egypt and Edom.

A great cloud of Locus come and destroys all the vegetation in the land. A great drought has had its effect on the land. God tells Joel, that these events have come about because of the people's actions. The destruction of Judah is prophesied. He tells them that God judgment is upon them but God made a conditional promise for the salvation of Judah. However, they do not repent, so the destruction of Judah will happen.
He tells of the day of Gods judgment and the outpouring of Gods spirit to all flesh. He describes the end times and the future restoration of Judah. He reminded the people that they were not fighting an earthly enemy, but, they were facing the Almighty God.

Book of AMOS Ultimate Universal Rule of David

Amos is the author of this book. He was a herdsman and pincher chosen by God to prophesy about catastrophes about Israel (northern kingdom) and other gentile countries. . His book was written after the separation of the kingdoms. Both kingdoms were on the road to destruction due to their idolatry. Jeroboam II and Uzziah were the kings. He prophesied around 755 B.C. He talks about the social sins of people who derive their wealth from oppression of others.

He tells of Gods future judgments concerning all the nations in the area including that of Israel and Judah. He delivers sermons concerning the present, past and future of Israel and her judgment for her actions. He tells of vision of Locust, Fire, Plumb line (god set between his people), and Opposition to Amaziah, summer fruit and stricken doorpost. He tells of the five promises of the restoration of Israel and the tabernacle of David.

Book of OBADIAH   Destruction of Edom

Obadiah was the author. He was a lesser-known prophet who prophesied against the Edomite's. He is considered a Minor Prophet. We know he wrote the book before, the taking or Jerusalem, and was most likely during the reign of Jehoram 841 B.C. The dating is difficult because the facts mentioned in the text happened 4 times. From 850BC—586 BC.

The Edomite's were the descendants of Esau who was Jacob's brother. They would rejoice at the taking of Jerusalem. However, they tried to keep the temple from being destroyed in 70 AD and were destroyed as a people.

Obadiah tells God's prophecy about the judgment of Edom because of their violence against Jacob's people, and standing by and not aiding their brother's people. The judgment is given to the Edomite's. They will be treated as they treated other and they would no longer be a people.

Book of JONAH   An Errand of Mercy to Nineveh

Jonah was the author of the book. He wrote it during the reign of Jeroboam II (782 B.C. to 753B.C.) The book of Jonah is considered as one of the books of the Minor Prophets. This book is a story of an event which took place with Jonah.

God decides that he wants the gentles of Nineveh to repent from their evil ways. God calls Jonah to preach repentance to the city of Nineveh. Jonah fears the preaching to the gentiles and tries to go to Tarshish to get away. He feels that he will be killed if he goes to Nineveh.
This brings the great story of Jonah and the whale. While on his way to Tarshish a storm appears and the sailors are distress and Jonah tells the sailors that he has brought about the storm because of his disobedience to God. Jonah tells the sailors to throw him over board to save themselves. Jonah is swallowed by a great fish and is in it for 3 days. While in the fish, Jonah prayed to the lord for his salvation. God has the fish vomit him on the shore. God again asks Jonah to go to Nineveh. He accepts and goes there and tells them that in 40 days they shall be overthrown. The king had the people repent of their evil ways. God then relented from the disaster. However, Jonah was angry because he thought God should destroy the city. Jonah was so distressed that he prayed to God for his death. God kept him alive by shading him with a plant and then taking it away I the morning. Jonah became angry again and wanted death. God explained that he had the right to have pity on these people just as Jonah had the right to be angry about the

taking away of the shade plant.

The Book of Jonah shows us that God loves all his creations, not just his chosen people. Yes even us gentiles! This was his first outreach to the gentiles in the Old Testament. He asks us all to repent in our ways. When we do, he gives us blessing or withholds disasters from us just as he did with his chosen people.

Jonah learned a valuable lesson through his experience. He learned that God loved all his creation and wanted them to repent. He also learned that God wanted obedience and you cannot get away from him.

Book of MICAH   Bethlehem to be Birthplace of the Messiah

Micah was the writer of his book. This book is considered to be part of the Minor Prophets. His prophecies were from 735 B.C. to 710 B.C. He came from the country near Jerusalem. He Knew Hosea and Isaiah. He believed in justice, kindness, and humility, which were disappearing in his time. He warned the people about oppressing others. He predicts judgments against Samaria, Judah the destruction of Jerusalem. He predicts a restoration and the coming of the Messiah. The book can be understood in 3 major parts. The first Chapter 1-3, predicts the destruction of Samaria and Jerusalem for their respective sins. . The next portion is about the promises to restore the Judean state. The final area is found in chapter 6 and 7 where it tells of dishonesty in marketplace and corruption in government. The Lord requires of man only to do justice, love many and walk humbly with God.

Micah speaks to both the northern and the southern Kingdoms. He speaks mainly to the leaders in the cities of Samaria the capital of Northern Kingdom and Jerusalem in the Southern Kingdom. He reminds people in the city of their sins and need to repent. He warns of the future destruction if they do not repent. He announces the coming kingdom and a ruler born in Bethlehem. The rulers will be rejected until the time when" she who is in labor has given birth." This time is noted as the time of Christ in revelations.
He records Gods pleads and his responses concerning the things God has done and why there is ingratitude, dishonesty, idolatry and possible punishment.

He also prophesied that Jesus would be born in Bethlehem and he will be in the majesty of the lord God. Jesus greatness would reach the ends of the world.

Book of NAHUM   Destruction of Nineveh

Nahum is the author of the book written about 664 B.C. His book is considered to be one of the Minor Prophets books. He lived near the city of Nineveh. He was given a vision of the destruction of Nineveh. It happened 100 years after Jonah to warn the gentiles of the Assyrian capital. The people had reverted to their sinful nature. Nahum records his vision for the destruction of Nineveh. He describes God's decreed, judgment, and how he will destroy the city. He also tells the reasons for destroying Nineveh and why it was deserved. He also, declares that there will be no restoration of the city.
Babylon and Medes destroy the city 20 year later

Book of HABAKKUK   The Just shall live by Faith

Habakkuk is the author of this book. His book is considered to be one of the Minor Prophet books. The book is written prior to the invasion of Judah by Babylonians. It was most likely written during the reign of Manasseh (686- 642 BC.) may be 609BC.

The book has to main thoughts. The first thought is in Chapters 1 & 2 concerning Habakkuk problems he has with the world and Gods reply to his problems. The other section is in Chapter 3 where he prays to Gods for mercy, and how he trusted in God's Salvation.

The book describes how Habakkuk faith is shaken so he takes problems concerning his country and its faith of God. He wants to know, how long shall I cry for help and you will not listen. God then replies. He requests to know why there is iniquity, violence and the law is powerless. He wants to know why a country more wicked then his own would be use to destroy his country. God tells him how he is raising the army to destroy Judah. He tells him the many woe's to man. God ensures him that justice is ultimately triumphing. Habakkuk understands and prays for God's mercy and rejoices in the Lord. He understands God's method and realizes he needs to continue to have faith in God. He writes a song of praise to the lord.

Habakkuk learns to accept Gods' judgment and live by faith instead of reason.

Book of ZEPHANIAH   Coming of a pure language

Zephaniah authored the book. He was the great-great Grandson of godly King Hezekiah. This book is considered as one of the Minor Prophets books. .
The Book was written around 630 B.C. to 625 B. C.

Zephaniah was given a vision by God, which concerned

with the Judgment day of the Lord and Salvation in the day of the lord.
He discussed the judgment of the whole earth and judgment of Judah. He describes the causes for the judgment. The book calls for repentance. The book describes judgment for nearby countries. It tells of the lord's justice and promises a restoration. Along with the restoration it promises to furnish a new pure language. He will change the speech of the peoples to a pure speech, that all of them may call on the name of the Lord and serve him with one accord.

Book of HAGGAI   Rebuilding the Temple

Haggai is the author of the book. He was the great-great Grandson of godly King Hezekiah. His name means "Festival". His message was around 520 B.C. This is book is considered as one of the Minor Prophets. The book is built upon prophetic revelations experienced by Haggai. The king of Persia allowed the people to return to build the temple. When the people returned they started building their homes and had other problems and didn't concentrate on the building of the Temple. The book was written to urge the people to rebuild the temple.
God tell Haggai that the temple must be completed. The foundation had been completed earlier but work had stopped. God told Haggai that the crops had been small because the work on the temple had been stopped. The people needed to build the temple in order to receive God's blessing. Haggai took this message to Zerubbabel, and the son of the High priest. They in turn took the message to the people. Then the work was restarted on the temple. After a while the people felt that the new temple would not be as glorious as the first.

Zerubbabel reminded the people that God was on their side and he could make it more glorious. God foretells of the future destruction of the nearby gentile nations. God honors Zerubbabel. Zerubbabel become the linage of Jesus and both of his parents.

Book of ZECHARIAH   Coming of the Messiah

Zechariah was the author of the book. His name means "Yahweh Remembers." He was a contemporary of Haggai and Zerubbabel, the governor. The time of the book is from 520 B.C to 470B.C. This book is considered a one of the Minor Prophets Books. During this time Esther had become the Queen of Persia. His ministry was longer and then that of Haggai. He and Haggai urged the rebuilding of the temple. It was completed in 515 B.C.

Zechariah has eight visions, which are interpreted by an angel. The visions are used to encourage the people with his giving them a magnificent future. The visions were: Horses among the Myrtle trees, Four Horns of Four Craftsmen, man with the measuring line, Cleansing of Joshua the high Priest, Golden lamp stand and olive tree, flying scroll, women in the Basket and the four chariots. The first 5 visions are to comfort the people. The other 3 are judgments. Zechariah tells the people that they must rebuke hypocrisy, repent of disobedience, restore Israel and rejoin in Israel's future. He also tells them of the coming Messiah. Three prophesies which Jesus fulfilled by his life are found here. (1) He tells of the first coming on a donkey in chapter 9:9, (2) Messiah's rejection in Chapter 11, (3)the betrayal of the messiah with 30 pieces of silver in chapter 11:12. He also prophesied the second coming of glory in Chapter 9:10.which we are awaiting. He tells of the coming rule of the Messiah.

Book of Malachi Final message to a disobedient people

Malachi was the author of the book. His name meant "My Messenger". This book is considered the last book of the Minor Prophets. It was written during the Persian domination around 432B.C. to 425 B.C. This is a period during the time that Nehemiah had returned to Babylon. He was the last of the writing prophets. The four hundred years of silence began after this book

It should be noted that God told Malachi that his name would be great among the gentiles. This shows that God had a future plan to give an inheritance to the gentiles. Malachi prophesied when the people were giving up on God and the prophecies of Haggai and Zechariah had not happened. God calls on Malachi and explains that the people are not following him and the priests do not honor him. The Lord curses the priests and the people continue to commit Idolatry. The lord tells he will judge the people. Those that fear the lord and meditate on his name he will make them his. There are prophecies of dealing with the destruction of the wicked and rewards to the one who fear his name. He then prophesied the return of Elijah before the coming of the great and dreadful day of the Lord when the sun shall be turned to darkness and the moon into blood.
Malachi's message informed the people that they were disobedient to God. They still did not repent, so God sent no more prophets to help them. Because of this God did not speak to his people until he was preparing the way for Jesus.

New Testament

The New Testament is composed of 27 Books. There are 5 Books of History (The Gospels-Mathew, Mark, Luke, John and Acts.). There are 21 letter or epistles and 1 prophetic book (Revelation).
Scalars have reconfirmed that, the original New Testament was written during the lifetime of the eyewitnesses of the life of Christ. The New Testament is an account of Jesus the Man.

Gospels

Matthew, Mark, Luke and John wrote these eyewitness accounts of the life of our Lord Jesus the Christ. In the old days it took two witnesses to assure it was true. The Lord left these accounts as witness of his first coming. Matthew and John lived as apostle of Jesus and they tell their witness. Luke gathered eyewitness accounts from others and wrote his book. Mark was the author of his book. He was in the company of Peter the apostle. It is felt that most of the witness accounts came from Peter and put into words by Mark.

The witness of each tells the personal remembrances of the life of Christ. Each author had a different emphasis on his testimonial. Matthew told Jesus the Messiah as for told by the Old Testament. He makes references to the Old Testament. Mark tells of the superhuman Power of Jesus that showed his deity by the miracles he performed. Luke describes the events showing the humanity of Jesus. John speaks to the Deity of Jesus by telling what he said rather than what he did. For more information concerning Jesus' life, teachings, and ministry you need to read the Gospels. (*For general information see the section on Jesus.*)

Book of MATTHEW   Jesus the Messiah

It is accepted that Matthew, the personal companion of Jesus, was the author of this book. It was probably written between 58 A.D. and 68 A.D. Matthew wrote mainly to the Jewish people. He proved that Jesus was the Messiah by referencing the Old Testament passages and how Jesus fulfilled the scriptures. The major teaching of Jesus related in this book are: Lessons from Sermon on the Mount, parables concerning the kingdom, Christian living and warnings concerning the end times.

He tells the Genealogy of Jesus being form Abraham and King David. He tells the birth and early life of Jesus. He tells about John the Baptist, Jesus' baptism and the tempting by the devil. Matthew records Jesus life and ministry as the messiah. He records Jesus' teaching in parables and teaching of his second coming. He then records the last week of Jesus' life, the death and resurrection.

Matthew demonstrated that Jesus is the promised Messiah. He depicts this by relaying the fulfillment of Old Testament scripture and recording the miracles showing that God sent Jesus. Jesus is the Savior, and the messiah for all people. . He also tells that changes will follow Jesus coming. The book quotes a large amount of Jesus words. It records Jesus sermons quite thoroughly and specifically the Sermon on the Mount and Jesus' second coming

Matthew Outline
Chapters 1-4 Genealogy, birth and beginning of public ministry
Chapter's 5-7 Ten Miracles
Chapter 10 Talk to the apostles
Chapters 11-12 Jesus rejection by the Jews
Chapter 13 Parables of the Kingdom
Chapter 14-17 The disciples acknowledge Jesus
Chaptetr 18 faith and forgiveness and instruction
Chapters 19-22 Instruction on how to live.
Chapters 23-25 Woes against hypocrisy
Chapters 26-28 Crucifixion, death and resurrection

Book of MARK   Jesus the Wonderful & suffering servant.

John Mark, the son of Mary who was a leader in the church in Jerusalem, with Peter the apostle, wrote the book. It is felt that this first book of the New Testament was written between 55A.D. and 65 A.D. with Peter's relating eyewitness experiences of Jesus Life. The book is centered in God's presence in the suffering of his son and the coming of the Son of man.

Mark describes the life and the teachings of Jesus. It starts at the beginning of his ministry when he was baptized by John the Baptist. He tells of Jesus first miracles, his parables and the five major miracles. The book turns to how the opposition grows against Jesus. He then spends the last third of the book to the last week and crucifixion of Jesus. He ends by telling of the resurrection and ascension of Jesus.

Mark emphasis was on Jesus superhuman qualities demonstrating his deity by his miracles He tell what Jesus did rather then things Jesus said. Mark also describes how Jesus came to earth to serve. The part that emprises the servant aspect is where Mark recorded "For even the Son of man come not to be served but to serve others and to give his life as a ransom for many. (Mark 10:45)

An outline of mark
Chapter 1-8 Jesus Ministry of Serving
Chapters 8-10 Jesus teachings about serving
Chapters 11-15 Jesus life was given as a ransom for others.
Chapter 16 Jesus ministry of service extended to his followers.

Book of LUKE Jesus the Son of Man

Luke was the author of this Gospel and the book of Acts. Paul referred to Luke as the "beloved physician." Luke worked with Paul, Timothy and Mark and he gathered other eyewitness events to write this book. He took the events of Jesus life and described them to show how God had ordered these events from beginning to end. He traces the divine design of salvation for all mankind through Jesus.

The book was written around 60 A.D. A great deal of information was gathered from the church fathers. It is believed that Luke also spent time with Mary, John and James the brother of Jesus who was the bishop of the Jerusalem church. He stayed with them at their home in Caesarea.

Luke describes events proceeding Jesus Birth and the events accompanying it. He then moves on to tell about Jesus' ministry. His description of the ministry is quite thorough. The book describes Jesus' power and Miracles. It tells of the teaching of the disciples and his attempts to teach the Pharisees. Jesus' miracles and the parables are described. The many ways the Jesus faced rejection are told. The last section describes the crucifixion, resurrection, and the ascension of the Son of Man.

The theme of the book is that Jesus came to rescue all who are lost. Luke's background was that of a Greek influence. He approached his book in an orderly manner and told about the life of Jesus from beginning to end. This Gospel is the most complete recording of Jesus life. It starts with the foretelling of Jesus, events of his birth, his ancestors. It records the facts of Jesus' ministry. It concludes with the death and resurrection of Jesus.

Outline
Chapters 1-2   Introduction and the infancy of Jesus.
Chapters 3-4 Preaching of John, Baptism, temptation
Chapters 4-9   Ministry of Galilee
Chapters 9-13   Samaria, sayings and parables.
Chapters 14-21 journey to Jerusalem. He also tell what Jesus is doing and why.
Chapter 22-23 The last week of Jesus life and his crucifixion
Chapter 24   Resurrection of Jesus

Book of JOHN   Jesus the Son of God

John, the disciple whom Jesus loved, was the author of

this gospel. He was the son of Zebedee. It appears that he may have been a cousin of Jesus and knew him when he was growing up. John wrote this book, the epistles of John and Revelations. John was a follower of John the Baptist and later became an apostle. After Jesus' ascension he was with Peter and James in the church in Jerusalem. He later lived in Ephesus. This book was written around 66 to 68 A.D. John portrays Jesus with his deity as the Son of God. John chooses incidents from Jesus life that explains that he is the Messiah and the Son of God.

John starts his book describing the Deity of Jesus and his work prior to becoming a man. He then tells of John the Baptist, who was a voice crying in the wilderness, telling that the Messiah is coming. Jesus then come to John and is baptized. After being baptized Jesus starts his ministry. He describes the first miracles of Jesus and the first introduction of Jesus to Galilee, Judea and Samaria. He discussed the significant events of Jesus as the Son of God. They are Christ changes water into wine, Christ heals the Nobleman's son, Christ heals the sick man at the Sheep Gate pool on the Sabbath, Jesus feeds the 5000, Jesus walks on water, healing of a blind man, and Jesus raises Lazarus from the dead. The opposition of the Pharisees increases and Jesus prepares the disciples for the future. This rejection of the Jewish leaders turns to the Crucifixion of Jesus. The Resurrection then proves the deity of Jesus as the Messiah and the Son of God. He further describes Jesus' appearances to various witnesses after the resurrection.

John's emphasis is on the deity of Jesus. He does this by telling about Jesus sermons and conversations. He had access to Jesus' teachings because he was one of the three inter circle disciples who Jesus would take aside and discuss items. John recognized that belief and faith in Jesus meat to trust him. The purpose of this Gospel is so you can believe in Jesus is the messiah; the Son of God and that by believing in him you will have life by the power of his name. John not only tells of his deity, he explains that Jesus was with God from the beginning of Man. John presents his case for Jesus deity by quoting seven of Jesus quotes. They are: I am the bread of life, I am the light of the world I am the door, I am the good shepherd, I am the resurrection and the life, I am the way the truth and the life. I am the true vine

Outline of John
Chapter 1 The incarnation and introduction of God the son.
Chapters 2-4 Presentation of the son of God
Chapters 5-12 The opposition to the Son of God
Chapters 13-17 Preparation of the Disciples by Jesus
Chapters 18-21 The crucifixion and resurrection of Jesus

Book of ACTS Formation of Christ's Church with the aid of the Holy Spirit.

The author was Luke, the beloved physician. It was written during the first century of the church. It was completed just prior to the death of Paul (63A.D.). Some feel it was use as a written defense of Paul in his trail before Caesar. The book is a history of the events of the first 30years of the Church.

It describes the appearance of the Holy Spirit and its anointing of the apostles as promised by Jesus Christ. It shows how the Holy Spirit empowered the disciples and

aided in the formation of the Church. Chapters 1-9 are the history of the church formation and its persecution in Israel. Chapters 9-12 shows how the Spirit leads the followers to spread the Gospel
Chapters 13 through 21 describe the history concerning the spreading of the word and formation of the church among the gentiles. Throughout the book is tells of the persecution of the newly formed Church. Chapters 21-28 tell about Paul while he is in prison. He is sustained by the Holy Spirit.

Acts of the Apostles really is the story of the coming of the Holy Spirit and the apostles as they continued the faith and fulfilled the task of witnessing to Jerusalem, Judea, and Samaria and to the end of the known world.

The book starts with appearances of the resurrected Jesus (Messiah/Christ). Jesus appeared to his followers and friends for 40 days. Jesus promised that after he left he would send the Holy Spirit. Jesus gives the great commission and ascended to heaven. Pentecost (sometimes called the Feast of Fruits) was celebrated 50 days after the resurrection and 10 days after Jesus ascension. The birthday of the church was on the Day of Pentecost. On that day, there appeared divided tongues of fire that sat upon the head each apostle. They were filled with the Holy Spirit as for told by the prophet Joel.

The Holy Spirit comes to us and writes God's Laws in our hearts. Some scholars feel that this book shows how the first century Christians followed and established Jesus instructions as noted in **Acts 1:8** "But you shall receive power when the Holy Spirit has come upon you; and you shall witnesses to Me in Jerusalem, and in all Judea and Samaria, and to the end of the earth" These were the last words Christ said just before his ascension to his father.

Peter immediately went to work and spread the Gospel to Jerusalem. He gives a sermon at the Jewish temple and he and John are put in prison. They are freed by an angle. Stephen preaches to the council trying to convince them to accept Christ. They don't and kill Stephen. He is the first martyr of Christ.

The book records the first sermons of the apostles, their miracles, first organizing the growth of the believers, the persecution and the death of martyr of the first Christians. It tells about the missionary work of the apostles and the establishment of the first churches of Asia and Europe. Throughout the book it tells how the Holy Spirit empowers the leaders of the church and its new members.

As many of the believers at the Pentecost were Jews that didn't live in Judea the Gospel next spread in Antioch which was a gentile city. Everywhere the Gospel was taken the believers they were persecuted. God use persecution to spread the Gospel to the ends of the world

On the road to Damascus, Jesus appeared to Saul, a man who persecuted the believers. He had orders from the Hebrew religious leaders to bring in the followers of Christ so they could try to destroy the Christian movement. Jesus blinds him and proves he is the Christ. Saul is then converted and becomes a follower and an apostle of Christ. With this change, he takes the name of Paul. It describes Paul's three missionary trips to the gentles. The book describes the work of the church from 30 A.D. to 60 A.D. It is the history of how God moved from the time of the Jews to the time of the Gentiles. It moves God's people from the Judean ritual law to the grace of God.

Peter is given a vision and learns that the eating rituals are no longer in effect and the Gospel is to be taken to the Gentiles. Peter goes to Caesarea to preach the Gospel to the Gentiles. He meets Cornelius and he becomes the first gentile to become a believer. Many gentiles are converted and speak in tongues.

King Herod, in an attempt to stop Christianity, kills James the brother of John. He Blasphemes God and an angel strike's him and he dies.

All the apostles and believer continued to witness to the Gospel through the known world. Most of the rest of the Book tell about Paul's efforts to spreads the Gospel to the gentiles. It describes the three Missionary journeys of Paul to Asia and Europe. He travels to many areas converting gentiles and Jews to Christianity. He preaches, performs miracles and sets up churches in Antioch, Cyprus, I conium, Lustra, Thessalonica, Philippi, Berea, Athens, Corinth, Crispus, Galatia, Ephesus and Macedonia. He is continually persecuted. While in Jerusalem he is arrested and imprisoned in jail. Paul decides to use his roman citizenship to resolve maters and take it before Cesar. He is sent to Rome to be tried as Roman. He is imprisoned there and tries to direct the churches by letters (Epistles). These letters are now part of the Bible. During his imprisonment, he is comforted and aided by the Holy Spirit.

Book of ROMANS   Nature of Christ's Work (statement of Christian doctrine)

The book of Romans is a letter written by Paul around 57 A.D. to the church that was in Rome. Paul wrote letters because of his constant moving around to preach the Gospel. He wrote it during his third missionary trip while he was in Corinth. Paul had not been to Rome but he knew he would because God told him that he would go to Rome. He wrote the letter in anticipation that he would go there later to preach to them. After Paul was converted to Christianity, He realized that there was a different way of understanding God and his Son, Jesus. Paul reviewed the scriptures in light of Jesus the Messiah. Romans reflect Paul's new understanding of God, Jesus and grace through the redemption that is in Christ Jesus. It describes the nature of the Gospel and the life of righteousness, which is justifies freely by grace through the redemption of Jesus.

Paul tells the need for us to live by faith. He discussed the guilt of the gentiles and the results of their guilt. He also tells of the Jews were guilty and how they were judged by their works. He shows that all are guilty before God. He then describes righteousness and its benefits, which are peace with God, Joy during tribulation and salvation. He tells how through the death of Jesus, we may have Gods' grace for our salvation. We should not let sin be a dominion over us but live in righteousness. He explains the problems that the Jew has had in accepting Jesus and how they will someday be restored to Jesus as the Messiah. Responsibilities toward God, society, higher powers and neighbors are explained. In contrast he then explains the Christian liberty.
Many people believe that this book explains Christianity to the Gentiles. It was a letter to the Gentiles in Rome

about salvation. Paul tells us that we all need to be right with God. But man has sinned and must turn to Jesus for righteousness with God. Through Jesus we can receive salvation according to Gods' New Covenant with us. When we do this we are provided with the Holy Spirit and a new changed life. In this changed life we will become righteous and will become reconciled to God.

Outline of Romans
Chapters 1-3 Reason we need Gods' righteousness
Chapters 3-5 How God provides salvation and righteousness
Chapters 6-8 Ongoing work of righteousness by God in us.
Chapters 9-11 God's freedom in giving righteousness
Chapters 12-16 Service is a practical expression of righteousness

Book of I CORINTHIANS Various Church Disorders and how to overcome them.

Paul was the author of this letter. It was written in Ephesus, to the church of Corinth around 56A. D. This church was in one of the busiest cities in Greece. It was a city of degraded culture and idolatrous religions. Paul had founded this church on his second missionary trip around 52 A.D. He heard from Chloe that the church was having problems due to the holding on of some of the idolatry and customs of the worldly city. Paul wrote this letter to help restore righteousness to the Corinthians.

The letter was written because the people in Corinth were straying from a righteous life like the nonbeliever that was around them. Paul, out of his love sent instruction on how they should live in accordance with God's will. He reminds them that they need to listen to the Holy Spirit and its use for guidance. The Holy Spirit empowers them to see the truth of God and his will for their righteousness. He asks them to put away sin and live in a loving and holy manner. He furnished exact instruction on how they should correct the problems that he heard about. One of the most import factors of how to live this righteous life was to have proper love for God and each other. He defines love as being patient and kind. Love is not jealous or boastful or proud, or rude, it does not demand its own way. It is not irritable, and it keeps no record of being wronged. It does not rejoice about injustice but rejoices wherever the truth wins out. Love never gives up, never loses faith, is always hopeful and endures through every circumstance. Loves last forever.

He discusses the reason for the divisions and the misunderstanding of the Gospel. He mentions the Gospel is not an earthly wisdom but a heavenly wisdom. He tells the responsibilities of the ministers. He explains how to handle disagreement, immorality certain practice, abuse of the Lords supper and spiritual gifts. He discusses the Gifts of the Holy Spirits and how they should be used within the church. He reiterated Christ died for our sins and he was buried and he rose again the third day according to the scriptures. He explains the resurrection of the dead and their new bodies.

Book of II CORINTHIANS Paul's Vindication of his Apostleship

Paul wrote a second letter in 56 A.D. to Corinth because he heard that the church had received much good from the first letter. However, there were some leaders there who were discrediting Paul. Paul writes the second letter in vindication of himself as an Apostle of Christ. He warns about deceitful teachers and reminds them that he founded the church and should have a say in its operations.

Paul describes his philosophy of ministry; triumph in Christ, changes lives, preaching of Christ, as Lord and we are servants. He explains motivation in the ministry. Paul discusses the way we cans be transformed by the Spirit and live in confidence and be reconciled to gods. By doing this we will live a new way of living under the new covenant He also discusses an appeal to forgive sinners, how joy can come from generous giving , the glory of the new covenant, how we will have new bodies in heaven and how we are God's ambassadors in our ministries.

Paul appeals for reconciliation of the church and separation from unbelievers. Paul answers his accusers and defends his apostleship. He tells them he will visit them. He asks that they examine themselves and their faith to prove to themselves that Jesus Christ is in them.

Book of GALATIANS   By Grace, not by Law

Paul started the church of Galatia on his first missionary trip. After Paul left the church, a Jewish teacher came to the church and discredited Paul as an apostle. They changed Paul's teaching by making the people feel that they could only be Christians if they obeyed the Jewish law and circumcision. The people were eager to follow to become Christians. When Paul heard of this false teaching he wrote this epistle, in 53A.D. to reassure that grace, not the works of the law, is the way to salvation. The Law was the tutor to bring us to Christ so that we might be justified by faith in him. It is the grace of God through our salvation that we are not governed by sin. We are set free from the bondage of law and the bondage of sin because of the indwelling of the Holy Spirit. The spirit did not come by the law but through faith in Jesus. Paul tells that the gospel of grace was given to him by a revelation of Jesus Christ. He defended his apostleship and informs them that the Jerusalem leadership agreed with the gospel of Grace. .

He explains that no one is justified in the sight of God, by the law. Jews and Gentiles are all sons of God through faith in Jesus Christ. Paul then explains how to live in faith and God's grace in our struggles with one another, love, bearing another's burdens and so fulfill the law of Christ. We need to live by the fruit of the spirit, which are; love, joy, peace longsuffering, kindness, goodness faithfulness, gentleness, self-control. This way we can walk in the Spirit.

Book of EPHESIANS Unity of the Church

Paul wrote this epistle while he was a prisoner in Rome around 60 A.D. Some scholars believe that this epistle was to be circulated to many churches. In it he discusses the privileges and responsibilities of a Christian. He tells of a need for one church where Jews and Gentile both be members of the church. He explains how the people of the Church should be united in Christ.

Paul tells about the spiritual blessing of God, Jesus and the Holy Spirit, which is upon them. He asked that there be a reconciliation of Jews and Gentiles. He wants them to pray to God, through the Holy Spirit, that Christ will dwell in the hearts of man. He asks them to walk in the way of the spirit. He tells how Christ's family should live together and resolve any conflicts. Believers should work together as a society in fellowship with Christ. Paul tells the believers to be united as one body and one spirit. He tells us the God equips the saints to bring others to Christ. So they should speak in truth and love and work in unity. He tells us how we can live in this society as husbands, wives, children, and as servants. He explains that we need to put on our armor of God to stand against the wiles of the devil. The armor is; gird your waist with truth, a breastplate of righteousness, Shod your feet preparation of the gospel of peace, shield of faith, helmet of salvation and sword of the Spirit (word of God).

Book of PHILIPPIANS   A Missionary Epistle (resources in suffering.)

On Paul's second missionary trip while in Greece he started the church with the aid of Lydia and others. Paul was persecuted and beaten while in prison.
The church wanted to support him during his trails. Later, they sent Epaphroditus with money and goods to support him in the Roman prison. Paul wrote this epistle while in a Roman prison (60 A.D.) to thank the Philippians in the church for their support
Paul wrote and thanked the church for their assistance in his time of need. He explained that in his affliction the Gospel was being promoted. He warned against living and having confidence in the flesh. Jesus' life showed us humility and service and we should live like him. He asked the people to have humility and be examples of Christ, Timothy and Epaphroditus (who came to be a servant to Paul). He asks them to know Christ and be at peace with each other and the lord at all times. He said don't worry about anything; instead, pray about everything. Then you will receive the peace of God.

Book of COLOSSIANS   Deity of Jesus

Paul wrote the epistle to the Colossae church, which was 100 miles east of Ephesus, while in prison in Rome around 61 A.D. Paul wrote this letter because he heard that certain teachers were corrupting the Gospel by adding angelic powers and special ceremonies and secret knowledge that portrayed a philosophy rather than a teaching of Christ. To rebuke this idea he made the center of the book the explanation of Christ.

Paul tells how Jesus was the image of God, the first born over all creation. He is the head of the body, the church and the firstborn from the dead. By him he will reconcile all things to himself through the blood of his cross. He tells the church is to reveal the mysteries of God to the Gentiles: which is Christ in you, the hope of Glory. Paul tells with Christ in us, we have freedom from the worldly philosophy the judgment of men. We need to put off our old ways and be new in Christ. In putting on the new way, he advises us to live holy as man, wife, child, work and in our public lives.

Book of I THESSALONIANS The Lord's Second Coming

Paul preached to the people of Thessalonica. Some of the Gentiles believed but there was a disagreement between the Jews. He was falsely accused of being an enemy of Rome and was run out of town. He went to Athens and sent for Timothy. Timothy told him about the good and bad situations and Paul was concerned and wanted to write a letter to encourage the believer who were suffering persecution and answer the concerns about the return of Christ and the fate of those who had died without seeing Christ. He wrote this epistle from Corinth around 50 A.D.

In this epistle, he tells how Timothy had told him of their faith and love they had for him. In response he tell them that he is sending Timothy to minister them concerning God and fellow labor in the gospel. Timothy will establish them and encourage them in faith. He tells them to live as the Holy Spirit leads them and not in passion of lust as the people who do not know God. He tells them, the dead who believed that Jesus is asleep in Jesus. The Lord will descend from heaven with a shout, with the voice of an archangel, and with the trumpet of God. And the dead in Christ will rise first. Then those who are alive and remain shall be caught up together with them in the clouds to meet him and always be with the Lord. The day of the lord is describe and we are told to live in the light of God and to be sober and wear the armament of faith, love, hope of salvation. He gives instruction for holy living. These were: Rejoice always, Pray without ceasing, in everything give thanks; for this is the will of God in Christ Jesus for you, Do not quench the Spirit. Do not despise prophecies, Test all things; hold fast what is good and Abstain from every form of evil.

Book of II THESSALONIANS The Lord's Second Coming

Paul wrote this epistle just a few months later then the first. It was in response that some in the church believe that Jesus had already come. He explained they should have hope for Christ reappearance soon. However, the second coming was still in the future and to live in faithfulness.

Paul realizes their persecution and encourages them in it. He prays for blessings. He then tells of the events preceding the return of Christ. Evil time and men shall come and deceive many. Jesus will give us everlasting consolation and good hope by grace. And comfort your hearts and establish you in good words. Be patient in Christ and withdraw from disorderly people. He reminds them that they need to continue working instead of just waiting for Christ's return.

Book of I TIMOTHY Pastors Care of the Church in Ephesus

In the first verse it states this is a letter from Paul. Some feel it is not written in the same manner as Paul normally wrote. In the time of the epistle (around 63 A.D.) it was common for others to write for a person to carry on their work. Most feel that Paul was the author.
Timothy was one of Paul's converts. He and Luke was his closest companion on his missionary trips. At times Timothy would stay to help a church. Paul sent for Timothy several times to aid him and then go help a church that Paul could not go to. Timothy worked with the churches of Ephesus, Crete and the Asian cities. It would be no surprise that, if Paul wanted to say something about the worship and leadership of a church, he would send it to Timothy. The epistles of I and II Timothy and Titus are considered to be Pastoral Epistles.

The epistle tells of the problems teaching the correct doctrine because the area of the churches had mystical teaching before they heard of Christ. He urged prayer in the church. Explained how everyone should conduct himself or herself in church. This included the women, Bishops and Deacons. He discussed false teachers and instructions for the true teachers. He told how to treat all people, including widows, elders. He says not to neglect the gifts of the spirit. He teaches the slave and the owner to help and serve his fellow Christian. He asks the rich to use their riches for good and share that they may lay hold on eternal life.

Book of II TIMOTHY   Paul's Final Word

The general background of the second epistle to Timothy is the same as first Timothy.
This epistle was written during the second imprisonment in Rome around 67 A.D. Nero had burnt Rome and was blaming the Christians for the fire and persecution was increasing. Some believe this lead to the demise of Paul and Peter.
The epistle is written to Timothy to thank him and remind him of his responsibilities. He tells him to be good teachers, enduring hard work, flee from lust and pursue righteousness, be a gentle servant of the Lord. Paul give a great instruction to Timothy "Preach the word of God, Be prepared, whether the time is favorable or not, Patiently correct, rebuke and encourage you people with good teaching He warns of future bad times and how unrighteous people will act and will become worse. He tell Timothy to preach the word with longsuffering. Paul then talks of his nearing death and his situation in prison. He tells how the Lord has stood with him and strengthened him and delivers him from evil work and preserves him for the heavenly kingdom.

Book of TITUS   The Churches of Crete

The authorship of Titus is similar to that of Timothy. The Greeting is still from Paul. It was written in 65A.D. Titus was another convert of Paul who he put faith in his leadership of the Church. He was a Greek who worked Macedonia. He also worked in Ephesus and was sent to Corinth and Jerusalem. He traveled with Paul many times and was with him at his last arrest in Rome.

Paul writes the epistle to aid Titus at the church in Crete. He tells him to ordain only qualified elders. He sets the qualifications. He discusses the false teachers again and to speak only proper doctrine. He reminds them to obey authorities and be ready for every good work. Paul furnishes instructions to Titus concerning leadership in the church, and how to set an example and live a Holy lifestyle. He reminds them of the renewing of the Holy Spirit and the hope of eternal life.

Book of PHILEMON *Conversion of a runaway slave*

Paul *wa*s the author of this epistle. It is believed it was written during his last imprisonment in Rome. It would most likely been around 60 A.D. Paul had converted a slave Onesimus, who belonged to an owner named Philemon. Philemon was a friend and fellow worker of Paul's. Onesimus had stolen from Philemon and gone to Rome where he met Paul. Paul wanted to correct the situation with forgiveness so he wrote this epistle. He then sent Onesimus and a friend named Tychicus with the epistle.

Paul tells Philemon how much he enjoys the work and friendship with him. Paul petitions for Onesimus with his discretion. He tells him he is returning Onesimus.

He tells him how Onesimus is a brother in Christ. Paul asks Philemon to forgive Onesimus, as he is now a brother in the Lord and charge anything that Onesimus owed to Paul's account. Paul asks Philemon to prepare a guest room for him for he wanted to be with him.

Book of HEBREWS   Christ the Mediator of a New Covenant

This letter or epistle is not addressed to any specific person or group. It is called Hebrews because it explains how the new covenant replaces the old covenant of the Hebrew people which were worshiping under the Levitical laws of Judaism. It justifies the new covenant with the scriptures found in the Old Testament. It instructs the reader to leave the Old Levitical ways of worships and use the new covenant to worship God.

The early Eastern Church attributed the epistle to Paul along with his other epistles. As you read the book, you can see, this message would be similar to what Paul may have preached when he went to a new city and talked to Hebrews in the synagogue. He would explain the new covenant to the people and use the old scriptures to prove it.
It is commonly felts that Hebrews was written between 64 and 68 AD. These dates are derived due to comments in the epistle.

The main discussions in the book are that Christ's majesty made him superior over men, angles, and God's other chosen men. Christ coming to us brought us a new and superior priest hood, a promised new covenant which put God's law in our hearts and a promise to be our God.

The writer tells the truths of the superiority of the Christian way. From start to finish, Jesus is presented as the center of God's purpose. It explains the Goal of God's dealing with Israel and all men. The epistle explains the superiority of Christ and the new covenant which was activated by Jesus Christ life, death and resurrection and Gods' proclamations in his scriptures. Jesus is our sanctuary and a sacrifice which sets us apart for sin and furnishes us salvation. Once we have accepted Jesus and have the laws in our hearts, we must live with our faith.

Hebrews tells us that Christ's' deity making him superior to Moses, prophets, Aaronic priesthood and angels. Jesus Christ suffered through his trials on the cross in obedience to God so we would have a new and better covenant. Many Old Testament scriptures were used to prove Christ's relationship to God. The writer used the Old Testament to show how Hebrews and all men should worship the Son (Christ).

The people of Judaism did not abide in Gods' original covenant which was promised and sealed with blood from the time of Moses. So they received the promised Curses. Gods' earlier covenant was voided because his people disobeyed the terms of the covenant. In the old covenant blood of animals was used to cleanse people's bodies from impurity so they could worship God. The sacrifice offered under the former covenant was repeatedly done. However, Gods' love for all of his people was so great he gave us a new covenant that is easier and more lasting than the first. God foretold of the new covenant in his scriptures of the prophets (Isaiah and Jeremiah). He told about Jesus' life and sacrifice 600 year prior to his birth.

In the New covenant, Jesus by the power of the eternal spirit offered body and blood to God as a perfect sacrifice for our forgiveness of sins. Jesus' sacrifice was offered only once to be forever valid God. Jesus death cancelled the old covenant and instituted the new covenant. Later God sent the Holy Spirit to complete furnishing the balance of the New Covenant, and the law was now in the hearts of man.

God made Jesus our Mediator and High Priest for our salvation. It is wonderful to have Jesus as a mediator. He understands us and gives us assurance of a place in Gods' kingdom. Jesus will always be merciful and faithful. As High Priest he is replacing the non-perfect Levitical priest system. Christ is our eternal High Priest. He identified with man and offered his self as a sacrifice on our behalf. Christ is presented as a divine human Prophet, Priest and King in Hebrews. His humanity and deity are asserted with the many titles describing his attributes and accomplishments. He is superior to all who were before him and offers the supreme sacrifice, priesthood.

Many Hebrew that accepted Jesus were still zealous for the old traditions. The writer was trying to explain that the Christ was the new temple and that their trying to maintaining the old temple was improper

We need to fix our thoughts on Jesus. He gives us confidence so we can go to him for mercy and grace. He will help us through temptation. Following Christ produces faith, self-discipline, love and Good works.

Seeing our Lord Jesus leads us to faith in God. Faith is an important part of the new covenant. It is substance of things hoped for the evidence of things not seen. Faith must be maintained as it was with Christ and the other great men in the Bible. We must have faith in Christ while enduring hostility and God's chastening. Chapters 10 & 11 give many examples of faith down through ages. With this faith and the new covenant we are assured an eternal life. Heb. 11:6 " But without faith it is impossible to please him for he who comes to God must believe that he is and that he is a reward of those who diligently seek him." He tells how we need to hold to our faith and how we should treat others and our fellow believers while doing the great commission

Warnings of falling away, danger of unbelief, and hardening of the heart are given to them and to us. We must keep Christ as the mainstay of your hearts.
There a peril in turning away from God. They are:
1. Neglecting or ignoring salvation furnished by Jesus Christ. Drifting away from the things we have heard. (2:1-4)
2. Do not harden your hearts in rebellion. (3:7-4:13)
3. Dullness of hearing to remain strong and mature in the ways of God. (5:11-6:20)
4. Don't drawback into sin willfully after we have received the knowledge of the truth, for there are no longer remains a sacrifice for sins. You will face judgment without Jesus' protection. (10:19-39)
5. Do not refuse God but serve God acceptably with reverence and fear. (12:25)
Hebrews also informs us that we need to live in brotherly love, obey Gods' laws, follow Jesus and have fellowship with other believers. We are not to forsake the assembly of ourselves together as is the manner of

some, but exhort one another to so much the more s we see the day approaching. We are to continue in brotherly love. In so doing we will obey God's laws and treat others as we would like to be treated. For who knows we may someday entertain angels? When we love Christ, we will be honorable, hospitable, and be more like him. Thus, we will be more pleasing in his sight and give Glory to Christ.

Outline

1:1-3   Christ greater than the prophets
1; 4-14   Superior due to his Deity, and Humanity
2:1-4   Danger of Neglect, Be more aware of the new covenant or we may drift away. Christ is superior because of his Humanity
2:5-16   Christ, greater than Satan
2:17-3:6   Christ, Greater than Moses
3:7-4:13   Dangers of unbelief, Hardening of Heart and a Challenge to enter His Rest

4:14-5:10   The High Priesthood of Jesus
5:11-6:20   Danger of not maturing are falling away.
     Need for Maturity in Christ
7:1-28   The superior covenant brought with Jesus Priesthood
Jesus superior priesthood is better than the one established by Moses.
8:1-6   Jesus superior ministries
A better Covenant 8:7-13 The superior covenant brought with Jesus Priesthood. Anew covenant as announced by Jeremiah The old is now obsolete and the new active.
9:1-10:18   New covenants concerning Sanctuary, Sacrifice

10:19-31   Hold fast to your confession of Faith
Hold fast to faith because there are dangers in losing it.
10:32-10:39 God's chosen had great faith
12:1-17   God's discipline and its results Christ endured life on earth as a man, we must also endure life. Even the chastening of our heavenly father to show us his way and prepare us for his kingdom. We must keep our eyes on Christ
12:18-24   A contrast of the Old Covenant and the Heavenly fellowship of the Church
12:25-29 Warning about the danger of refusing God
13:1-25   Practical advice and closing words.

Book of JAMES   Good Works

James wrote this epistle. As there were four James mentioned in early writings, it is not certain which wrote this epistle. However, most believe that it was the brother of Jesus who was the leader of the Jerusalem church. The Sanhedrin executed him when he refused to deny Christ. This meant that the epistle had to have been written before 62 A.D. James wrote this epistle in and attempts to help the scattered twelve tribes that were scattered abroad.

James writes this epistle to the Christians of the twelve tribes of Israel which a no longer in the country. It recognizes the various trails they are facing. He knows that their faith is being tested. He encourages them to continue in their faith, which would make a difference in their life. Faith can inspire action and good works for the Lord. He asks them to pray with faith for wisdom on how to handle their trails. He tells them, when they endure temptation they will receive the crown of life as the Lord promised. Most of the text is based on how faith and the word are to be used to become a mature Christian. Faith aids in controlling our speech, wisdom, controls our fleshly wants, gives grace and humbleness. We must maintain our faith and endure until the Lord returns.

Book of I PETER   To a Persecuted Church

Peter is the author of this epistle. It is felt that he may have had assistance to put it in the Greek form. He saw how the Christians were being persecuted throughout the Empire and wanted to encourage them through their trials and strengthen their faith. It is felt that he wrote his epistle just after Paul was martyred and just before his death. Some believe that he was crucified upside down in Rome. The book must have been written around 64 A.D.

Peter writes to most of the known churches of the time. Thus the epistle was to be sent to all Christians of the time. Peter sent it because he knew that they were being persecuted. He wanted them to be encouraged and remember to maintain their faith to face their persecuted.. He reminds them that through the resurrection of Jesus from the dead that they will reserve a place in heaven.   He tells them they will have salvation. He asks them to be holy and love the brethren. He reminds them to obey the word which makes them special people. He asks them to conduct themselves properly with the Government and in business, and in their marriage. He tells them how to conduct themselves during suffering and how to minister to others during suffering. He encourages those suffering by telling them they will receive future Glory.

Book of II PETER Prediction of Apostasy

The early church felt that Peter was the writer of this epistle. Some people doubt this and say it was written by another using Peter's name. It is believed that it was written in 64 A.D. just before Peter's death. Peter hears of false teachers who are changing the doctrine of Christ. He wanted to warn the churches to stay to the God new taught by the disciples. The first epistle was to aid in the suffering of persecution. This epistle was written to assure the teachings.

Peter tells how divine power was given to all through the knowledge of Christ. It aids with self-control, kindness, love and knowledge. Peter recognizes that his death is near and tells of the power and coming of our lord and that he was an eyewitness of his majesty. He reminds them of the prophetic word spoken of Christ. He discusses the false teacher and how God has destroyed them in the past. He tells how the false teacher was in according to the flesh and in lust. He then warns of the last days. There will be scoffers stating that God no longer exists. But the day of the lord will come as a thief in the night. We must continually look toward the Lord and ignore the false teachings. This will help us grow in grace and knowledge of our Lord

John' Epistles

John the apostle wrote the Gospel of John, Revelations and three epistles (I John, II John, III John). John wrote these epistles to the second generation of Christians prior to 95 A.D. John lived and cared for Jesus mother in Jerusalem until her death. After the destruction of

Jerusalem he resided in Ephesus where he wrote his three epistles.

Book of I JOHN   Fellowship Love

The main theme of I John is fellowship. It tells how we should love God, and love other as God loves us. We need to conduct ourselves in love for one another and follow the light that God gives us through the scriptures and the Holy Spirit. He tells about the characteristics of fellowship. They are Purity of life, practice of righteousness, love in deed and truth and love as Jesus did. John asks the believers to hold fast to their basic Christian beliefs.

He tells that God is light; God is Love; and God is life. We need to walk in the light, confess our sins and keeps the word of the lord. We are to love one another and not the things of the world. The antichrists will come among us. Beware and let the Son of the Father abide in you so you will not sin or be deceived. When we are born in the Son of God we need to be righteousness in love and truth. God abides in us when we abide in him. In this relationship we are assured salvation. We are warned about sin and to rely on Christ for eternal life.

Book of II JOHN   Caution against False Teachers

John tells of his delight that children are walking in truth and commandments of the father while loving one another. He warns of false teachers, which are appearing in the church. He reminds them to look to themselves, that they do not lose their reward in Christ. He asks them to stay away from false teachers who may share in evil deeds.

Book of III JOHN — Rejection of John's Helpers

This epistle was written to Gaius, brethren in Christ. He thanks him for his generosity toward the brethren and strangers. He had borne witness of his love before the church. He tells how Diotrephes is talking foolishly against him and some followers with malicious words. He reminds him to do good and not evil. Those who do good know God but those who do evil have not seen God.

Book of JUDE — Imminent Apostasy

It is believed that the author Jude was the brother of Jesus. He identifies himself as a servant of Jesus Christ and brother of James. It appears that he was converted after the resurrection of Christ. This epistle was written sometime between 66 and 80 A.D. It mainly deals with False Teacher of the past and future.

Jude tells how ungodly men have turned the grace of god into licentiousness and denies the Lord Jesus Christ. He reminds them how God has judged the type of people down through the ages (Destroying non-believers going to the promise land, Sodom and Gomorrah etc.). These people are murmurers, complainer, walking according to their own lusts; and they mouth great swelling words, flattering people to again advantage. He tells us to defend ourselves from these people. To defend ourselves, we must keep in the love of God and build ourselves up in faith and praying in the Holy Spirit.

Book of REVELATIONS — Unveiling or Ultimate Triumph of Christ

The resurrected Lord Jesus Christ called his Beloved

Disciple John, in a vision. He told him write the things which you have seen, and the thing he would show him. John wrote down what he saw and named it Revelation or Apocalypses. The reason for this name was it was in the style of the apocalyptic literature and was a prophecy for the future. John had been banished to the Isle of Patmos under the persecution of the Roman Emperor Domitian in the year 95 A.D. He had the vision while he was on the island.

Revelations is a book of prophecy. It reveals the course and destiny of the Church. It assures us again that God is in control with an everlasting life in our future. It tells God's plan for the last days.

A great deal of symbolism is used in this book. Thus, interpreting it is difficult. The Historical interpreters believe the book was designed to forecast a general view of the whole period of history. Futurists center the book around Jesus return and the end of the world. Spiritualists believe it is great principles of Divine Government applicable to all times. Most believe that it is a combination of Historical and futurist interpretation. Some common beliefs concerning the symbols are as follows. Maybe they will help you with your understanding.

Bible Symbols

For Good

1. Throne — Power of God
2. 4 living creatures — Holiness
3. 7 spirits of God — Fullness of God's Holy Spirit
4. 24 Elders — prophets—12 apostles

5. Bowls of incense	Prayer of the saints
6. Two witnesses	Elijah and Moses
7. Martyrs	
8. 7 lamp stands	7 churches of Asia
9. Male Child	Jesus
10. 7 Angels	Bishops of 7 churches
11. The women	The Church (Jesus bride)
12. Child	Jesus
13. Morning Star	Jesus
14. Son of Man	Jesus

For Evil

1. Bottomless pit	Hell
2. Beast	Devil, demonic power, slanderer
3. Dragon	Devil
4. Babylon	world political system or world power
5. Harlot	Idolatry
6. 7 Heads	Great Intelligence or governments.
7. 10 Horns	Great Power
8. 7 Diadems	Worldwide Power
9. False Prophets	Worship of philosophy or intellectual system opposed to God.
10. Image	Power of Cesar
11. Leopard-Beast	World Power.
12. Lamb-Beast	False Prophet

13. Seven Heads and ten horns   The dragon, leopard-Beast, and Scarlet beast of Babylon had them. The seven heads may have been the seven world governments of the past.
14. Women Great city that rules over the kings of the earth

The color white represents purity

Numbers

1/3 Partial (Judgment)
3   Solidity, Divine perfection, God head
4   Creation
5   Grace
6   Man's work
7   Divine, complete, perfection, Holy, Totality
10 World Powers
12   Gods people
666 Man pretending to be God; concentrated human pride, number of the Beast
144,000 Complete number of God's people on earth.
Many things in the book are done in groups of 7. It appears that the divine completion is done with the seven items. Item's, which are grouped, in 7's are: Letters to the church, seals, trumpets, veils, candlesticks, stars, and angels. Spirits, a lamb with 7 horns, lamps, thunders, dragon with seven heads, crowns, leopard beast with 7 heads, scarlet beast with 7 heads, mountains and kings. There are also 7 times that blessed is used with those who honor and obey God.

The book has two main parts. The parts tell of things of John's time (the seven churches) and the things of the future (end times).
The book opens with a greeting form John and the telling of how Jesus gave him the vision and asks him to write what he sees.

He then gives messages to the 7 churches of Asia. In the messages he describes their nature and warns them that they can be destroyed if they don't continue to conduct themselves properly. The messages are organized with a command, a commendation and /or condemnation, a correction, and a challenge. Some people feel that these messages fit all churches and people. There are some scholars that believe the letters to the churches is the future history of the Church.

Then the predictive part of the book starts with the description of God in heaven in his glory and rule. Items described are: the Throne of God, the 24 elders, four living creatures, the sealed book and songs of Praise to God. Then the seven seals are opened telling of the tribulation. They were about: Conquering, taking peace from the earth, high price of grain. Death to 1/4 of the earth, a delay of revenge for the martyrs, the coming of the Lord with wrath and the bringing of the seven angles with their trumpets with noise, thundering, lightning's and an earthquake.

Then there was the sounding of the seven trumpets. After the sounding of each trumpet, great events took place. They were: 1/3 of the trees and grass were destroyed, 1/3 of the sea was destroyed including the ships and the creatures, 1/3 of the waters of the world were made bitter, 1/3 of the stars were darkened, the bottomless pit is opened and all the people who did not have the seal of God on their forehead would be stricken and take 5 months to die. The four angels were released to kill a third of mankind. 1/3 of mankind is killed with fire and smoke and brimstone. And at the seventh trumpet, the angles proclaimed the kingdom of the Lord and of his Christ shall reign forever and ever.

Prophecies using images are given. These images are a woman, war in heaven, war on earth, beast of the sea and the earth, the chosen 144,000, announcement of the three angles and a harvest judgment. The full wrath of God is the sent to earth by the pouring of the wrath form 7 Bowls. The wrath composed of the following: sours on those who had the mark of the beast, every living creature in the sea dies, waters on the land are turned to blood, men were scorch with fire, the beasts kingdom became full of darkness, Euphrates river is dried up in preparation of the Armageddon, and the last bowl cause great earthquakes and there were no islands or mountains.

Other images are given. The images are of Babylon and it fall, doom to the Beast followers, Harvest of the earth, marriage supper of the lamb, the white horse and armies of heaven, final doom of Beast and False prophet, the binding of Satin for 1000 years and the millennia reign of Christ.

Satin is release after the millennia and a final attack of the saints of God begins. Satin is defeated with his earthly army. All evil influences are put away. God now has the final judgment of all souls and those with their name in the book of life are saved and The Devil (Satin) and his followers are cast into the Lake of Fire for the final death.

A new heaven and a new earth with a New Jerusalem are created. Heaven and its glory with the tree of life, our Most High God, are described.

Jesus again warns that his coming will be quick and blessed is he who keeps the words of the prophecy of this book.

Using the symbolism stated above may help you understand these prophecies. However, the above definitions of the symbols are some present thinking and may be incorrect. Many scalars have written book about the interpretation of this book. A look at other resources may be helpful for further study.

Special Events in the Bible

Following is a list of many major events, which are described in the Bible and the location where they can be found. Jesus' miracles and those of the early Church are listed here also. It is hopeful that this list will aid you in finding the events.

Event	Location
Creation	Genesis 1 & 2
The fall of Adam & Eve	Genesis 3
Flood	Genesis 6-8
Tower of Babel	Genesis 10, 11: 9
Abraham's covenant	Genesis 13:14
Destruction of Sodom & Gomorrah	Genesis 19
Birth of Isaac	Genesis 21
Abraham's sacrificial test	Genesis 22
Life of Isaac	Genesis 25
Life of Jacob	Genesis 27
Life of Joseph (leading to Egypt)	Genesis 37-50

Joseph's Brothers selling him in to slavery
Genesis 37

Egyptians killing of the Israel men-children & saving of Moses
Exodus1: 15

Moses request Pharaoh to let his people go.
Exodus 7-13

Parting of the Red sea   Exodus 14:13

God Covenant with Israel   Exodus 19:5

10 Commandment   Exodus 20
                                                      Deuteronomy 5:6

The setting of the boundaries of the Promised Land
Deuteronomy 34:1

Crossing of the Jordan River with the Ark of the Covenant
Joshua 3

The 12 tribes of Israel boundaries
Joshua 13-18

Joshua battle at Jericho   Joshua 6

Passover   Exodus 12: 43

Pentecost First fruits of the Week   Deut. 16: 9

Trumpets (Rosh Hashanah)	Deut. 16: 9
Day of Atonement (Yom Kippur)	Lev. 23:26
Tabernacles (Booths or Ingathering)	Neh. 8: 13
Dedication (lights- Hanukkah	John 10:22
Purim (lots)	Esther 9:18
Gideon	Judges 6-9
Samson & Delilah	Judges 13-16
David & Goliath	1 Samuel 17
David and Bath Sheba	2 Samuel1 1
Construction of the temple (Solomon) 1 Kings 5, 2 Chronicles 3	
Ministry of Elijah Miracles during ministry	1 Kings 17
Ministry of Elisha Miracles during Jehoram reign	2 Kings 4 –6
Queen of Sheba visits Solomon	2 Chronicles 9
Isaiah predicting the crucifixion	Isaiah 53
Shadrach, Meshach and Abend-Nego survive the furnace	Daniel 3: 19
Daniel in the lion's Den	Daniel 6: 16

70 weeks of Daniel.	Daniel 9: 24
Jonah and the whale (Great Fish)	Jonah 1: 15
Haggai (genealogy of Joseph & Marry through Zerubbabel)	Matt. 1:12 Luke 3:27

Genealogy of Jesus

Thru Joseph	Matt.1
Thru Mary	Luke 3:23

Jesus

Birth (Christmas)	Matt. 1: 18 Luke 2
Baptism	Matt. 3:13 Mark 1: 9 Luke 3:21 John 1: 29
Temping by the devil	Matt. 4 Mark 1:12 Luke 4
Sermon on the Mount	Matt. 5
Jesus Transfiguration	Matthew 17:1 Mark 9:2 Luke 9:28
Triumphal Entry (Palm Sunday)	Mark 11 Luke 19:28

Last supper (First communion)	Matt.26: 20 Mark14: 22 Luke 22: 14
Crucifixion	Matt. 27: 26 Mark15: 24 Luke 23: 26 John 19:17
Resurrection (Easter)	Matt. 28 Mark 16 Luke 24 John 20
Ascension	Act 1: 9 Mark 16:19 Luke 24: 49

Notes from Bible Scholars

Following are some interesting facts gathered from various sources. Some of these sources are Bible with commentary, Halley's Handbook of the Bible, Holman Bible Atlas, and other scalars such as Chuck Missler. Some scholars may disagree upon the source of the data and the timing of these facts. However, they demonstrate that God is still active and is guiding our universe.

1. Septuagint a translation of the Old Testament

72 Hebrew scholars translated the Old Testament into the Greek language in 270 BC. This was done because many of the Jewish people had been displaced from Israel. The world language was Greek. This translation is called the Septuagint. Copies of the Septuagint are still in existence

2. Jesus declared as the Messiah

Jesus was recognized as the Messiah when he made his triumphal entry in to Jerusalem. We know this because the people sang **Psalm 118:26, Luke 19:40**. "

3. Following are some symbols, anniversaries and specific locations

1. Sacrifice of Abraham's son Isaac /Lamb and Jesus may have been on the same spot
2. Enoch never died and was taken to heaven and Jesus was resurrected on the anniversary of the date.

3. The flooding of the earth was prophesied 4 generations prior the flood. God promised that Enoch that the flood would not occur until his son Methuselah

died. When Methuselah died, Noah completed the arc and the flood came. (Noted in a history book about Enoch)

4. The Hebrews celebrates 7 feasts. Some scholars believe that the 1st three are predictive of the 1st coming of Christ. And the other 3 predict the 2nd coming.

5. Christ's resurrection occurred on the anniversary of the Ark resting on the land (Hebrew calendar Masson14.)

4. The Genealogy from Adam through Noah.

The names of the people listed in Noah's genealogy have special meanings. If you put the meaning of these names together in the order of birth, a message reads as follows.
 Man   appointed, mortal sorrow but blessed God   shall come down, (Adam) (Seth) (Enos) (Cainan) (Mahalaleel) (Jored)teaching that His death shall bring forth despairing, bring relief or comfort.
(Enoch) (Methuselah) (Lamech) (Noah)

5. The sign on the Cross

The inscription of Jesus accusation, which was displayed on the cross, was: "The King of the Jews. It was written in three languages. The Hebrew version was acrostic. If you take the first letters of each word, it spells Yahweh (the name of God.)

6 Nebuchadnezzar dreams. of the future of world power. (Daniel 2:31) The dream was of a man who was made of different kinds of materials. Daniel interpreted the dream with the aid of God. It told that there were to be several world kingdoms and then they would be destroyed and scattered to many nations.

1. The head was of Gold and it represented Babylon Empire (Winged Lyon).

2. The Chest and arms was silver (the next world empire was the Persian (Bear)

After you another kingdom not as strong

3. Next kingdom was represented as Bronze bellies and thighs. This was the Greeks (Leopard).

4. The Legs strong as iron represented the Roman Empire (Great & Terrible Beast). Iron breaks in pieces and shatters all things

5. Feet and toes were partly of iron and partly of clay, so the kingdom shall be partly strong and partly fragile. This is the fallen Roman Empire, which became many nations some strong and some fragile.
 A stone was cut and hit the image in its feet and broke them in pieces. Then the iron, clay, bronze, silver and gold was crushed together. The wind carried them away.

7. Some of the Problems related to Evolution vs. Creation

1. All supposed missing links between animal and man have been found out to be hoaxes.
2. DNA code cannot be evolved. DNA is passed from parents to child.

3. Matter cannot be created or destroyed according to theory of Relativity (EMC squared).
4. World is in bondage to decay. No new mater is being produced.
5. Human artifacts are found throughout the Geologic Column.
6. Populations statistics continue to grow at a consistent rate even though there have been catastrophes to humans. If evolution of man was as far back as claimed the population would be greater the earth could support.
7. A living cell has to many proteins and in different specific organization that it is incomprehensible that it could happen due to evolution.

8. Satan
1. He has access to God.
2. Satan's mind is open to God
3. Satan is not omnipresent or. Omnificent.
4. Satan cannot do anything that God doesn't approve.
5. He wants to ascend into heaven and exalt his throne above the stars of God. Isaiah 14:13
6. He fell from heaven. Isaiah 14:12
7. Satan will be tormented forever Rev.: 21:10
8. Jesus had the following names for Satan. The enemy. The evil one, The Prince of this world, A liar, the father of lies, a murderer.
9. God's interaction with Satin (Lucifer) Isaiah 14.
10. God describes covering cherub (possibly Lucifer) before the fall in Ezekiel 28:13-19

9. The 7 Dispensations (Gods dealing)

1. Age of innocents. (Garden of Eden.)
2. Conscience (After Fall of Man)
3. Human Government (after Flood)

4. Abraham's Promise (the Call of Abraham.)
5. Law (Exodus and formation of a nation.)
6. Church (Age of Grace.)
7. Kingdom. (To come)

10. God's <u>Plagues against the Egyptians Gods</u>
Nine of the plagues of were found in nature. The tenth and final was one not found in nature but only could be directed by God (pass over). It appears that the plagues were directed toward the god's of found that the original religion of Egypt. Sir Flinders Petrie an Egyptian archaeologist states that Egypt's original God was monotheistic. But before the dawn of history it had changed which each tribe had a god that was represented by animals and things of nature.

No & Description	What happened	Result	Egyptian God.
1. Blood	River was changed to Blood The River smelt, Fish died, no drinking water	Pharaoh's Magicians turned water into blood Pharaoh denied Moses	Nile river Khnum, Sati, Hapi Osiris Sobek Apepi
2. Plagues of Frogs	Frogs came from the water and covered the land	Pharaoh's Magicians produces frogs. Pharaoh denied Moses	Heka Thoth
3 Gnats or Lice	The dust becomes full of lice	Magicians could not bring lice.	Seth Geb.

	all over the land	Pharaoh denied Moses	
4. Flies	Swarms of flies covered the land	Pharaoh promised to let the people go but then changes refuse them	Vatchit, Beelzebub
5. Livestock &Cattle	Egyptian livestock died Israel livestock did not die	Pharaoh investigated the deaths but refused to let the people go.	Ptah, Apis, Hathor
6. Boils	Boils break out on the people	Magicians are struck by boils and cannot respond Pharaoh denies	Sekhmet, Imhotep, Serapis
7. Hail	Hail came and destroyed animals & crops and men who didn't take protection as God warned	Pharaoh felt bad but still denies	Geb, Nut, Amun-Ra, Osiris
8. Locusts	Locusts come and eat all vegetation after the hail	The people want Pharaoh to let the people go. Pharaoh denies	Sobek, Ra, Shu, Geb, Osiris

9. Darkness	Darkness fell on the Egyptians so bad that they could not see. God's people had light	Pharaoh call Moses and ask him to leave without the livestock. He would not so Pharaoh aid he didn't want to see Moses again.	Nut, Hathor, Amun-Ra
10 Death of 1ˢᵗ born (Passover)	The angle of death killed the first born of the family if they were not protected by the Passover.	Pharaoh and the Egyptians urge Israel to leave quickly After they left Pharaoh changed his mind and came after God's people.	None

11. Family Tree of the Patriarchs
 (Not under the direction of God.)

Abraham with Hagar (Sara's maidservant) begot Ishmael. God blessed him and made him fruitful, and multiply him exceeding. He had begot twelve princes, and God said, "I will make him a great nation (Edomite's)

These are the names of the sons of Ishmael, listed in the order of their birth: Nebaioth the firstborn of Ishmael, Kedar, Adbeel, Mibsam, Mishma, Dumah, Massa, Hadad, Tema Jetur, Naphish and Kedemah

(**Those Bless by God.**)
Abraham and Sarah (wife) begot Isaac. (Son)
Isaac married Rebekah and there were two sons
Esau & Jacob
(Jacob received the Patriarch blessing)
Jacob fathered sons with four different women.
Following is a list of the women and the Sons of Jacob.
(Genesis 35:23)

Leah (wife)
 Reuben, Simeon, Levi, Judah, Issachar and Zebulun
Zilpah (Leah's handmaiden) Gad and Asher

Rachel (wife)
Joseph and Benjamin, Bilhah, (Rachel handmaiden) Dan and Naphtali.
Jacob adopted Joseph Children. (Genesis 48:19)
Ephraim and Manasseh.

However, when the tribes were allotted Land, Joseph' portion was given to his sons Ephraim and Manasseh. Levi was not given an allotment because they would be God priest and live among all the tribes. Thus the Tribes that were given Land were: Asher, Naphtali East Manasseh, Zebulun , Issachar, West Manasseh, Gad, Ephraim, Dan, Benjamin, Reuben Judah and Simeon.

12. The New Testament was written in one generation.

The New Testament contains 27 books composed of 5 historical (Gospels and Acts), 21 epistles (letters to the churches), and 1 on prophecy (Revelation). As time has passed with modern technology, it has proven that the New Testament was written with one generation after Christ. This was the time when there were eyewitnesses to Christ's life and resurrection. If, there were any lies in the New Testament, the people would have known and would not believe. However, more and more people became believers.

Another factor, which demonstrates that the New Testament was written in the first century is the fact that the only persecution of the Christians mentioned in the New Testament is that of the Jews. The persecution by Rome came later after the writings.

13. The exact date of the coming on the Messiah was prophesied (Daniel's 70 weeks)

In Daniel 9 there is a prophecy for 70 weeks. The Hebrews grouped days, weeks, and years into groupings of 7 units. It says: That from the going for the of the command to restore and build Jerusalem until Messiah the Prince there shall be seven weeks and sixty two weeks (total of 69 weeks of years which becomes 483 years) Sir Robert Anderson research this time using the 360 day calendar used by the Hebrews and determined that there would be exactly 173,880 days until the coming of the Messiah. This turns out to be the exact day that Jesus allowed him to be call King and enter Jerusalem on a donkey. This is further explained in his book "Coming Prince."

Other Scholars such as Halley states that there were three dates where the Persian kings decreed that the city should be built. They were 536 BC, 457BC, and 444BC. They felt that the 457BC date was the most meaningful date. If you add the 69 years X 7 = 483years to that date, it would be.26AD. This was the very year that Jesus was baptized and began his public ministry.

14. God's Exile of his people from the Promised Land. Until 1948-1967.

Chuck Missler furnished some information that he called a prophetic Simile. It is concerned with God's promises to his people where God said "But if your heart turns away and you are not obedient, and if you are drawn away to bow down to other gods and worship them, I declare to you this day that you will certainly be destroyed. You will not live long in the land you are crossing the Jordan to enter and possess. "(Deuteronomy 30:17). His people disobeyed and he decided to send them away to Babylon in captivity for 70 years. During the captivity, there was still disobedience. So he told Ezekiel that he would punish his people for 430 years. At the end of the 70 years they were release them from captivity. When the people returned to Jerusalem to build the temple they still disobeyed, so God enforced his other statue of 7 times the punishment. This kept them from having a nation. After this period he gave them a nation again in 1948 and their city of Jerusalem in 1967..

Chuck Missler related this in his Learn the Bible in 24 Hours.
It contains his computations with the 360 Jewish calendar and general outline of the events.

15. The Ark of the covenant

It was a chest, 3-3/4 feet long, 2-1/4 feet wide, 2-1/4 high. It was made of acacia wood and overlaid with gold. It contained the two tablets of the Ten Commandments, Aaron's rod and a pot of Manna. Its top was called the Mercy seat. A Cherub was at each end. The Cherubs faced each other with their wings spread looking down toward the Chest. The mercy seat was above the Ten Commandments. This represented the meeting place of Law and Mercy. The Ark was placed in the Holy of Holies. This was a place for God in the Tabernacle and later in the temple. (See Exodus 25:10)

16. Symbolisms used in the Bible

Many of the Bible authors used objects and numbers to represent the meaning of their narratives, poetry and Metaphors. To the people of the time they may have more meaning that they do today. Following are some of the objects and numbers are as follows:

Objects

Some of the following symbols are noted in a book Chuck Missler, Arthur Custance, Web Hulonl and A.B. Simpsons titled "Devine Emblems"

Gold = Deity; highest quality; heavenly perfection

Silver = representative of blood, redemption or its price

Bronze/brass = a container of fire; related to sin

Clay = ritually corruptible, weakened, man-made

Rock = place of safety, military advantage

Gates = the seat of judgment and decision-making in a city

Living Water = running water; ritual purification

Leaven = sin or pride (puffs up to appear more than it really is)

Sheep = God's people

Goat = antithesis of sheep; often demonic or Gentile leader

Raven = representative of unclean birds (sometimes a term for demons)

Dove = clean, ritually pure; the Holy Spirit

(At one's) Right hand = position of highest privilege

Sackcloth (burlap) and ashes = deep mourning

Sword = war or judicial authority

Trumpet = awakening from normal routines

Light = revelation, truth

Oil = the Holy Spirit

Numbers
E. W. Bullinger's Number in Scripture Book (Grand

Rapids: Kregel, 1967) furnishes an understanding of how numbers are used in scripture.

Hebrew (and sometimes Greek) letters with numerical values also signify themes.

1 = Unity; primacy; sufficiency; beginning

2 = Division; different ness; opposition, or intensification; doubling

3 = Solidity; divine perfection; entirety; substantive ness; Godhead; concentrated essence

4 = creation; created ness; material completeness

5 = Grace; favor; healing; supernatural strengthening; forgiveness
5's = nearly all dimensions and articles of the tabernacle come in multiples of 5

7 = spiritual perfection; God's choice vs. mans'

9 = end; conclusion of a matter
10 perfection of the divine order; assurance of completion

40 = (5 x8) = probation; trail; discipline; or enlarged dominion, extended rule

50 = (5 x 10) perfect deliverance; (7 x 7 +1) = continued deliverance following the perfect   consummation of time.

70 = (7x10) spiritual order carries out with spiritual

power

666 = man pretending to be God; concentrated human pride

17. Hebrew Offerings

Offering	Purpose	Reason for offering
Burnt – Killing and burning animals	Make payment for sins	Make self-dedication to God.
Grain or meal-burn some grain, flour, Balance to priests	Show honor and respect to God in worship	Special gift to God
Peace Parts of the animal are burnt.	Giving gratitude to God	Having peace and fellowship with God
Sin-Performing a sin against god's commandments.	Deal with unintentional sin or anything that violates of the commandments	Restore fellowship with God.
Guilt- sin against another	Payment of sin and injury to another & forgiveness of sin from God	Provide and compensate the other person

18. Sinners prayer

The Sinners Prayer was created by scholars and clergymen. It is not found in the Bible. However, it has many Bible truths in it. Some of the beliefs that are brought into the prayer are:
• Jesus Christ is the only way to have the new covenant with God.
• Forgiveness is through Jesus' blood sacrifice.
• We need to confess our sins and repent for salvation and redemption through Jesus Christ.
• Committing our life to God and Jesus is the way we will be born again (spiritually).
• We will receive the Holy Spirit.

It is used as a prayer outline for a new believer so they can tell God that they acknowledge their belief and accept Jesus as their Lord and savior. They ask for forgiveness of their sins and the aid of the Holy Spirit A pledge is made to do God's so they will be new creation.
The prayer should remain simple because it is between the person praying and God. It is helpful if they understand what they are committed to. If God is happy with their commitment, that is all that matters. He will continue to work in their hearts and care for them. Just saying the prayer will not save anyone. It is the change of heart and a commitment to God that saves you.
Some scriptures that is involved with this prayer are as follows.
Romans 10:9 John 3:36 Romans 3:22 2C.orinthians 5: Ezekiel 36:25 Titus 3:4   Ephesians 1:13 Ephesians 1:7 Matthew 26:28

19. 4 laws

1. God Loves you and offers a wonderful plan for your life. . John3:16, John 10:10

2. Man is sinful and separated from God therefore he cannot know and experience God's love and plan for his life. Romans 3:23, Romans 6:23

3. Jesus Christ is God's only provision for man's sin. Through him you and know and experience God's love and plan for your life.
Romans 5:8, John 14:6
4. We must individually receive Jesus Christ as savior and Lord; then we can know and experience God's love and plan for our lives.
John 1:12
Ephesians 2:8.

11. Romans Road

Romans 3:10 As it is written: "There is no one righteous, not even one
Romans 3:23 for all have sinned and fall short of the glory of God.
Romans 6:23 For the wages of sin is death, but the gift of God is eternal life in Christ Jesus our Lord.
Romans 5:8 But God demonstrates his own love for us in this: While we were still sinners, Christ died for us
Romans 10:9-10 that if you confess with your mouth, "Jesus is Lord," and believe in your heart that God raised him from the dead, you will be saved.
For it is with your heart that you believe and are justified, and it is with your mouth that you confess and are saved
Romans10:13 for, "Everyone who calls on the name of the Lord will be saved."

Special Scriptures

LORDS PRAYER

Matthew 6: 9 Luke 11: 2

'Our Father in heaven,
Hallowed be your name,
Your kingdom come,
Your will be done
On earth as it is in heaven.
Give us today our daily bread.
Forgive us our debts,
As we also have forgiven our debtors.
And lead us not into temptation,
But deliver us from the evil one
(For yours is the kingdom and the
power and the glory forever. Amen (KJ)

Beatitudes

Matthew 5: 3

Blessed are the poor in spirit, for theirs is the kingdom of heaven.
Blessed are those who mourn, for they will be comforted.
Blessed are the meek, for they will inherit the earth.
Blessed are those who hunger and thirst for righteousness, for they will be filled.
Blessed are the merciful, for they will be shown mercy.
Blessed are the pure in heart, for they will see God.
Blessed are the peacemakers, for they will be called sons of God.

Blessed are those who are persecuted because of righteousness,
 For theirs is the kingdom of heaven.
"Blessed are you when people insult you, persecute you and falsely say all kinds of evil against you because of me.
Rejoice and be glad, because great is your reward in heaven, for in the same way they persecuted the prophets who were before you.

John 5:24
"I tell you the truth; whoever hears my word and believes him who sent me has eternal life and will not be condemned; he has crossed over from death to life.
.

John 3:16-18
 "For God so loved the world that he gave his one and only Son, that whoever believes in him shall not perish but have eternal life. For God did not send his Son into the world condemn the world,
 but to save the world through him.
Whoever believes in him is not condemned, but whoever does not believe stands condemned already because he has not believed in the name of God's one and only Son.
.

10 Commandments
 (Briefly stated) Exodus 20 also in Deuteronomy 5

1. You shall have no other gods before me.
2. You shall not make for yourself any carved image. – You shall not bow down to them.
3. You shall not take the name of the Lord your God in Vain.

4. Remember the Sabbath day, to keep it holy.
5. Honor your father and your mother.
6. You shall not murder.
7. You shall not commit adultery.
8. You shall not steal.
9. You shall not bear false witness against your neighbor.
10. You shall not covet your neighbor.

Greatest commandment

Mark12: 29
"The most important one" answered Jesus, "is this: 'Hear, O Israel, the Lord our God, the Lord is one. Love the Lord your God with all your heart and with all your soul and with your entire mind and with all your strength.' The second is this: 'Love your neighbor as yourself.' There is no commandment greater than these

Great Commission

Matthew 28:18
Therefore go and make disciples of all nations, baptizing them in the name of the Father and of the Son and of the Holy Spirit, and teaching them to obey everything I have commanded you. And surely I am with you always, to the very end of the age."

Create a clean heart

Psalm 51: 10
Create in me a pure heart,
O God, and renew a steadfast spirit within me.
Do not cast me from your presence
or take your Holy Spirit from me.
 Restore to me the joy of your salvation

And grant me a willing spirit, to sustain me.

Numbers 6: 24

The Lord bless you and keep you; the Lord make his face shine upon you and be gracious to you; the Lord turn his face toward your and give you peace.
The LORD bless you and keep you;
The LORD make his face shine upon you
and be gracious to you;
The LORD turn his face toward you and give you peace.

Golden rule
Matthew 7:12, Luke 6:31
So in everything, do to others what you would have them do to you

Love

1 Corinthians 13: 4
Love is patient, love is kind. It does not envy, it does not boast, it is not proud.
It is not rude, it is not self-seeking, it is not easily angered, it keeps no record of wrongs.
Love does not delight in evil but rejoices with the truth.
It always protects, always trusts, always hopes, and always perseveres.
Love never fails.

Saving eternal life

Matthew 16:24
Then Jesus said to his disciples, "If anyone would come after me, he must deny himself and take up his cross and

follow me. For whoever wants to save his life will lose it, but whoever loses his life for me will find it. What good will it be for a man if he gains the whole world, yet forfeits his soul? Or what can a man give in exchange for his soul?

Love
Deuteronomy 10: 12
what does the LORD your God ask of you but to fear the LORD your God, to walk in all his ways, to love him, to serve the LORD your God with all your heart and with all your soul,

Philippians 2:4 Each of you should look not only to your own interests, but also to the interests of others. Your attitude should be the same as that of Christ Jesus: Who, being in very nature God, did not consider equality with God something to be grasped, but made himself nothing, taking the very nature of a servant, being made in human likeness. And being found in appearance as a man, he humbled himself and became obedient to death —even death on a cross! Therefore God exalted him to the highest place and gave him the name that is above every name, that at the name of Jesus every knee should bow, in heaven and on earth and under the earth, and every tongue confess that Jesus Christ is Lord, to the glory of God the Father

Beware of False Teaching.

Matthew 7: 15 "Watch out for false prophets. They come to you in sheep's clothing, but inwardly they are ferocious wolves. By their fruit you will recognize them. Do people pick grapes from thorn bushes, or figs from thistles?

1 John 1: 8-10
If we claim to be without sin, we deceive ourselves and the truth is not in us.

If we confess our sins, he is faithful and just and will forgive us our sins and purify us from all unrighteousness. If we claim we have not sinned, we make him out to be a liar and his word has no place in our lives.

Divine Shepherd
Psalm 23
The LORD is my shepherd; I shall not be in want.
He makes me lie down in green pastures; he leads me beside quiet waters,
he restores my soul. He guides me in paths of righteousness for his name's sake.
Even though I walk through the valley of the shadow of death, I will fear no evil, for you are with me; your rod and your staff, they comfort me. You prepare a table before me in the presence of my enemies. You anoint my head with oil; my cup overflows. Surely goodness and love will follow me all the days of my life, and I will dwell in the house of the LORD forever

Child rising

Proverbs 22: 6 Train up a child in the way he should go and when he is old he will not depart from it. Train child in the way he should go, and when he is old he will not turn from it.

Ecclesiastes 3
Time to Do.

There is a time for everything,
and a season for every activity under heaven:
a time to be born and a time to die,
a time to plant and a time to uproot,
a time to kill and a time to heal,
a time to tear down and a time to build,
a time to weep and a time to laugh,
a time to mourn and a time to dance,
a time to scatter stones and a time to gather them,
a time to embrace and a time to refrain,
a time to search and a time to give up,
a time to keep and a time to throw away,
a time to tear and a time to mend, a time to be silent
and a time to speak,
a time to love and a time to hate,
a time for war and a time for peace.

Isaiah 61: 10
I delight greatly in the LORD; my soul rejoices in my God. For he has clothed me with garments of salvation and arrayed me in a robe of righteousness, as a bridegroom adorns his head like a priest, and as a bride adorns herself with her jewels.

Matthew 16: 24
"If anyone would come after me, he must deny himself and take up his cross and follow me.
 For whoever wants to save his life will lose it, but whoever loses his life for me will find it.
 What good will it be for a man if he gains the whole

world, yet forfeits his soul? Or what can a man give in exchange for his soul?

Rules of kingdom
Luke 6: 27-38 "But I tell you who hear me: Love your enemies, do good to those who hate you, bless those who curse you, pray for those who mistreat you. If someone strikes you on one cheek, turn to him the other also. If someone takes your cloak, do not stop him from taking your tunic. Give to everyone who asks you, and if anyone takes what belongs to you, do not demand it back. Do to others as you would have them do to you. "If you love those who love you, what credit is that to you? Even 'sinners' love those who love them. And if you do good to those who are good to you, what credit is that to you? Even 'sinners' do that. And if you lend to those from whom you expect repayment, what credit is that to you? Even 'sinners' lend to 'sinners,' expecting to be repaid in full. But love your enemies, do good to them, and lend to them without expecting to get anything back. Then your reward will be great, and you will be sons of the Most High, because he is kind to the ungrateful and wicked. Be merciful, just as your Father is merciful. "Do not judge and you will not be judged? Do not condemn, and you will not be condemned. Forgive, and you will be forgiven. Give and it will be given to you. A good measure, pressed down, shaken together and running over, will be poured into your lap. For with the measure you use, it will be measured to you."

Lords supper

Luke 22:17
After taking the cup, he gave thanks and said, "Take this and divide it among you.
For I tell you I will not drink again of the fruit of the vine until the kingdom of God comes."
And he took bread, gave thanks and broke it, and gave it to them, saying, "This is my body given for you; do this in remembrance of me." In the same way, after the supper he took the cup, saying, "This cup is the new covenant in my blood, which is poured out for you.

I am the Good shepherd
John 10 "I tell you the truth, the man who does not enter the sheep pen by the gate, but climbs in by some other way, is a thief and a robber. The man who enters by the gate is the shepherd of his sheep. The watchman opens the gate for him, and the sheep listen to his voice. He calls his own sheep by name and leads them out. When he has brought out all his own, he goes on ahead of them, and his sheep follow him because they know his voice. But they will never follow a stranger; in fact, they will run away from him because they do not recognize a stranger's voice." Jesus used this figure of speech, but they did not understand what he was telling them. Therefore Jesus said again, "I tell you the truth, I am the gate for the sheep. All who ever came before me were thieves and robbers, but the sheep did not listen to them. I am the gate; whoever enters through me will be saved. He will come in and go out, and find pasture

Come to Me (Jesus)

Matthew 11: 28
"Come to me, all you who are weary and burdened, and I will give you rest. Take my yoke upon you and learn from me, for I am gentle and humble in heart, and you will find rest for your souls. For my yoke is easy and my burden is light."

Love I Corinthians

13:2 If I have the gift of prophecy and can fathom all mysteries and all knowledge, and if I have a faith that can move mountains, but have not love, I am nothing. If I give all I possess to the poor and surrender my body to the flames, but have not love, I gain nothing. Love is patient, love is kind. It does not envy, it does not boast, it is not proud. It is not rude, it is not self-seeking, it is not easily angered, it keeps no record of wrongs. Love does not delight in evil but rejoices with the truth. It always protects, always trusts, always hopes, always perseveres. Love never fails.

Giving
2 Corinthians 9: 6
Remember this: Whoever sows sparingly will also reap sparingly, and whoever sows generously will also reap generously. Each man should give what he has decided in his heart to give not reluctantly or under compulsion, for God loves a cheerful giver. And God is able to make all grace abound to you, so that in all things at all times, having all that you need, you will abound in every good work

Do not grieve the Holy Spirit.

Ephesians 4: 30
And do not grieve the Holy Spirit of God, with whom you were sealed for the day of redemption.
Get rid of all bitterness, rage and anger, brawling and slander, along with every form of malice.
Be kind and compassionate to one another, forgiving each other, just as in Christ God forgave you.

Husband and wives responsibilities
Ephesians 5: 22
Wives, submit to your husbands as to the Lord. For the husband is the head of the wife as Christ is the head of the church, his body, of which he is the Savior. Now as the church submits to Christ, so also wives should submit to their husbands in everything. Husbands, love your wives, just as Christ loved the church and gave himself up for her to make her holy, cleansing her by the washing with water through the word, and to present her to himself as a radiant church, without stain or wrinkle or any other blemish, but holy and blameless. In this same way, husbands ought to love their wives as their own bodies. He who loves his wife loves himself. After all, no one ever hated his own body, but he feeds and cares for it, just as Christ does the church— for we are members of his body. "For this reason a man will leave his father and mother and be united to his wife, and the two will become one flesh." This is a profound mystery—but I am talking about Christ and the church. However, each one of you also must love his wife as he loves himself, and the wife must respect her husband

Children obey and Fathers bring up

Ephesians 6: 1.

Children, obey your parents in the Lord, for this is right. "Honor your father and mother"—which is the first commandment with a promise— "that it may go well with you and that you may enjoy long life on the earth." Fathers, do not exasperate your children instead, bring them up in the training and instruction of the Lord.

Armor of God

Ephesians 6: 10
Finally, my brethren, be strong in the Lord and in the power of His might. Put on the whole armor of God that you may be able to stand against the wiles of the devil. For we do not wrestle against flesh and blood, but against principalities, against powers, against the rulers of the darkness of this age, against spiritual host of wickedness in the heavenly places.
Therefore take up the whole armor of God, that you may be able to withstand in the evil day, and having done all, to stand.
Stand therefore, having girded your waist with truth, having put on the breast plate of righteousness, and having shod your feet with the preparation of the Gospel of peace; above all, taking the shield of faith with which you will be able to quench all the fiery darts of the which one. And take the helmet of salvation and the sword of the Spirit, which is the word of God. Finally, be strong in the Lord and in his mighty power. Put on the full armor of God so that you can take your stand against the devil's schemes. For our struggle is not against flesh and blood, but against the rulers, against the authorities, against the powers of this dark world and against the spiritual forces of evil in the heavenly realms.
Therefore put on the full armor of God, so that when the day of evil comes, you may be able to stand your

ground, and after you have done everything, to stand. Stand firm then, with the belt of truth buckled around your waist, with the breastplate of righteousness in place, and with your feet fitted with the readiness that comes from the gospel of peace. In addition to all this, take up the shield of faith, with which you can extinguish all the flaming arrows of the evil one. Take the helmet of salvation and the sword of the Spirit, which is the word of God.

Confession of Sin.
1 John 1: 9
If we confess our sins, he is faithful and just and will forgive us our sins and purify us from all unrighteousness

Jesus makes us Sons
Galatians 4: 4
But when the time had fully come, God sent his Son, born of a woman, born under law,
to redeem those under law, that we might receive the full rights of sons. Because you are sons, God sent the Spirit of his Son into our hearts, the Spirit who calls out, "Abba, Father." So you are no longer a slave, but a son; and since you are a son, God has made you also an heir

Matthew 4: 4 It is written Man shall not live by bread alone, but by every word that proceeds from the mouth of God.

Instructions of Holy Living
I Thessalonians Chapter 5:15

Make sure that nobody pays back wrong for wrong, but always try to be kind to each other and to everyone else. Be joyful always; pray continually; give thanks in all circumstances, for this is God's will for you in Christ Jesus. Do not put out the Spirit's fire; do not treat prophecies with contempt. Test everything. Hold on to the good. Avoid every kind of evil.

Rev. 22: 12 Jesus said:" And behold, I am coming quickly, and my reward is with Me, to give to every one according to his work. I am the Alpha and the Omega, the Beginning and the End, the First and the Last." "Behold, I am coming soon! My reward is with me, and I will give to everyone according to what he has done I am the Alpha and the Omega, the First and the Last, the Beginning and the End. **Rev. 3: 20** Here I am! I stand at the door and knock. If anyone hears my voice and opens the door, I will come in and eat with him, and he with me

Being Saved (Roman Road)

Romans 3:10 As it is written: "There is no one righteous, not even one
Romans 3:23 for all have sinned and fall short of the glory of God
Romans 6:23 For the wages of sin is death, but the gift of God is eternal life in Christ Jesus our Lord.
Romans 5:8 But God demonstrates his own love for us in this: While we were still sinners, Christ died for us
Romans 10:9-10 That if you confess with your mouth, "Jesus is Lord," and believe in your heart that God raised him from the dead, you will be saved.

For it is with your heart that you believe and are justified, and it is with your mouth that you confess and are saved

Romans 10:13 for, "Everyone who calls on the name of the Lord will be saved."

Exhortations for a Christian life

Hebrews 13:1-21
Keep on loving each other as brothers. Do not forget to entertain strangers, for by so doing some people have entertained angels without knowing it. Remember those in prison as if you were their fellow prisoners, and those who are mistreated as if you yourselves were suffering.
Marriage should be honored by all, and the marriage bed kept pure, for God will judge the adulterer and all the sexually immoral. Keep your lives free from the love of money and be content with what you have, because God has said, "Never will I leave you; never will I forsake you." So we say with confidence, "The Lord is my helper; I will not be afraid. What can man do to me?"
Remember your leaders, who spoke the word of God to you. Consider the outcome of their way of life and imitate their faith. Jesus Christ is the same yesterday and today and forever. Do not be carried away by all kinds of strange teachings.

It is good for our hearts to be strengthened by grace, not by ceremonial foods, which are of no value to those who eat them. We have an altar from which those who minister at the tabernacle have no right to eat. The high priest carries the blood of animals into the Most Holy Place as a sin offering, but the bodies are burned outside the camp. And so Jesus also suffered outside the city gate to make the people holy through his own blood. Let us, then, go to him outside the camp, bearing the disgrace he bore. For here we do not have an enduring city, but we are looking for the city that is to come.

Through Jesus, therefore, let us continually offer to God a sacrifice of praise—the fruit of lips that confess his name. And do not forget to do good and to share with others, for with such sacrifices God is pleased.

Obey your leaders and submit to their authority. They keep watch over you as men who must give an account. Obey them so that their work will be a joy, not a burden, for that would be of no advantage to you.

Pray for us. We are sure that we have a clear conscience and desire to live honorably in every way. I particularly urge you to pray so that I may be restored to you soon. May the God of peace, who through the blood of the eternal covenant brought back from the dead our Lord Jesus, that great Shepherd of the sheep, equip you with everything good for doing his will, and may he work in us what is pleasing to him, through Jesus Christ, to whom be glory for ever and ever. Amen.

Rules for Christian Households
Colossians 3:18-4:1
Wives, submit to your husbands, as is fitting in the Lord. Husbands love your wives and do not be harsh with them. Children, obey your parents in everything, for this pleases the Lord.

Fathers, do not embitter your children, or they will become discouraged.

Slaves obey your earthly masters in everything; and do it, not only when their eye is on you and to win their favor, but with sincerity of heart and reverence for the Lord.

Whatever you do, work at it with all your heart, as working for the Lord, not for men,

Since you know that you will receive an inheritance from the Lord as a reward. It is the Lord Christ you are serving.

Anyone who does wrong will be repaid for his wrong, and there is no favoritism.

Masters, provide your slaves with what is right and fair, because you know that you also have a Master in heaven.

Time line of the Bible

Dates in this Timeline are derived from the historical record note in the Bible and the Calendar using Christ's birth (A.D.) as the starting time. Times noted B.C. is before the birth of Christ. Many dates relating to history may vary in other documents. In many cases, there is no complete historical link to the present calendar. Many of the dates are related to events and people. Using people, their events and other item related to time we can make some approximate times. The Bible figures that creation was around 4000 years before Christ.

Using the events and times noted in the Bible does not have and exact relation to the present calendar system. There are two different view of the length of time noted in the Bible and the B.C. Calendar. One states that there were 3569 years and the other 2384 years between Adam and Abraham. The dates for Abraham to Exodus vary from 645 B.C. to 430 B.C. Many people Use round off number of time and use state that Adam was 4000 B.C., Flood was 2400 B.C., Abraham was about 2000 B.C., Exodus was 1400 B.C., David was 1013 B.C, Judah captured by Babylon was 600 B.C.

The present dating system was changed from the time of the start of Rome, to the birth of Christ. There are minute differences in the solar year and the calendar. There have been mistakes due to the leap years. In earlier time they had problem with the leap years, which had to be corrected.

These dates are approximate due to the lack of written history. They were gathered from several sources. They were gathered from the Bible references to historical events and archaeology studies. *See the Books of the Bible section for the dates of the authorship.*

Dates before the written record are approximate. However, they show the sequence of the events in relation to the people.

People & Events of the Bible   World events & Times

Adam   Creation of Universe   4000 B.C.

People started Cities   3300-2200 B.C.
                                         Early Bronze Age

The flood   2400 B.C. After Flood
Noah's sons disbursed.
Shem to Asia
Ham to Africa
Japheth to Europe

Tower of Babel   2247B.C.

Abraham   2100 B.C.
   Beginning of the Patriarchs Period   (Ended with the 12 tribes in Egypt)

Bronze age   2000-1550 BC

Egypt Dynasties   200BC to 600 BC.

Destruction of Sodom
and Gomorrah   2085 B.C.

Sodom & Gomorrah	1898 B.C.
Jacob	1900 B.C.
Joseph	1800 B.C.
Egypt world Power	1600-1200B.C.
Moses	1400 B.C
Exodus	1491 B.C.

Bible begins with Genesis, Exodus, Leviticus, Numbers, &Deuteronomy.

Battle of Jericho	1360 BC

Israel's 12 tribes enter in the promised

Promise land is divided into 12 tribal Areas	1385 B.C.
Joshua dies	1380 B.C.
Judges rules Israel	1380-970

Time of the Judges and their history

Ruth lives	1175-1125 B.C.
Book of Ruth written	1150B.C.
Samuel	1100B.C.
Saul	1053 B.C.

Saul's reign	1053-1010BC
United Israel Kingdom	1050 to 931 B.C.
King Saul and his son are killed	1010 B.C.
David	1013 B.C.
Assyria World power	900-607 BC
David reign	1000-960 BC
Solomon	973 B.C.
Solomon's reign	970-930 BC
Solomon's Temple is completed	959 B.C.
Division of Israel	933 B.C.
Northern Kingdom	931 to 722 B.C.
Southern Kingdom	931 to 586 B.C.
Elisha and Prophets	854 B.C.-444 B.C.
First Olympic games	776 B.C.
Rome is started by the unity of local villages	753 B.C.
Galilee Captivity	734 B.C.
Captivity of Israel	721 B.C.
The Great Wall of China was built	700-600 B.C.
1st siege of Jerusalem	

Beginning of the servitude of the nation. It was the first Captivity of the people by Babylon	605 B.C.
Babylon world power	606-536BC
2nd siege of Jerusalem Jehoiachin's Captivity	598 B.C.
3rd siege of Jerusalem Destruction of Jerusalem And the Holy Temple	586 B.C

Israel in captivity in Babylon 604 BC-538BC

Return to Israel	538 B.C.
Persia world power (Cyrus Decree)	550-330BC
2nd start of rebuilding Temple	520 B.C.
Completed the New Temple	515 B.C.
Ester (Queen of Persia)	478 B.C.-465 B.C.
Ezra Goes to Jerusalem	457 B.C.

Nehemiah rebuilds Jerusalem wall 444 B.C.

Greek Rule begins	330BC

Greek Empire	330-146BC
Dead Sea scrolls were written	200B.C.-67 A.D.
Maccabean period	167-63BC
Rome rule begins	146 BC
Roman world power	146BC-476AD
Herod the Great ruled	37-4 BC
Christ's Birth	00AD
Jesus' Baptism and Start of his ministry	27AD
Jesus Resurrection	30AD
Birth of the Church Pentecost (Baptism Of 3000 people)	30AD
Beginning of the Church Age	
Church persecution	032-313AD
Conversion of Saul	42AD
Salvation of Gentiles In Antioch	42AD

Founding of churches
By the apostles   30-63AD

Paul's 1st. Missionary trip   45-48 AD
He went to Galisa and Cyprus,
(Salamis, Paphos, Antioch in Pisidia, Iconium, Lystra, Derbe, Attalia. Perga,

Paul's 2nd Missionary trip   50-53 AD
He revisited the Galatian Churches and Troas, Philippi, Thessalonica, Berea, Athens, Corinth & Ephesus.

Paul's 3rd.Missionary trip   54-57AD
He Revisited the Galatia Churches,
 Ephesus, Corinth, Philippi, Illyricum.
Troas, Patra, Miletus. He wrote Romans, Galatians, and I & II Corinthians during this trip.

Execution of Paul   65AD

Rome Burns and destroys most of the city. 64 AD

The New Testament was written   30-95AD

1st generation of eye witness of Christ
 and the beginning of the Church.   33 AD.

Emperor Constantine
Conversion   312 AD
He sees a cross in the sky and is told to follow it and he will win the battle.

End of Christian
Persecution by Rome   313 AD

Constantine proclaims Christianity

Prominent People in the Bible

(Listed in alphabetical order)

Name
Description (Time of Events) (Bible References)

Aaron
Moses older brother and 1st Hebrew priest (15th Century) (Exodus 4:40)

Abdon
God's judge of Israel (11th Century) (Judges 12: 13)

Able
Adam's second son who was killed by his brother Cain (1st century after creation) (Genesis 5)

Abraham
His given name was Abram. God changed his to Abraham. He is the Father of the Israelites. Abraham was a man of faith in the Holy God who called him. He never wavered in his faith. Abraham was called by God to be the father of a new nation that would believe the Holy God. His faith was so strong that he left his family land and followed God to start this new nation. There was no instruction on Righteousness so he had to learn by experience and messages from God. God would point out his mistakes so he would learn as He did with the Egyptian king. God blessed him and gave benefits to aid his life. In return Abraham became stronger in his relationship with God. God made promises (covenants) with Abraham. As Abraham had a good relationship with

God, he maintained his faith even though some promises were for his descendants.

His faith was tested when God asked him to sacrifice his son Isaac. Abraham passed the test and he didn't lose his promised son.

When Abraham couldn't handle a situation by himself, God worked miracles in his life. He aided him in recovering his captured nephew by defeating Kings in war. He was warned about the destruction of Sodom and Gomorra and aided his nephew, Lot, to survive. His wife Sarah had his son Isaac well after her child bearing years. He did become the father of the Israel nation. And was an example of faith that God wants of us. He gave him the experiences of having contact with local leaders. The most important one was Melchizedek, the king and great high priest of God Most High. Abraham had reverenced for him and gave him one tenth of the spoils he received when he defeated the kings and rescued Lot. Through these experiences he taught him to love his fellow men and God. (2200 B.C.) (Genesis Chapters 11-26)

Adam
1st Created human. He lived in the Garden of Eden. God created Eve to aid and comfort him. He and Eve were the first to sin and cause men to die. (6th day of creation) (Genesis 1)

Andrew
Apostle of Jesus, Brother of Peter, and taught about Jesus. (1st Century A.D.)

Barak
God's Judge of Israel (Foreign Oppression) (12th Century B.C.) (Judges 4:5)

Bartholomew
He was a disciple of Jesus. He worked with the early church and went east and it is believed that he was flayed alive in Armenia. (1st Century A.D.) (Matthew 10, Mark 3: 18)

Bilhah
She was Rachel's servant and Bilhah gave her to Jacob to have children. She bore Dan, Naphtali. (18th Century B.C.)(Genesis 29)

Cain
He was Adam's first son and the first murderer. (1st Generation after Creation)(Genesis 4)

Caleb
He and Joshua were the only ones who survived the 40 years in the wilderness because of their faith in God.. He was a spy for the Promised Land. (15th Century B.C.) (Numbers 14)

Caiaphas
He ruled as Jewish high priest (18-36 A.D.) He gathered the Sanhedrin, (Jewish court) which led to the crucifixion of Jesus.

Daniel
God's righteous Prophet in Babylon and an Administrator. He and three other friends were in the first group of captives to go the Babylon. Daniels had his name changed to Belteshassar. His friend became Shadrach, Meshach and Abednego. Daniel and his friends achieved government position in Babylon. His friends were placed in a fiery furnace because they refused to worship the king's idol.

However, with the aid of and angle miraculously survived. Daniel was placed in a lion's den, to die, because he worshiped God when there was an edict to worship no one except the King for a month. He also survived the threat of the lions.

God gave him the ability to interpret dreams about future events. In these dreams prophecies were received about the time of Jesus would be with the Israelites, the rise and fall of the next three world kingdoms that were to prepare for the coming of the Gospel (Persian, Greek and Romans.) and the fall of The Babylon empire. (6th Century B.C.) (Book of Daniel)

David

He was the 2nd King of Israel, mighty warrior and follower of God. David was a great king for forty years. He made Israel a strong military, political and an influential nation. He was a passionate person loving others and God. He also was a musical person who wrote Psalms and poetry. He was loyal and filled with humility. As with all men, he had success and failure. God aided in taking care of his chosen people. He defeated other nations and united the Promised Land. He made Jerusalem the capital city because he wanted unite the Chose people and have a place of worship God.

The most memorable events showing his success were: 1. Killing Philistine giant armored warrior Goliath by stunning him with a stone from his sling and then killing him and winning the war. As A result he became Israel's hero. 2. Honoring God's appointed king, who was his adversary, and didn't kill him when he had two chances. 3. Obtaining their promised land from the Philistines Moabites, Ammonites and Jobsites. 4. Bringing unity to the Israel nation and setting the boundaries of the Promised Land. 5. He set up the city of Jerusalem as the capital of the country and the center of Gods worship. He initiates the preparation of the Holy Temple. As with all men, he had flaws that affected his life so God reduce his help. He had an affair with Bathsheba resulting in a pregnancy and then arranged for her husband to be killed so he could have her. Nathaniel the prophet came a told him about God knowing about his actions. David severely repented. From then on he had problem within his family (1003 B.C.-970 B.C.) (1st Samuel Chapter's 16-31-2nd Samuel 24, 1st Kings, Chapter 1and 2)

Deborah
She was God's Judge for Israel. She was the first women to have leadership in Israel. (12th Century B.C.) (Judges 4:5)

Ehud
He was God's Judge that killed King Eglon and then subjugates Moab assuring peace for 80 years. (13th Century B.C.) (Judges 3)

Elijah
He was the 1st leading profit & great Miracle worker in the Norther kingdom. At that time the people were worshiping God and Baal. Elijah told the king that God was placing a drought on the kingdom because of them not worshiping God. He lived with a widow and her son and the birds brought them food. Later the widow's son died and Elijah brought him back to life. Elijah went to the king and set up a challenge between him and 450 Baal prophets. He also asked the people to believe in God or Baal as a result of the challenge. The challenge was to cut up a bull and place it on wood without fire and God would send down fire to burn the wood and bull. The Baal prophets could not arouse their god to action even when they showed their faith by cutting themselves. Their attempts were futile. Then Elijah had water put on the wood and then called God to send fire and

destroy everything. The Baal prophets were killed. He then announced that the drought would be removed by God. The Baal worshiping queen was upset and wanted to kill Elijah. He later went to Mt. Sinai with Elisha to talk to God. God told him he was going to heaven and Elisha was to take his place. Elisha received a double portion of Elijah abilities. He was taken to heaven in a Fiery Chariot. (9th Century B.C.) (1st Kings 17-19, 2nd Kings2)

Elisha
He was the 2nd leading prophet and protégé of Elijah. His duty was to bring God's people away from other gods and back to God. Elisha was a more social prophet and worked in many campsites. He associated with other prophets and kings. He performed many miracles. He stopped a river, healed bad water, give an overflow of oil to help a widow, restored boy back to life. He fed hundreds, healed leprosy. He performed many other miracles that are noted in 2nd Kings. (9th Century B.C.) (1st King 19, 2nd Kings Chapters 2-13)

Elon
God's Judge who ruled for 10years. (12th Century B, C.) (Judges 12:8)

Ephraim He was Joseph's son who became a tribal leader. (19th Century B.C.) (Genesis 49)

Esau
Non- blessed Son of Isaac. God told their mother that the second would serve the first. Esau was the first born of the twins. To assure the prediction, Jacob and his mother deceived Isaac and received the blessing. However, He was the founder of Edom and other nations that God gave to him. (20th Century B.C.) (Genesis 25)

Ester
She was the Queen of Babylon who aided in the protection of God's People that were about to be killed because they were Israelite's. (483 BC.to 473 B.C.) (Book of Ester)

Eve
She was the first women and Adams Wife. Satan convinced her to sin by eating from the forbidden tree. (Part of Creation)(Genesis2)

Ezekiel
He was God's prophet and a priest who was in Babylon during the exile. One of his prophecies was the destruction of the temple. He aided in the return of Israel He wrote his book (592 B.C.-570 B.C.) (Book of Ezekiel)

Ezra

He was a priest who aided in the return of the Israelites to Jerusalem. (538 B. C. - 473 B.C.) (Book of Ezra)

Gabriel

He is the archangel that sent messages and helped men. He told Mary, even though she was a virgin, she would have Jesus. He assisted men in the Old Testament. He will also assist in the future. (Samuel 8:16-27, 9:20-27, Luke 1:11-38, 1 Thessalonians 4:16, Revelations 9:1, 20:1)

Gideon

He was God's Judge and warrior who led armies against the Midianites and led his people away from idolatry. He refused to be their king and remained a judge. (12 Century

B.C.) (Judges 6-8)

God

He is our eternal God who created the world as we know it. He is the father of Jesus our Lord. He has other names such as Jehovah, Yahweh etc. (For further information see the God section of notes.) The Bible tells us all about him. You will get to know him through the Bible and the actions of all His followers.

Jesus said if we see him we see his father It appears that we can get the best understanding by reading about Jesus in the gospels. He also is in the background supporting all the other people mentioned in the Bible. He is the eternal God is the beginning and the end and ruler of the Universe. He is eternal and the Bible is his word to man. When you read through the Bible you see his love for us and know why we need to love and respect him. With this understanding we look forward to be with him in his eternal kingdom. *(For further information see the God section in the notes.)*

Hagar

She was Abraham's second wife, who was Sarai's servant. Her son was Ishmael who started many nations. (22nd Century B.C.) (Genesis 16)

Ham

He was Noah's second son who settled in Africa and Egypt after the Flood. (11th generations after Adam) (Genesis 5, 7, 9&10)

Ibzan

He was God's Judge and leader for seven years.(11 Century B.C.) (Judges 12:8)

Isaac

He was Abraham and Sarah's promised blessed son. He was born to Sarah well after her child bearing age. God tested Abraham by asking him to sacrifice Isaac. Abraham started the sacrifice but God stopped him due to his faith He was the father of Jacob and Esau. (21nd Century B.C.) (Genesis 21)

Isaiah

He was one the greatest Israel prophets. His beginning was when he had a vision where God was looking for a prophet who was willing to speak God's word. He said "hear am I. Send me" This was the beginning of 50 years of service to God during the reign of four Kings. He was involved in Political and military issues and spent most of his time in Jerusalem. During which there were two attacks by foreign countries He and other prophets warned the people to be righteous and follow God and not their plans for their nation. The people disregarded the poor and stopped following God. With this disobedience God allowed the destruction of Jerusalem. As a prophet he foretold God's plans for the future. He is best known for his foretelling of the coming messiah (Jesus) and his life and trails'. Jesus proclaimed the fulfillment of his prophecies when he read Isaiah's words in the synagogue Later Jesus fulfilled those concerning him.

Ishmael

He was Abraham and Hagar's son. As Hagar was not part of God's plan he did not receive God's blessing of the Israel nation. However, God promised his descendants to have other kingdoms. (22nd Century B.C.) (Genesis 16)

Jacob

He is Abraham's grandson who received God's blessing from Isaac. His brother was Esau. They were to be divided and have separate kingdoms. God later changed his name to Israel. He was the father of the 12 tribes of Israel (20 Century B.C.) (Genesis 25, 35:10)

Jair He was a Judge leader for 22 years. (12th Century B.C.) (Judges 10:3-5)

James

Jesus's Brother, It is believed he wrote the Book of James. He was a strong worker in the early church and was executed by the Sanhedrin (1st Century A.D.) (Galatians 1:18)

James (2)

Son of Alpheus was an apostle of Jesus.(1st Century A.D.) (Matthew 10:3)

James (3)

He was the son of Zebedee and John's brother. Both were Jesus apostles. (1st Century A.D.) (Matthew 10:3)

Japheth

Noah's son, who survived the flood, settled in the eastern

end of the Mediterranean Sea. (11th Generations after Adam) (Genesis 10)

Jephthah

He was a ruling Judge for more than 6 years. He defeated the Ammonite's and lost his daughter. (11th Century B.C.) (Judges 11:1)

Jeroboam

He was the 1st king of the North Kingdom. (930 B.C. - 909 B.C.) (1st Kings 11:26-14:20, 2 Chronicles 10:12-12:20)

Jeremiah God's Prophet. God told him that He put His words in Jeremiah's mouth. He was the last prophet to reside in Israel before the final captivity by Babylon. He continued to warn the people to return to God. He wrote the Book of Jeremiah and Lamentations. (His ministry was 627 B.C.-580 B.C.) (2nd Chronicles 35:25.)

Jesus

He is Gods son, who lived a prophesized life so that man would know that he was sent by God to bring the Gospel for our salvation and eternal life. His life was sacrificed to institute God's new covenant (Gospel). He is the Hebrew Messiah and Greek Christ. His life shows us the image of God his father. His teachings were so great that Christians around the world follow them. His impact was so great that the calendar is based around his birth. His main teaching was that we need to love God and our fellow men. By doing this we can all get along and our leaders will lead in righteousness. (He had many names and they can be found in the Jesus name section.) He lived from 0 A.D to 33 A.D.

The Gospel books (Matthew, Mark and Luke) tell us about him and his life. *(Further information is furnished in the Jesus section of the Notes.)*

Job

He was a righteous man who was persecuted by the devil to see if he would stop believing in God. His faith overruled the devils temptations and God rewarded him. (1900 B.C. - 1800 B.C.)(Book of Job)

John

He was the brother of disciple James. He was a close friend and disciple of Jesus. He authored the Books of John and Revelations. (1st Century A.D.) (Mentioned in the other Gospels)

John Baptist

He was the baptizing prophet who was called to proclaim the coming of Jesus the Messiah. His title was John the Baptist. (1st Century A.D.) (Matthew 3}

Jonah

He was God's prophet that was sent to prophesize to Nineveh and he refused and ran away. His refusal was met with his internment in a large fish for 3 days. He then returned and went to Nineveh and gave them Gods message. (8th Century B.C.) (Book of Jonah)

Joseph

He was Jacob's favorite Son. He was sold in slavery and sent to Egypt. He was persecuted for many years but he maintained his faith in God. He was finally rewarded and made second in command of Egypt. He later sent for his brothers. The Israelites were in Egypt for centuries. (18th Century B.C.) (Genesis 37-47)

Joseph 2

Jesus adopted earthly father. He was in the King David linage and was aware of his wife and her virgin birth of Jesus. Later, he fathered Jesus' brothers and sisters. Brothers (James, Joses, Jude and Simon) and Sisters (Salome and Mary) (1 Century A.D.) (Matthew 1)

Joseph 3 Jesus's younger brother (1st Century A.C.) (Matthew 13:55)

Joshua

He was the Son of Num. He left Egypt when the Israelites were allowed to leave. He had faith in God when many of the chosen people didn't when God told them to take their land and they saw the strength of the people living there. Because of his faith, God allowed him to live while the other died in the wilderness. God allowed him to enter the Promised Land. Moses trained him to be a leader of the Israelites while they were returning to their promised land. He led the people while they fought for the land. He led the battle of Jericho and other cities as they acquired their promised land. (15th Century B.C.) (The Books of Exodus, Deuteronomy and Joshua)

Judas

Jesus's younger brother. Judas is a Greek form of the name Judah. After the resurrection he became a stronger believer and wrote the Book of Jude (1st Century A.D.) (Matthew 13:55)

Judas 2

He is the son of James and a disciple of Jesus. (1st Century A.D.) (Luke 6:16, Matthew 2:4 & Mark 3:16-19)

Judas 3

Judas Iscariot was a disciple of Jesus who betrayed him. (1st Century A.D.) (Matthew 2:4, Betrayal -Matthew 24:16, 26:47-50, Matthew 27)

Jude

Jesus Brother who's Greek would be Judas. (1 Century A.D.) (Matthew 13:55)

Lazarus

He and his two sisters were great friends with Jesus. He always spent time with them when he went to Bethany. Jesus came later and raised him from the dead. (Luke 16) (John 11:1-44)

Leah
She was Jacob's first wife due to deception. She gave Jacob 6 sons for the tribes of Israel (Ruben, Simeon, Levi, Judah, Issachar, Zebulun and a daughter Dinah

Luke
He is the Doctor friend of Paul that interviewed and witnessed the events of Christianity and wrote the Books of

Luke and Acts. (1st Century A.D.)

Manasseh He was one of Joseph's sons. Later an Israel tribe was made for his descendants. (19th Century B.C.) (Genesis 48)

Mark
He was also called John. He was a leader in the Jerusalem church and a friend of Peter and Barnabas. He, with Peter's input wrote the Book of Mark (1st Century A.D.) (Acts 12:12, 15:37)

Mary
She was the mother of Jesus who God honored because she was in the linage of King David as prophesized for Jesus's birth. (1st Century A.D.) (Luke 2:1, Matthew 1:18-25)

Mary 2
Mary Magdalene was deliver form demon position by Jesus. She felt indebted to Jesus and followed him and served him and the disciples throughout Jesus's ministry. She witnessed the crucifixion and resurrection of Jesus. She was one of the first people. (Matt. 27:56 -28:10)

Mary 3
Mary and Martha were Lazarus's brother. Jesus loved this family and spent a great deal of time with them in Bethany. They were there when he resurrected Lazarus from the dead. (Luke 10:39)

Matthew
He was a disciple of Jesus. He was also call Levi. He was a tax collector for Rome when Jesus called him. He wrote the

Gospel of Matthew. (1st Century A.D.) (Mathew 9:9, Mark 2:13, Luke 6:15)

Matthias
He was elected to take the twelfth disciple position vacated by Judas Iscariot. (1st Century A.D.) (Acts 1:12-26)

Melchizedek
He was the King of Salem and Abraham honored him as God's Priest. He has been compared many times in the Bible because of his righteousness. (22th Century B.C.) (Genesis 14:18)

Michael
Archangel
He has other angels under his authority. He fights battles for God, and will fight Satan in the final battle for earth. (He is eternal). (Daniel 10:13, Jude 1:9, Revelations 12:7-9)

Moses
Moses was chosen by God to lead the chosen people out of captivity in Egypt to their Promised Land. He was aided by God's miracles to gain their freedom. He was their leader while they were in their 40 years in the wilderness. God aided him and his people during this stressful time. (15th Century B.C.) (Book of Exodus)

Nebuchadnezzar
He was the Babylon King that Captured Israel and took them captive to Babylon. (604 B.C.- 562 B.C.) (2 Kings 24, Daniel 2)

Nehemiah
He was the Persian king Artaxerxes cup

bearer. He was upset that his home land was not being rebuilt. He convinced the king to let him get the Wall of Jerusalem rebuilt. He later returned to Jerusalem and tried to keep it in repair so people would return to Gods temple and city. (6th Century B.C.)(Book of Nehemiah,)

Noah
God wanted to destroy men because they had become evil, but he saw Noah's righteousness and decided to start over again with him and his family. Noah built the ark that God told him to build and then God flooded the earth destroying the evil in it. After the flood receded, Noah and his family went to different areas to repopulate the earth.(10th Generation after Adam) (Genesis, Chapters 6 through 9)

Othniel
Caleb offered his daughter to the man who would drive out the people in his portion of the Promised Land. God aided Othniel and won his wife. Othniel became the Lord's Judge of Israel Through his leadership there was peace in the area for 40 years.. (14th Century B.C.) (Joshua15:16, Judges 3:7-11)

Paul
He was known as Saul of Tarsus and a Pharisee who persecuted the Christians. Jesus appeared to him and charged him to take the Gospel to the gentiles. This Changed his life and he repented and changed his name to Paul. He then travel in most of Europe and brought the Gospel to the gentiles. Paul made three missionary trips through Europe. During this time he overcame obstacles but kept spreading the word of God. Most of his efforts are recorded in the book of Acts. He also sent his teaching letters to various churches (Epistles). (34A.D.- 67A.D.)

(Acts, Romans, 1 Corinthians, 2 Corinthians, Galatians, Ephesians, Philippians, Colossians, 1Thessalonians 2Thessalonians, 1 Timothy, 2 Timothy, Titus, Philemon.)

Peter

His name was given to him by Jesus. It describes a rock. The Greek for rock is Cephas. His given name was Simon. He was a close friend and disciple of Jesus. One day, Jesus asked who do you say I am? "Simon Peter answered, "You are the Christ, the Son of the living God." Jesus replied, "Blessed are you, Simon son of Jonah, for this was not revealed to you by man, but by my Father in heaven. And I tell you that you are Peter, and on this rock I will build my church, and the gates of Hades will not overcome it." (Matthew 16:16-18)

After Jesus ascended to his heavenly Father, Peter was the mainstay of the teaching the Gospel to the Jews. He later talked at the coming of the Holy Spirit during Pentecost. He also was the first to go to the gentiles and realize they could become Christians. He was the strongest member of the church councils. He performed miracles to prove he was speaking the truth about Jesus.

Many of his action are also found in the Book of Acts. His actions with Jesus are recorded in the Gospel Books. He also wrote the books of Peter. Many believe that Mark gathered his information from Peter for his Gospel book. (His life efforts were between 30AD-64A.D. It is believed that He was crucified by the Romans.) (Acts, the 4 Gospel's, and Peter's two letters)

Phillip

He was a disciple of Jesus and a fisherman friend of Peter and Andrew. He followed Jesus throughout his ministry. He served as one of the seven to aid in spreading the word. He also converted an Ethiopian to Christianity (1st Century A.D.)(Matthew 10:3.Act 1:13, Acts 6:5, Acts 8:26-40)

Rachel
She was the wife of Jacob who he loved dearly. Her son was Joseph who took Israel to Egypt. She died giving birth to son Benjamin (18th Century B.C.)(Genesis 29)

Rahab
She was a prostitute in Jericho who aided the Israel spies. The Israelites honored her for her help and she later became an Israelite. (15th Century B.C.) (Joshua 2 & 6)

Rebekah
She was Isaac's wife who aided Jacob to obtain the blessing that he need to be the younger and stronger son as she was told in a dream before she gave birth to her children. (21st Century B.C.) (Geneses 24)

Rehpboam
He was Solomon's Son and ruled form 930B.C.-913B.D. His harsh rule caused the separation of Israel. He was the `1st king of the southern Kingdom. (1 Kings 11:43-12:17)

Samson
He was a Nazirite who became a judge with great strength. He used his strength to protect his people. He broke his Nazirite vows by marring a Philistine woman. She wanted to help Her Philistine people and tried to find the basis of his strength. God finally gave up on him when he violated the Nazirite code by the cutting of his hair. He lost his strength. They blinded him so he could

not attack them. Later God gave him the chance to redeem himself. He was put between to two towers in a building. He grabbed them and brought down the building, killing many Philistines and himself. (11th Century B.C.) (Judges 13 thru 16)

Samuel

He was one of Gods' Judges and became the 1st noted Prophet. His mother Hannah was childless and she made a pledge to God that if she was given a child she would consecrate him to God's service. She bore Samuel and then took him to be raised by Eli (The priest). One night God called Samuel and he thought it was Eli and went to him. It wasn't. It was God calling him.

Later God told Samuel that Eli sons were corrupt and He would let the philistines defeat them at Aphek. Eli died and the Philistines defeated the Israelites. They acquired the Ark of the Covenant and it became troublesome to them because God cursed them for them having it Samuel gathered the people and asked them to return to God and Samuel but the people want a king. God finally gives in to the people and selects Saul to be king of Israel. Samuel continues to be the spiritual leader of Israel. He anoints Saul. God later realizes Saul's faults and has Samuel anoint David to be King. He is a hero of faith to God. The events of his life and those of the kingdoms are written in the Books of Samuel. (11th Century B.C.)

Sarah

Her given name was Sarai. She was the Wife Abraham. She was childless and gave her servant to have children for her. This didn't work out well. After her child bearing year, an angel of the lord told that she would have the promised Son. She bore Isaac who became the promised son that would have God's blessings. (22nd Century B.C.) (Genesis 11:29-30, 18:10, 21:1-6)

Saul
He was the 1st King of Israel. He was chosen by God and anointed by Samuel. At first he is a successful king and protects his people. Later he strayed from God and his instructions, so God told Samuel to anoint David as the next king. David honored Saul's appointment and did not respond to Saul trying to kill him. While losing a battle and he killed himself by falling on his sword. (1050B.C.-1010 B.C.) (1st Samuel 7:15-31:13)

Shamagar
He was a Judge of Israel that struck down six hundred Philistines with an Ox goad. (11th Century B.C.)(Judges 3:31)

Shem
He was Noah's son and survivor of the Flood. He settled in the Middle East and the father of most of the people of that area. (11th Generation of Adam) (Genesis 5:32, 10:22)

Simon 1
He was a disciple of Jesus. They called him Simon the Zealot. He was with Jesus in the final day and saw his assertion to Heaven. (1st Century A.C.) (Mark 3:16, Luke 6:15, Acts 1:1-13)

Simon 2
Jesus's earthly brother (1st century A.D.) (Matthew 13:55)

Solomon

He was King David and his wife Bathsheba's son and the 3rd King of Israel. God granted him his request for wisdom and made Israel great through this wisdom. People came to Israel just to admire and verify his great wisdom. He was in line with God and built his temple. He wrote 300 proverbs and 1000 songs. However, power and money can lead man away from God's righteousness. He was changed due to his life style with his 700 wives and 300 concubines. God had promised King David that he would continue supporting Solomon. Things got worse and when He died the nation of Israel was split into two parts. (970B. C. - 930B.C.) (2nd Samuel 12:24, 1st Kings Chapters 1-11, 2nd Chronicles Chapters 1-9).

Thaddaeus

He was a one of the twelve disciples.(1st Century A.D.) (Matthew 10:2-4).

Thomas

He was one of Jesus's 12 disciples He is best known as a doubter. This is because he didn't see Christ when the other disciples saw Jesus after his resurrection. Later Jesus confronted him and he believed. Jesus told him, "Because you have seen me, you have believed; blessed are those who have not seen and yet have believed. (1st Century A.D.) (Matthew 10:2-4, John 24:24-29)

Tola

He was the son of Puah and a Judge of Israel for twenty three years. (12 Century B.C.) (Judges 10:1-2)

Zechariah

He was a priest and prophet that aided in the return from

Babylon captivity to the Promised Land. He received vision that aided in convincing his people to return to their home. Some of his prophecies told about the redemption of Israel. (520 B.C.- 470 B.C.)   (Ezra 5-1, his Book of Zechariah)

Zephaniah

He was a prophet of Israel. He predicted the fall of Jerusalem. He also talked against the leader of the time because they were not following God's will.
(630 B.C.- 625 B.C.) (The Book of Zephaniah, 2nd Kings 25:18, Jeremiah 21:1)

Words of the Bible

Abide: To maintain and to remain faithful and remain satisfied.

Abomination: To hate extremely; to abhor; to detest, to loath. The act of abomination or state of being: detestation; extreme aversion; that which is abominated or hateful vice.

Anoint: Poring oil upon to consecrate in a sacred rite.

Antichrist: An Opponent of Christ; a person or power antagonistic to Christ.

Apostle: A messenger. One of the Twelve Disciples of Christ

Baptism: Sacramental, ritual, or religious ceremony signifying spiritual rebirth, admission or purification. It is accomplished by immersion in water. It is an experience that initiates or sanctifies

Believe: To be convinced of the truth dependability, or existence of something without demonstrable evidence.

Born Again: See John 3: 3-21. One is born of water and the spirit.

Christ: One anointed as ruler; the appellation given to Jesus of Nazareth by the Christian world; deliverer, a Messiah; a first proper name.

Covenant: An agreement between two or more to do

or refrain from doing something.

Crucify: To put to death by nailing or otherwise affixing to a cross; excruciate or torment; treat with grievous severity.

Deliverance: The act of delivering from captivity, oppression, or danger.

Demons: An evil spirit; fiendish; possessed by an evil spirit. One seemingly possessed by a demon or evil spirit.

Devil: An evil spirit or being. He is represented in scripture as the traducer, tempter, deceiver and leader or ruler of hell.

Epistles: Message, letter. A letter of formal or morally instructive.. It is one of the apostolic letters of the New Testament.

Faith: Confidence or trust to God; loyalty; fidelity belief not substantiated by proof. It is Spiritual acceptance of truth or realities not certified by reason. It is belief in God, belief in the doctrines or teaching of a religion. Faith is the substance of things hoped for, the evidence of things not seen.

Faithful: Strict in the performance of duty; unswervingly devoted; loyal to one's promises; trustworthy adhering to fact or true to an original the believing members of the Church.

Fast: To go without food for a period of time. A person

abstains from food for religious reason. It is usually done during a long duration of prayer.

Fornication: Sexual acts outside the marriage resulting in sin.

Gentiles: In the time of god using Israel-- A clan, race or people that is foreign, pagan, and heathen.

Glory: Praise, honor or distinction accorded by common consent; thanksgiving expressed in adoration; a blessing from heaven.

Gospel: The body of doctrine taught by Christ and the apostles; Christian revelation; glad tidings, concerning salvation and the kingdom of God as announced to the world by Christ. The Gospel books are first four books of the New Testament. Something infallibly true or implicitly believed.

Grace: A special dispensation or privilege; the unmerited love and favor of God.

Hades: The abode or state of the dead.

Hallelujah: Praise ye Jehovah, Praise the Lord, a song of praise to the Lord.

Heaven: The final place where the blessed go after death and meet God.

Holy: Consecrated to god; dedicated by religious authority; having qualities compelling worship and adoration; exalted by dedication to service of the church or of the religion.

Hosanna: An exclamation, used as an acclamation of praise to God or Christ. It is a joyful expression of praise or adoration.

Hope: The belief that one's desires may be attained and trusting with expectations of attainment.

Jesus: He is the divine Son of God. He was born of God and the virgin women (Mary). He was sinless. He performed miracles (nature, sickness, death and power or evil spirits.) He died on a cross for our sins as for told years before the event. His body was resurrected three days after he was killed. He is now in Heaven with God He will come again to rule the world.

Love
Agape love: The benevolent affection of God for his creatures, or the reverent affection due God form them. Christians love, brotherly love of one another. It is a feeling of warm personal attachment or deep affection, as for a friend, parent, or child.

Eros love: A passionate affection for a person of the opposite sex; sexual passion or desire, or its gratification.

Other love: A strong predilection or liking for anything (material things such as; books, music, Etc.)

Lord: A person possessing supreme power and authority. Supreme Being; God; Jesus Christ, esp. in the expression Our Lord.

Messiah: "anointed one" Someone anointed with a particularly blessed by God for a particular task Greek word for anointed one is Christ. Jesus was anointed by God to bring salvation to all the people.

Minister: One authorized to conduct religious services, as a pastor or clergyman.

Miracles: A wonder; a marvelous thing something which seems to go beyond the known laws of nature and is held to be the act of a supernatural being.

Omnipotent: All powerful

Omnipresent: Everywhere at all times

Omniscient: All wise and knowing

Pass over: A seven-day festival of the Jews during which no foods made with leaven may be eaten, occurring in the spring of the year to commemorate the escape of the Hebrews from slavery in Egypt.

Redemption: Deliverance from sin and its consequences through the atonement of Jesus

Rejoice: To experience joy and gladness in a high degree, to be joyful, to exult.

Revelation: The last book of the Bible. A striking disclosure as of something not before realized. God's disclosure of himself and of his will to his creatures

Righteousness: A person acting in accordance with the

dictates of morality; agreeing with right; just; equitable.

Rise: To Come back from the dead. Christ rose on the third day.

Sabbath: The seventh day of the week, Saturday, as the day of rest and religious observances among the Jews and certain Christian sects. The first day of the week, Sunday, similarly observed by most Christians and in commemoration fo9 the resurrection of Christ. It is to be a period of rest or quiet.

Sacrifices: The offering of an animal or a possession to a deity in propitiation or homage; that which is so offered; the surrender or destruction of something praised or desirable for the sake of something considered as having a higher or more pressing claim; the thing so surrendered or devoted.

Salvation: The redemption of man from the bondage and penalty of sin; redemption. It is being "born again". God wipes the slates of our lives clean by the blood of Jesus.

Sanctify: To make holy or sacred, to set apart for holy or religious use, to purify from sin.

Satan: The chief evil spirit; the great adversary of man; the devil.

Savior: One who saves rescues or delivers; a title of God and Christ.

Hallelujah: Praise ye Jehovah, Praise the Lord, a song of praise to the Lord.

Sin: The voluntary or willful departure of an individual from a custom prescribed by divine law, divine command, or society in general; moral depravity; wickedness; iniquity; a transgression; on offense against a standard.

Holy Spirit Is the third person in the Trinity. It is also known as the Holy Ghost. A spirit, by whose indwelling the Christian is enabled to live a Godly life.

Stewardship: Being wise and faithful while managing finances or other affairs of the owner. In many churches it is giving and redistribution of moneys for Gods work needed here on earth.

Synagogue: A congregation of Jews assembled for the purpose of worship.

Tabernacle: A tent used by the Israelites as a portable sanctuary in the wilderness during the Exodus

Tribulations: Great Trouble. It is a time in the Future when God schedule a disaster for men on earth in the end times. It has been called by many names in the Bible. They Are: The Day of The Lord. That day of Vengeance, the great day of God Almighty, The day of wrath, the day of trouble and The day of the Lord's anger.

Wages of Sin: Spiritual death with no eternal live

Worship: Worship singing praises to God, prayer, thanksgiving and listening to him speak through his word and giving praise to God.

Maps of Bible Times

Following are maps of Bible times.

Ancient near East

Israel's Tribal lands

Important areas in Israel

Egyptian Empire 1600-1200 B.C.

Assyrian Empire 900-607 B.C.

Babylonian Empire 606-536 B.C.

Persian Empire 536-330 B.C.

Greek Empire 330-146 B.C.

Roman Empire 146 B.C. – 476 A.D.

The Early Churches

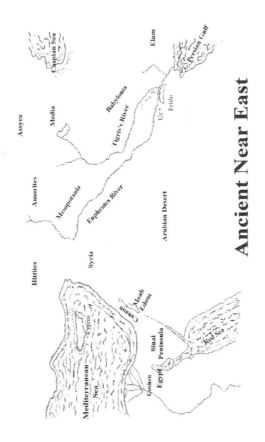

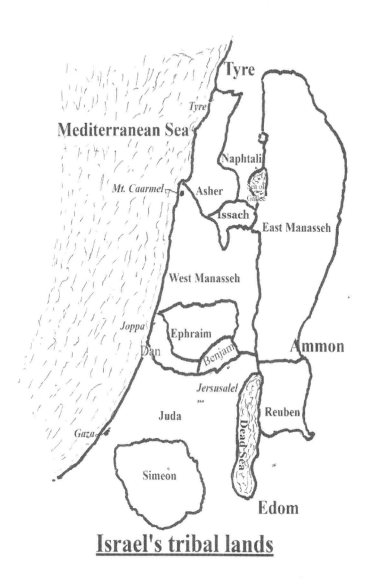

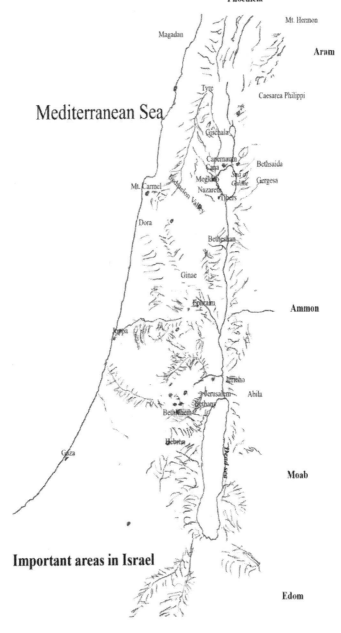

Assyrian Empire 900-607 B. C.

Babylonian Emmpire 606-536 B.C.

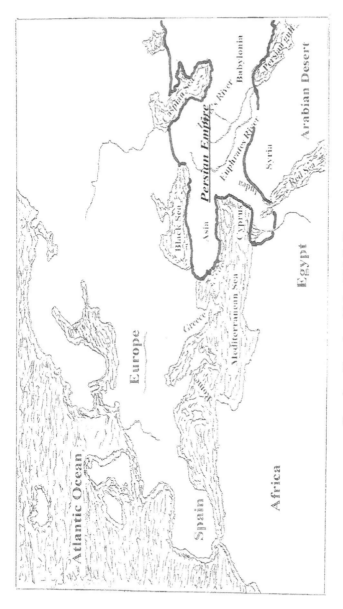

Persian Empire 536 - 330 B C.

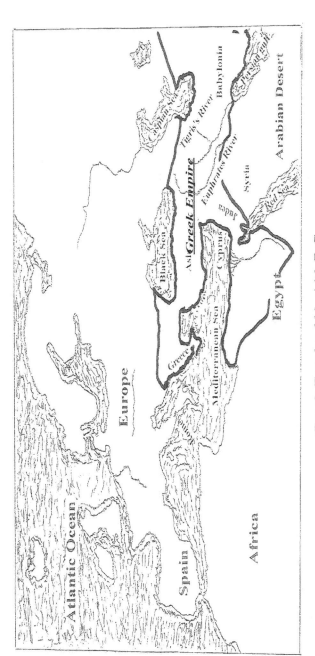

Greek Empire 330 -146 B.C.

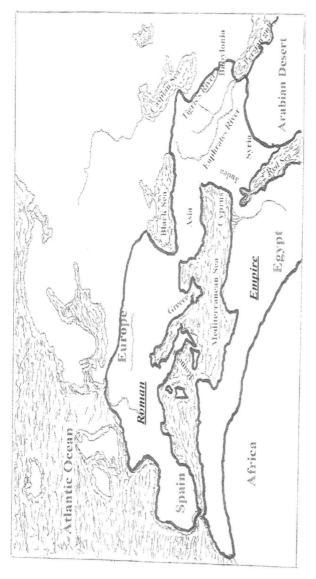

Roman Empire 146 B.B. - 476 A.D.

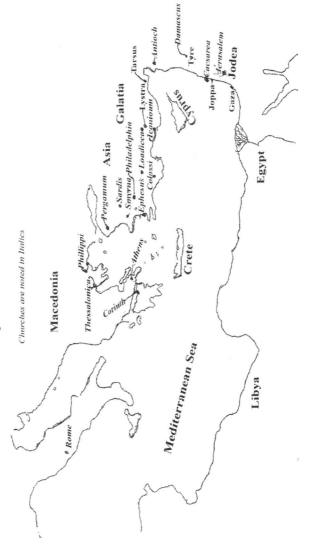

Subject index

This is an index of some of the major notes in the book. Each section has additional notes that you may want to read for your understanding.

10 Commandments 330	Book of HEBREWS 291
4 laws 327	Book of HOSEA 260
400 years of silence 163	Book of I THESSALONIANS 286
Aaron 355	Book of I CHRONICALES 244
Abraham 355	
Adam 356	Book of I CORINTHIANS 281
Antichrist 379	
Apostolic Age 50	Book of I JOHN 299
Ark of the covenant 323	Book of I KINGS 242
Armageddon War 148	Book of I PETER 297
Armor of God 340	Book of I SAMUEL 240
Baptism 89	Book of I TIMOTHY 288
Basic Bible Notes 8	Book of II CHRONICALSE 244
Beatitudes 329	
Believe 80	Book of II CORINTHIANS 282
Bible Books (*Descriptions*) 225	
	Book of II JOHN 299
Bible Symbols 301	Book of II PETER 298
Book of ACTS 276	Book of II SAMUEL 241
Book of AMOS 261	Book of II THESSALONIANS 287
Book of COLOSSIANS 286	
Book of DANIEL 258	Book of II TIMOTHY 289
Book of DEUTERONOMY 235	Book of III JOHN 300
	Book of ISAIAH 253
Book of ECCLESIASTES 251	Book of JAMES 296
Book of EPHESIANS 284	Book of JEREMIAH 254
Book of ESTHER 248	Book of JOB 249
Book of EXODUS 228	Book of JOEL 261
Book of EZEKIEL 256	Book of JOHN 274
Book of EZRA 246	Book of JONAH 263
Book of GALATIANS 283	Book of JOSHUA 236
Book of GENESIS 225	Book of JUDE 300
Book of HABAKKUK 265	Book of JUDGES 237
Book of HAGGAI 267	

Book of KINGS 242
Book of LAMENTATIONS 256
Book of LEVITICUS 232
Book of LUKE 273
Book of Malachi 269
Book of MARK 272
Book of MATTHEW 271
Book of MICAH 264
Book of NAHUM 265
Book of NEHEMIAH 247
Book of NUMBERS 233
Book of OBADIAH 262
Book of PHILEMON 290
Book of PHILIPPIANS 285
Book of PROVERBS 251
Book of PSALMS 250
Book of REVELATIONS. 300
Book of ROMANS 279
Book of RUTH 238
Book of SONG OF SOLOMON 252
Book of TITUS 289
Book of ZECHARIAH 268
Book of ZEPHANIAH 266
Books of the Bible 213
Books of the Bible-written 220
Born of the spirit 68
children 107
Christian Fellowship 109
Christmas 119
Church 97
Communion 117
Confession of Sin 341
Crucifixion 28, 32
Daniel 357
David 358
Days of Creation 165
Devil, ... 56
Divorce 106
Easter 121
Elijah 359

Elisha 360
End Times Prophecies 126
Esau 360
Eve 361
exact date of the coming on the Messiah 321
Exhortations 343
Facts about the Bible 1
Faith 81, 380
Fall of Jerusalem 152
Forgiveness 88
Fruits of the Holy Spirit 55
Genealogy from Adam through Noah 314
Genealogy of Christ 126
Genealogy of Jesus 53
Gifts of the Holy Spirit 55
Giving (Tithing/use) 115
God 11, 362
God repeals some Hebrew ritual laws 95
God's appearances 15
God's Covenant with his people and Nation 59
God's Exile of his people from the Promised Land. Until 1948-1967 322
God's Grace 111
God's new covenant with man 65
God's preparation for the Gospel 69
Gods' Attributes 18
Golden rule 332
Gospel—Good News --Gods' plan for salvation and Reconciliation 74
Great Commission 331
Greatest commandments .. 331
Hear the word of God. 79
Heaven and Hell 93
Hebrew Calendar 161

Hebrew Calendar, Festivals and celebrations 159
Hebrew Offerings 326
Holy Spirit 54
Husband and Wives Relationship 104
Husband and wives responsibilities 339
Isaac 363
Isaiah 363
Ishmael 363
Israelites Captivity 154
Jacob 364
James 364
Japheth 364
Jeremiah 365
Jerusalem 165
Jesus 21, 365
Jesus is the Son of God 24
Jesus' Apostles 49
Jesus' Deity and Humanity 45
Jesus' Family 53
Jesus's End Time Prophecy 130
Job 366
John 3:16-18 330
John Baptist 366
Jonah 366
Joseph 366
Joshua 367
Judas 367
Judgment 150
Lazarus 368
LORDS PRAYER 329
Lords supper 336
Love 83, 332, 333, 338, 382
Lucifer 56
Luke 368
Maps of Bible Times 387
Marriage 101
Mary 369
Melchizedek 370

Messiah: 383
Michael 370
Millennium 147
Miracles 196
Monies and weights 164
Moses 370
Nebuchadnezzar 370
Nebuchadnezzar dreams. World governments 314
Nehemiah 370
New Creation 90
Noah 371
Noah and the Flood 154
Oldest men in Bible 165
Parables 26
Paul 371
People & Events of the Bible 348
Peter 372
Phillip 372
Plagues against the Egyptians Gods 317
Prayer 91
problems related to Evolution 315
Prominent People 355
Prophecies /fulfillment 168
Prophecy 96
Psalm 23 334
Rachel 373
Rapture 143
Repentance 87
Resurrection 37
Rewards 100
Romans Road 328
Rules for Christian Households 344
Rules of kingdom 336
Sacred vessel of the sanctuary 158
Salvation 151
Samson 373

Samuel 374
Sarah 374
Satan 56, 316
Saul 375
Second coming of Christ ... 65, 141
Septuagint 216
Sexual Immorality 111
Shem 375
Signs of the End Times 128
Signs of the second coming 140
Sin 87
Sinners prayer 326
Solomon 376
Special Events in the Bible 307
Spiritual Maturing 90

Symbolisms used in the Bible 323
Tabernacle 157
-*The 10 Commandments* 162
Thomas 376
Time to Do 335
Times, People and when Old Testament books were written 217
Tower of Babel 156
Tribulation 144
Twelve tribes of Israel 162
Two Witnesses 136
What is the Bible? 2
Zechariah 376
Zephaniah 377

Made in the USA
Middletown, DE
07 July 2018